BANK INDONESIA
AND THE CRISIS

The **Institute of Southeast Asian Studies (ISEAS)** was established as an autonomous organization in 1968. It is a regional centre dedicated to the study of socio-political, security and economic trends and developments in Southeast Asia and its wider geostrategic and economic environment.

The Institute's research programmes are the Regional Economic Studies (RES, including ASEAN and APEC), Regional Strategic and Political Studies (RSPS), and Regional Social and Cultural Studies (RSCS).

ISEAS Publications, an established academic press, has issued more than 1,000 books and journals. It is the largest scholarly publisher of research about Southeast Asia from within the region. ISEAS Publications works with many other academic and trade publishers and distributors to disseminate important research and analyses from and about Southeast Asia to the rest of the world.

J. Soedradjad Djiwandono

BANK INDONESIA AND THE CRISIS

An Insider's View

Institute of Southeast Asian Studies
Singapore

First published in Singapore in 2005 by
ISEAS Publications
Institute of Southeast Asian Studies
30 Heng Mui Keng Terrace
Pasir Panjang
Singapore 119614

E-mail: publish@iseas.edu.sg
Website: http://bookshop.iseas.edu.sg

The responsibility for facts and opinions in this publication rests exclusively with the author and his interpretations do not necessarily reflect the views or the policy of the publisher or its supporters.

ISEAS Library Cataloguing-in-Publication Data

Djiwandono, Joseph Soedradjad, 1938-
   Bank Indonesia and the crisis: an insider's view.
   (Local history and memoirs ; 13)
   1.   Bank Indonesia.
   2.   Banks and banking, Central—Indonesia.
   3.   Financial crises—Indonesia.
   4.   Structural adjustment (Economic policy)—Indonesia.
   5.   Economic stabilization—Indonesia.
   I.   Title
   II.   Series: Local history and memoirs (Institute of Southeast Asian Studies); 13.
DS501 I595L no. 13   2004

ISBN 981-230-246-7

Cover photo by Suparlan USF (Bank Indonesia)
Typeset by International Typesetters Pte Ltd
Printed in Singapore by Utopia Press Pte Ltd

For Bianti, Tommy, Mulan, Mazel and Budi

Contents

Acknowledgements   *ix*
Glossary   *xi*

Prologue: The Crisis and Me   1

1   Introduction   13

2   Origin of the Crisis and Early Responses   22

3   Stabilization and Reform Programmes   76

4   Poor Programme Implementation   108

5   Stronger Programme with Weak Commitment   142

6   Bank Indonesia and the Crisis   165

7   Lessons from the Crisis   218

8   Epilogue   249

Postscript   258
Notes   262
References   276
Index   283
About the Author   291

List of Tables

Table 1   Chronology of Events, July 1997–May 1998   19

Table 2   Bank Indonesia's Intervention Band, 1992–97   38

Table 3   Indonesia's Official Reserves   50

Table 4   Number of Banks before Crisis   53

Table 5   Pre-Crisis Monetary and Banking Policy   54

Table 6   Official Reserves, Gross Reserves and the   87
             Difference, 1993–98

Table 7   Impacts of the Crisis: Indonesia, Thailand and   116
             Korea

Table 8   Bank Indonesia's Liquidity Support, 1997–99   176

Table 9   Vulnerability Indicators   219

Table 10   Impacts of Crisis   221

Table 11   Indonesia's Letters of Intent   233

Table 12   Indonesia's Financial Position in the Fund as of   245
             31 March 2002

Acknowledgements

Many individuals have been instrumental in providing me with generous support, advice and assistance that helped this long-drawn endeavour get started, proceed and finally completed. I would like to express my deep gratitude to all friends and colleagues who contributed one way or another to inspiring, pushing and encouraging me to write and publish this book. They are too many to list individually. However, it is my honour to specifically thank the following persons and institutions that have contributed to the completion of this book:

- The late Professor Sumitro Djojohadikusumo who gave me moral and intellectual support from the start, during the writing process as well as the finishing of the Bahasa Indonesia version.
- The then Director of the Institute of Southeast Asian Studies (ISEAS), Professor Chia Siow Yue, and Ambassador Kesavapany, the current ISEAS Director; Professor Jeffrey Sachs at the now defunct Harvard Institute of International Development (HIID); and Ambassador Barry Desker, at the Institute of Defence and Strategic Studies (IDSS) for generously inviting me to join their respective institutions as a Visiting Fellow to research and write this manuscript and other papers.
- My colleagues and friends at Bank Indonesia, the former managing directors, directors and staff who participated in the thinking and formulating of policies within Bank Indonesia through countless board meetings, morning and evening calls, steering committee and other meetings, especially immediately before and during the crisis.
- Colleagues and friends in the three prestigious research institutions that bore with me in the last several years, sharing ideas at seminars and conferences.

- My anonymous referees; the ISEAS Head of Publications, Triena Ong; and my editor, Dayaneetha De Silva.
- Since February 2001 up to the completion of this English edition I have been Visiting Senior Research Fellow with ISEAS, while the rewriting has been done at the IDSS. Both institutions provided me with an intellectual environment, excellent libraries and the necessary wherewithal during my research and writing.
- I received grants from the Ford Foundation, New York while working as Development Associate at the HIID and OPO-JFK School of Government, Harvard University from 1998–2000 while working on the Bahasa Indonesia version of the book.

I know that I will never be able to thank enough those closest to me during the agonizing period of the crisis and our lives afterward, including countless stressful days and nights in the last six years. These are my wife Bianti, my two sons Tommy and Budi, and my daughter-in-law Mulan in more recent years, plus my little grandson Mazel, together with close relatives and friends, whose love, affection and support have become my pillar of strength to work and finish the manuscript in periods that have been tinted with distractions from our normal lives.

J. Soedradjad Djiwandono
Singapore

Glossary

ADB	Asian Development Bank
AGO	Attorney General's Office
BI	Bank Indonesia
BLBI	Bantuan Likuiditas Bank Indonesia (BI liquidity support)
BOJ	Bank of Japan
Bulog	Badan Urusan Logistik, State Food Distribution Agency
CAR	capital adequacy ratio
CBS	currency board system
CFF	Compensatory Financing Facility
CGI	Consultative Group on Indonesia
EA	Extended Arrangement
EEF	Extended Fund Facility
ERM	Exchange Rate Mechanism
ESAF	Enhanced Structural Adjustment Facility
GDP	gross domestic product
GIC	Government of Singapore Investment Corporation
GRA	General Resource Account
HIPC	Highly Indebted Poor Countries
IBRA	Indonesian Bank Restructuring Agency
IFRCL	International Reserve and Foreign Currency Liquidity
IGGI	Inter-governmental Group on Indonesia
IIF	Institute of International Finance
IMF	International Monetary Fund
INDRA	Indonesian Debt Restructuring Agency
JIBOR	Jakarta Inter-bank Offered Rate
KLBI	Kredit Likuiditas Bank Indonesia
LLL	legal lending limit
LOI	letter of intent

MAS	Monetary Authority of Singapore
MEFP	Memorandum of Economic and Financial Policy
MRNIA	Master Refinancing and Note Issuance Agreement
MSAA	Master Settlement and Acquisition Agreement
NIR	Net International Reserves
NPL	non-performing loans
PGRF	Poverty Reduction and Growth Facility
SBA	stand-by arrangement
SBI	Bank Indonesia certificates
SBPU	Surat Berharga Pasar Uang (Money Market Securities)
SDR	Special Drawing Rights
SEACEN	Southeast Asia Central Bank Governors
SRF	Supplementary Reserve Facility

Prologue: The Crisis and Me

During the Wahid era Indonesians started to get used to news about the dismissals of government officials, including cabinet ministers and generals, beginning with the dismissals of the then Minister for Trade and Industry Jusuf Kalla and the Minister of Public Enterprises Laksamana Sukardi in July 2000. To make things worse, a dismissal was usually preceded by rumours and media reports.

However, my dismissal as Governor of the Bank Indonesia by President Soeharto several weeks before the end of my term attracted unusually widespread public and media interest. At the same time, the reasons for this unprecedented sacking of a Central Bank governor have remained a mystery, hence my justification for writing this book.

Dismissed as Bank Indonesia Governor

I was dismissed from my post as Governor of Bank Indonesia through a presidential decree on 11 February 1998. Official release from the post took place at the installation of my successor, Dr Sjahril Sabirin, on 19 February 1998. The new governor and myself undertook the legal transfer of authority at Bank Indonesia on 23 February 1998, thus formally ending my tenure, which had begun upon the installation of Development Cabinet VI on 21 March 1993.

My dismissal was unusual because on previous occasions, at least since 1983, the replacement of the central bank governor had usually been in tandem with the change of cabinet ministers. Since 1983, the position had also been accorded a state minister of cabinet status. Indeed, in this system the post of Central Bank Governor was equivalent to the posts of the Attorney General and the Commander of the Armed Forces — all three had state ministerial status. On one or two occasions the handovers were one or two days later than those of the cabinet ministers, but never weeks apart. The new cabinet, Development Cabinet VII, was installed on 16 March 1998 but my dismissal and the legal transfer of authority were all several weeks prior to this.

What seemed to be the reason behind the President's haste? Some government officials immediately made the standard comment that the replacement of an official was the prerogative of the President and that it was "normal".

It is indeed true that there is no regulation that forbids an Indonesian president to replace any cabinet minister at any time. However, to argue that it was "normal" for President Soeharto to have done so then would be misleading.

Actually granting the governor of central bank a cabinet ministerial status was *also* not "normal" because it effectively underscored the absence of an independent central bank in Indonesia.

Articles 8 and 9 of the Law of the Republic of Indonesia Number 13 of 1968 concerning the Central Bank (henceforth the Central Bank Law No. 13, 1968) explicitly states that Bank Indonesia implemented monetary policy that was formulated by the Monetary Board. This board should be comprised of several ministers, and chaired by the Minister of Finance. The governor was only a member of the board. However, there was a stipulation that, should he/she have different views from the board he/she could bring the issue to the President.

Since the governor of Bank Indonesia was now a cabinet member, the President was legally allowed to dismiss the governor. However, the Central Bank Law had a stipulation that could legally complicate the President's decision. Article 17 of the Central Bank Law 1968 included some rules on the release of the Bank Indonesia governor prior to the end of the term:

> The President could dismiss the governor and managing directors prior
> to the end of their terms, in cases of the decease of the person, certain

conduct or behavior that caused losses to Bank Indonesia or the interest of the state, something that caused the inability to perform the duties, or his/her personal wish.[1]

In the explanatory notes it was further stated that in case the dismissal was due to alleged wrongdoing, the dismissal would be temporary in nature. The governor could come up with a defence. If the President did not respond to the defence within one month, the temporary dismissal would be void. If a criminal act were the reason for the dismissal he/she would be dismissed with dishonour.

At issue was not just my dismissal. It also involved all the managing directors from my original team in 1993. Their dismissals were carried out two months before my own in the case of four, a week after for one, and a month after for another two. Except for one person, all were dismissed before their terms ended. However, according to the documents, all of us were dismissed with honour.

The decision on my dismissal was signed on 11 February 1998. The President officially told me on 17 February. But I learned about the decision one day after it was made on the morning of 12 February — in Indonesia a secret can only last one or two days.

I learned about the President's decision from my wife, on the morning of 12 February. Upon hearing the news my wife called me at my office around 8:30 that morning. I was in the middle of receiving Professor Widjojo Nitisastro in my office. My wife informed me that, according to a trusted friend, President Soeharto had signed a decree to fire me the night before. She asked me to check the news with my guest. So, after I hung up the telephone, I asked him. He awkwardly told me that actually it was his intention to tell me about it. In fact, Minister Moerdiono had been the first to know. He might not have had the heart to tell me in person, and he had asked Professor Widjojo to tell me instead.

Almost five years before, I had learned about my appointment to the post from the President directly also through a phone call in the early hours of 12 March 1993. I received a call from an adjutant of the President at about 3:30 am, asking me to call the President. I was Junior Minister of Trade then, so even though it was strange to have to call the President, it was not bizarre. Still I asked the adjutant when I was expected to call his answer was "right now". I learnt later that it was President Soeharto's habit during the fasting month to work after the end of the period of breaking the fast, *sahur*.

Playing Governor

My immediate problem that morning was whether I should carry on with my scheduled appointments or make changes. My schedule that day was to see the President with three other Ministers and Professor Widjojo to report on the plan to submit the names of problem banks to the Indonesian Bank Restructuring Agency (IBRA). In the late afternoon I was scheduled to leave for Bali to host the Southeast Asia Central Bank (SEACEN) Governors' meeting from 13 to 14 February 1998.[2]

Although the President had already signed the decree to dismiss me the night before, he allowed me to host the conference in Bali. During the meeting with the President, which also included the Ministers of Finance, Trade and Industry, State Secretariat and Professor Widjojo, the government's adviser, I explained to the President the plan to submit a list of 54 problem banks to IBRA to be restructured.

As a consequence, during the conference in Bali and after my return to Jakarta up till the day I was summoned to see him on 17 February, I had to pretend that I was still the governor. This was a little tricky. While in Bali, there were reports that I was to be dismissed in the Jakarta media. When journalists asked me to comment on the news, I told them that I did not know anything about it since I was in Bali. I told them to go and check with their sources in Jakarta.[3]

Hosting an international conference with full knowledge of my impending dismissal was a unique experience. Worse still, the conference was marred by a tragic aircraft accident that caused the demise of Governor Yuan-Dong Sheu together with Madame Sheu, a Deputy Governor and two officials from the Central Bank of China-Taipei.

Last Meeting with President Soeharto

Losing a job is an unpleasant experience. Officially, the President told me about my dismissal at a meeting at his private residence in Jalan Cendana, central Jakarta.

The night before a presidential adjutant informed me that the President would receive me at his residence on 9:30 am, 17 February 1998. However, I had a commitment in the morning at the Department of the Interior to give a briefing on the monetary and financial problems and the crisis to a conference of all the provincial governors together with some other cabinet ministers. I therefore asked the Minister of the Interior, who was to chair the meeting, to let me give my presentation early so that I could manage to be on time for the meeting with the President.

I met the President alone and the whole meeting took about an hour. I started the discussion by reporting on what had happened at the SEACEN Governors' meetings, including the accident that killed Governor Sheu and his entourage.

Afterwards, the President was very business-like, telling me about his decision to release me. I cannot remember his exact words. However, he told me approximately the following. He said that he was in the process of making changes in his government such as the one the day before, when he had replaced the Commander of the Armed Forces. He said that the other three government officials who had cabinet ministerial rank were also being replaced.

Then he added, "I want to replace you with Syahril Sabirin. The installation will be done in two days, on Thursday, 19 February". He continued saying, "You have been assisting me for ten years with heavy responsibilities, especially lately. I am grateful for your service to the government to help me all these years".

I too tried to be straightforward in response. I told him that I accepted his decision, and that I was also grateful to him for trusting me to serve in important posts in his government. I also apologized for the many problems in monetary and banking matters that must complicate his job as the national leader. And that basically ended my governorship of the central bank.

The whole process lasted about five minutes. But I asked the President for more time to discuss some issues that I wanted to talk to him about, since I knew that this would be my last chance. In fact, I had a chance to discuss with him pending issues that included Bank Indonesia's finalization of issuing the new 10,000 rupiah note and the possibility for repayment of deposits with banks that were liquidated. I also discussed accusations that I had not reported to him about the ownership of the liquidated banks. I also managed to tell him about my plan to write some books, including this one.

Of these four issues my priority was actually the third one, i.e. the rumour that he did not know that, among the liquidated banks, three were partly owned by his brother and children. In other words, that the

President had agreed to my proposal to liquidate these banks without knowing that his family partly owned three of them. And that he did not know this because I had not told him.

My colleagues were merely curious about this but the President's family used this argument to base their legal suits against me. Until then, I told my colleagues that during this era I would not be daring enough to liquidate banks without telling the President about their ownership, precisely because I knew that some of the candidate banks belonged to his family. But the argument of the family members was absurd. They may have thought that, had I told him that these banks belonged to his family, he may not have let the liquidation plan go ahead.

What I told the President at the meeting was just to remind him about what I did during the negotiations with the IMF, which included the bank closures in late October 1997. I did that to check whether he would acknowledge that I had indeed reported everything to him. From his reaction, it was clear that he acknowledged that I had reported everything to him. And that was good enough for me. However, he indirectly also admitted that he approved his family's legal suit against the Minister of Finance and myself because it was within their rights as citizens. In answer to my query, he said that he did not want people to think that he was changing the decision just because he wanted to save the family's business interests.

Although it was a sad meeting for me since it ended my long career in the administration, it was a productive one nonetheless because I was mentally prepared. Deep inside, I was hoping that the President remembered our discussion five years earlier in the wee hours of the month of Ramadhan in March 1993. Even though I had not been fully awake I had managed to convey my concerns about Indonesia's banking problems before accepting the job as Bank Indonesia's governor.

I had stated then that it would be a tough assignment to be at the Bank of Indonesia at that juncture. The President was a bit surprised and asked me why. I replied that there were a lot of bad debts in the banking sector and that there must be other problem banks beside Bank Summa, which was liquidated in 1992. I told him that I had talked to members of the Coffee Exporters Association, who told me that they would face problems with financing due to declining exports. Again, apparently surprised, he reminded me that my field of expertise was monetary economics. And I told him, yes indeed, but also international economics. He did not want to continue the discussion and ended the conversation by saying that I should coordinate the efforts to deal with these problems in my new job. He said that the new cabinet would be in place in about a week, then hung the phone up.

Relief and Disappointment

As someone who served long in the bureaucracy, I had been lucky to be posted to different institutions within the government that were never far from my main fields of interest. I had been involved in work that always related to international economics, monetary economics, public finance, or development economics.

However, being released from a post that had a lot of association with my long career in the government of course left me deeply disappointed.

In the protracted crisis, the period that I was involved in policy-making was short, albeit critical. I was released from my post early in the event, yet some seemed to argue that I should be responsible for problems arising from the crisis. My statement in the media after the dismissal was widely quoted. I was frank in responding to journalists' questions that I was disappointed and feeling like a general who was ordered to retreat from a battle before the war was over.[4]

My career in government with its formal basis in academic institutions had a long history. After graduating from Gajah Mada University with a degree in Economics (1963), I worked in the National Economics and Social Research Institute (LEKNAS) of the Indonesian Institute of Sciences (LIPI) from early 1964 until 1978. This period included studying at the University of Wisconsin, Madison, for an M.Sc. degree in Economics (1966). In 1978 my employment was transferred to the Faculty of Economics, the University of Indonesia up to the present. This period included graduate study leading to a Ph.D. in Economics (1980) at Boston University. But, in the tradition of the New Order, I worked in the government bureaucracy in several institutions. I was one year at the Department of Finance (1968), three years at the Department of Trade (1969–72), sixteen years at the National Development and Planning Agency (BAPPENAS), and for four years subsequently, Assistant Minister Coordinator for Economy, Finance and Industry (EKUIN). In the Cabinet I was Junior Minister of Trade (1988–93) for five years, and the Governor of Bank Indonesia for a similar period (1993–98).

I learned what contagion was all about through the battle against the onslaught on the rupiah that originated from the Thai baht crisis. The problem spread with frightening speed, ultimately affecting almost all aspects of Indonesian life. But I had not expected that the crisis would hit me personally in an equally rapid manner.

I told my colleagues about a joke among economists: a recession was when an economy experienced negative growth rates for two consecutive quarters with increasing unemployment rates. But a depression occurred when the economists were also becoming unemployed.

I had of course realized that the post of central bank governor in Asia since the crisis broke had become very risky. Of the 10 SEACEN governors who attended the Bali meeting, Governor Sheu of Taipei passed away two days after the meeting was over; I was out from my post either before the meeting (if one considered the signing of the decree as the date of my losing the job) or several days after; and then came the sackings or resignations of several Asian central bank governors in rapid succession. It started with Chaiyawat Wibulswasdi (Thailand), followed by Ahmad Muhammad Don (Malaysia) and Kyung Shik Lee (Korea). Also, not due to the crisis, but coincidentally just before the Bali meeting, the Managing Director of the Monetary Authority of Singapore (MAS) Lee Ek Tieng retired. Outside SEACEN, Governor Matsushita of the Bank of Japan also retired around this period.

Although being released from my post was unpleasant and disappointing, the overwhelming feeling after the fateful meeting with the President was a great relief from the heaviest burden of my long career. While I met with the President, my eldest son and my wife were already waiting for me in my office. That afternoon, I had lunch together with my family in a Japanese restaurant to "celebrate" the lifting of this burden.

Indeed, for several weeks afterward, I received much-appreciated wishes of support and congratulations from close friends, acquaintances, and relatives who wanted to show their moral support for me and my family.

Speculating on Reasons for my Dismissal

In the government announcement on the matter, Minister of State Secretary Moerdiono was quoted as saying:

> The President had thanked Mr. Soedradjad for what he had done all this time while reiterating that his past tasks had been very demanding. On the reasons for the dismissal Minister Moerdiono said, "It has been the custom in our system that the term of a Governor is approximately five years. In view of the ending of the Development Cabinet VI in the next few weeks, this replacement is being done". On a future post that may be given to the former Governor, Minister Moerdiono admitted that he did not know what was on the President's mind. However, in the discussion with the Minister of State Secretary Mr. Soedradjad told him that he wanted to concentrate on conducting research and to continue his teaching in the university".[5]

Most media reports in Indonesia and abroad tended to associate my dismissal with public perceptions of my disagreement with the President over the plan to adopt a fixed exchange system with a currency board system (CBS). Others argued that I was dismissed due to a failure to fight the crisis. Some also associated the dismissal with the previous dismissals of Bank Indonesia managing directors and alleged irregularities in the provision of liquidity support to the banking sector during the crisis.

It was also reported that I had been asking to be released from my post since the dismissal of four central bank managing directors without being consulted by the President. There was another rumour that I had been asking to resign due to the increasing job pressures since the bank closures.

With respect to the possibility that my view on the CBS had something to do with the dismissal, it should be noted that indeed I never said publicly that I was against the adoption of a CBS. And certainly, I was never against the CBS for fear of losing my job, as some media reports claimed. But it was also correct that I never implicitly or explicitly stated that I supported the adoption of a CBS for Indonesia.

What I did say in public about the issue was that "we have to study carefully the pros and cons and their implications". I made this statement several times, including after the Minister of Finance made a statement confirming the plan to adopt the CBS during a parliamentary hearing on 11 February 1998.[6] On several occasions I added that any system could be used effectively as long as it was implemented consistently and supported by the necessary institutions.

On 11 February 1998, the day the President signed the decree to dismiss me, *Suara Pembaruan*, a respected Jakarta daily, carried three items that had some reference to the crisis. First, a report on President Soeharto officiating the Perkasa Heavy Industrial Complex belonging to the Texmaco Group. In his speech the President lamented currency speculators who had ruined the national economy. Second, a report on Minister of Finance Mar'ie Muhammad answers to members of Parliament that the government would adopt a CBS. The report also mentioned that Prof. Steve Hanke made a statement that the rupiah could be pegged to the dollar at 5,000 rupiah to a dollar but he was still waiting for additional information from Bank Indonesia. It was also reported that, according to Mr. Abdul Gafur, Deputy Speaker of the House, the Parliament would assist the government in smoothing the process of the enactment of the law for adopting a CBS. Third, the paper also reported my speech in a programme for civics instructors explaining the Fund-supported programme to fight against the crisis, without any mention of a CBS.[7]

Why did I not state my objection to a CBS? I have to admit that I was afraid to publicly air my differences with the President on the matter. However, I also knew that being vague was the best technique in that peculiar environment to send a message to the President.[8]

I was not alone in using vague language. Even high-ranking officials from Western countries and the Fund used similar techniques. Their comments on the issue of adopting CBS were just as unclear, at least this was how they were reported in the Indonesian press. The following are some samples of their statements, as reported in the newspapers in February 1998:[9]

- Mr. Michel Camdessus stated that the CBS had a lot of advantages, but it had some shortcomings as well, while reminding the Indonesian government not to rush its adoption. Dr. Stanley Fischer similarly commented that the Indonesian government's plan to adopt a CBS was premature.
- Secretary Robert Rubin made a similar statement, while Chairman Greenspan said that a CBS could be very useful, but it had high risks.
- Even German Minister of Finance Theo Waigel, after meeting

President Soeharto, was quoted making a statement that the plan to adopt a CBS had to be carefully studied.

All the above were not straightforward statements asking President Soeharto to cancel his plan to adopt a CBS. But was there any doubt about their disapproval of the plan then? I do not think so.

The plan's supporters at that time were the vocal ones. Amongst them were several business persons, the Indonesian Chambers of Commerce and Industry (KADIN), some members of Parliament, and a number of economists. However, when the plan was aborted, none of them voiced their complaints.

A Unique Way of Firing

As noted above, it was explicitly stated that I was discharged with honour. This had also been the case with all the Bank Indonesia managing directors under me who were fired prior to or after my dismissal.

It is difficult to get to the truth of the matter. With the lack of transparency and minimal certainty it is also difficult to know whether anything reported in the media at the time can be believed.

There were two publications, one a magazine, *Prospek*, and the other a tabloid, *Xpos*, which wrote about my dismissal and offered analyses. "The Fall of CBS Victim" in *Prospek* said that my "sins" were threefold. The first one was related to the three managing directors who were interrogated by the police immediately after their dismissals in December 1997. It stated that I was too adamant in fighting for the three former managing directors both on legal as well as moral grounds. The second one was related to the bank closures that included three banks partly owned by the Soeharto family. And the last one was my stand on the CBS issue.[10]

The second publication came up with articles entitled, "Refusing CBS, Soedradjad was Fired"; "Soedradjad versus the Palace Family"; and "An Honest Man that was Sidelined". These articles reported that President Soeharto decided to adopt a CBS as his political responsibility in a meeting of the Economic Resiliency Council. In one, I was considered to be an obstacle in the President's scenario, so I had to go. The second discussed the decision to liquidate banks, which included three banks that were partly owned by the President's family. The last detailed the 50-point letter of intent that was signed by the President, which included steps to abolish monopolies such as the clove monopoly and the national car project. These points were the work of the economic team, in which the Minister of Finance and the Governor of the Central Bank were prominent members. The bank closures and agreement with the Fund seemed to be perceived by the Soeharto family as defamatory. The articles stated that the Governor was known as a clean official, not corrupt, even though he was criticized about his indecisiveness for not firing corrupt fellow officials. And since it was difficult to attack him on grounds of corruption, his enemies attacked him using religion.[11]

It is my contention that President Soeharto in his 32 years of rule never dismissed officials for merely one single reason even if it was a "cardinal sin" in his view. There were rumours that he would even grant a pardon if the official showed some remorse. He must also have thought that his decision about me would raise questions.

Be that as it may, the issue of why he could not have waited for another two weeks — when the cabinet was declared a "lame duck" anyway — or a month to the formation of the new cabinet, is irrelevant. In my opinion, it was precisely this untimely dismissal that indicated his intention to show the public his determination to punish his official for violating his unwritten rule about not embarrassing his family. The reports that I cited above seemed to be reflecting that all those requirements had been broken, and punishment had to be carried out. However, in typical New Order government style, the decision was couched in humane terms, thus the accolade "with honour" in my letter of dismissal.

The Western media used more telling terms in their reports about the dismissal. Some reports or analyses appearing in newspapers abroad used the terms "dismissed" (*New York Times* and *Strait Times*), "sacked" (*Asian Wall Street Journal*), "dumped" (*Financial Times*), and "fired" (*Washington Post* and *International Herald Tribune*). A book on the political economy of the Asian crisis also used the word "fired" in its discussion about the matter (Haggard 2000, p. 69). The Indonesian English daily, *Jakarta Post* used the term "summarily dismissed" in its editorial on 19 February 1998.

1

Introduction

The idea of writing an assessment and analysis of what had been developing in Indonesia's economics and finance had been with me for some time. It started around the middle of my five-year term as Governor of Bank Indonesia, when the Bank commissioned a team to write a history (Rahardjo 1995). The idea was to write about my experience as well as assessment of the management of the national economy, as viewed from the Indonesian central bank.

Due to the crisis that struck Indonesia in early July 1997, I decided to work on the Indonesian crisis first. With my dismissal, I wanted to write about what I had observed, analysed, and decided during the crisis in my capacity as one of the key Indonesian economic policy-makers. I told President Soeharto about this plan during my last meeting with him at his residence.

I ultimately wrote a book, *Mengelola Bank Indonesia dalam Masa Krisis* (Managing Bank Indonesia during the Crisis) and *Bergulat dengan Krisis dan Pemulihannya* (Fighting the Crisis and Its Recovery). Both were written in Bahasa Indonesia, and were published in October 2001. The present book is a revised English version of the first book.

The Indonesian crisis as a part of the Asian crisis has been analysed and reported on extensively. It has also been widely discussed at many conferences and seminars. Many have argued that the Asian financial crisis was the worst since the Second World War. Meanwhile, the Indonesian crisis has been portrayed as the worst case in the Asian crisis as measured in terms of different economic and social indicators and the depth and spread of its negative impacts.

The Indonesian crisis originated from an external shock in the foreign exchange market that contagiously caused a drastic depreciation of the rupiah, then became a total crisis. The shock in the foreign exchange market that originated from the Thai baht crisis produced a chain of effects that exposed structural weaknesses in Indonesia's economy, and its socio-political fabric, which were hitherto hidden by high economic growth.

Structural weaknesses were widespread in the Indonesian economy, both in the financial sectors, banking in particular, as well as the real sectors, in investment, production, and consumption activities. Weaknesses had also become embedded in Indonesia's social and political system. All these problems were known and even felt by the general public. However, the public did not seem to be too concerned, as if everyone had been mesmerized by Indonesia's high economic growth.

This book aims to explain and assess what happened during the crisis as an historical record of a very important, albeit difficult period, such that some lessons can be derived in the efforts for national development.

Since this is a personal assessment, the materials being used may be far from adequate. It is only hoped that what is written here will add to the existing record, while the analysis and assessment presented will stimulate more studies. It is my hope that this book will contribute to decision-makers in the government, bankers, academics, and the interested public in understanding and appreciating the issues and problems as well as policies adopted by the Central Bank and the government with respect to the crisis in Indonesia.

Outline of the Issues

The issues emanating from the Indonesian crisis are the following:

- **First**, the monetary policies adopted by the government through-out the period. Before adopting a free-floating exchange system, Indonesia relied on a managed floating system that was combined with a creeping depreciation of the rupiah to maintain realistic exchange rates. In its implementation, the exchange rate management was aimed at avoiding overvaluation of the rupiah that complicated exports or undervaluation that could encourage capital flight. This system was adjusted to market conditions, whereby the rupiah was allowed to float more freely by adjusting the intervention bands of Bank Indonesia, in the nature of John Williamson's "adjustable peg" (Williamson 1996). The intervention bands were widened seven times before the government decided to free-float the rupiah in mid-August 1997.

- **Second,** issues related to the Indonesian experience in restructuring the banking system in the context of comprehensive programmes to deal with the crisis. There is a detailed assessment of the closing of 16 banks as a priority action of Indonesia's IMF-supported programmes. The closure of banks in November 1997 is associated with issues and problems that have not been well explained to the public. A relevant question here is why a government policy aimed at bringing back public confidence in the banking sector ended up in the total loss of it? This question lingers on. I will present here my assessment about how this policy evolved and how it affected the national economy.

- **Third**, the Indonesian experience with the implementation of IMF-supported programmes that has also raised questions about the merits and demerits of asking the IMF for help in resolving the crisis. The polemic on the advantages and disadvantages of adopting Fund policies to fight the crisis ultimately boils down to questioning the government's decision to invite the Fund. Why did Indonesia rush to ask for the Fund's help when the government had not done so since the early 1970s?

- **Fourth**, my experience of Bank Indonesia's crisis management. Legally as well as in its actual operations, the central bank did not have autonomy even in the extraordinary circumstances of a devastating crisis. They included incidents such as my being sued in court by the Soeharto family for bank closures that were agreed upon by the President; being kept in the dark on some important monetary and banking policies; and finally, being summarily dismissed for reasons that were never clear.

I headed Bank Indonesia with high hopes of improving its organization and its working rules to prepare the institution to support the integration of the national economy with the global economy. I thought I had built a strong foundation for Bank Indonesia to face a more demanding task by pushing it to become a *centre of excellence*. Bit by bit these efforts seemed to bear some fruit.

However, with the onset of the crisis, these efforts seemed like building sandcastles on a beach washed away by a tsunami. I am sure my feelings were shared by my colleagues, the managing directors of Bank Indonesia, every time I think back of all the hardworking staff at that institution whose efforts were wiped out by the crisis. It is a little ironic that former President Soeharto also stated several times in my presence and that of others that he felt that the achievements of close to three decades of development were wiped out by the crisis.[1] As if he wanted to tell me that the financial crisis, which the monetary authorities could not solve, was the sole problem that ruined his vision.

I used the above metaphor when I was interviewed shortly after my dismissal, including one co-written by Sander Thoenes, a Dutch journalist for the *Financial Times* in Jakarta, who, not long after, was murdered mysteriously in East Timor.[2]

Bank Indonesia as an institution suffered heavily from public criticism. Even its Senior Deputy Governor, prior to his appointment to the post, used to refer to Bank Indonesia as "the den of thieves". This is a tragedy with Bank Indonesia as the victim.

Thus, one aim of this book is to assist readers to imagine that before the crisis struck, there was this institution that had some hope of becoming a good foundation for Indonesia's economic globalization.

During my tenure as Junior Minister of Trade (1988–93) on behalf of the Golkar party I visited different regions of the province of East Nusa Tenggara many times. In December 1992, or a little over three months before my transfer to the central bank, I was flown in a helicopter observing the devastation of a tsunami that had struck Flores, one of the many islands encompassing the province. The flight passed through a tranquil sea that did not show any signs of the fact that a week before, there was a small island off the coast of Flores Island with villages. I could not forget the eeriness of thinking that there had been people living on that little island before, but how it was all just sea-water now.

I am afraid only those who survived a tsunami can appreciate the actual meaning of the metaphor.

TABLE 1
Chronology of Events
July 1997–May 1998

Date	Event
1997	
2 July	*Baht is floated and depreciates by 15 to 20 per cent*
First week of July	Rupiah is under pressure
11 July	Bank Indonesia widens its intervention band from 8 to 12 per cent. From 1994–97 the band was widened six times, from one per cent in 1994 to 8 per cent in 1997
11 July	*Peso is floated*
24 July	Heavy pressure on ASEAN currencies — *currency meltdown*
5 August	Thailand freezes operations of 42 finance companies
14 August	Rupiah is floated; the government abolishes the intervention band
The week following 14 August	BI's intervention in the foreign exchange market starts with forward sales, followed by spot sales. Liquidity is tightened through doubling interest rates, expenditure reduction and Ministry of Finance's instruction for state enterprises and semi-government foundations to transfer their bank deposits into BI certificates (SBI).
20 August	*3-year SBA for Thailand is approved*
August 25	*Korean government guarantees banks' external liabilities*
3 September	The government announces a package of steps in the monetary, fiscal and real sectors, a precursor of the IMF-supported programme.

TABLE 1 (*continued*)
Chronology of Events
July 1997–May 1998

Date	Event
8 October	The government announces its decision to ask for IMF assistance.
14 October	*Thailand announces a strategy for financial restructuring, establishing an asset management company and strengthening blanket guarantees.*
31 October	The government submits the first letter of intent (LOI) to the IMF for SBA, preceded by two weeks of negotiations.
1 November	Closing of 16 banks with more than 400 branch offices all over Indonesia.
5 November	Approval of a three-year SBA by the Executive Board. The IMF loan is SDR 7.3 billion (approximately US$10 billion). Together with loans from the World Bank (US$4.5 billion), the Asian Development Bank (US$3.5 billion), Bank Indonesia reserves (US$5 billion) and lines of credit from a number of countries. This loan was known as the US$43 billion bail out for Indonesia. The first withdrawal of the loan, US$3 billion, takes place almost immediately after the approval.
Mid-November	*Change of government in Thailand*
19 November	*Korea widens its foreign exchange band, followed by sharp* won *depreciation*
4 December	*Approval of SBA for Korea*
8 December	*Thailand closes 56 finance companies*
Mid-December	Rumours surrounding the deteriorating health of President Soeharto. Deposit runs on banks. Bank Indonesia liquidity supports increase rapidly.
18 December	*Change of government in Korea*
23 December	President Soeharto replaces four Managing Directors of Bank Indonesia with candidates of his own choice.

TABLE 1 (*continued*)
Chronology of Events
July 1997–May 1998

Date	Event
27 December	President Soeharto agrees to the conversion of Bank Indonesia liquidity support to banks during the banking crisis and banking crisis following the bank closures and the floating of the rupiah. Different forms of liquidity support of 36,5 trillion rupiah (approximately US$7.5 billion) are converted into more secure bank certificates.
31 December	*14 merchant banks in Korea are suspended, and 2 large commercial banks taken over by the government.*
1998 6 January	The announcement of the 1997/98 budgets, which was negatively received by the market. The budget is a "balanced budget" in the Indonesian concept that included foreign loan receipts as government revenue. Thus, the budget actually contained a deficit of around one per cent of GDP. This was in violation of the first LOI, which required the budget to produce one per cent surplus instead. The rupiah comes under pressure.
15 January	A second LOI is signed by President Soeharto himself.
Mid-January	President Soeharto signals that he will choose Dr. B.J. Habibie as his Vice President. The market reaction to the new uncertainties about the budget, the new LOI and the choice of Dr. Habibie brings the rupiah to its lowest level of over 16,000 rupiah to US$1, albeit just for a very short period. Bank Indonesia liquidity support increases very rapidly.
20 January	*Malaysia introduces blanket guarantees for all depositors.*
21 January	President Soeharto establishes a new economics team, the "Council for Strengthening

TABLE 1 (*continued*)
Chronology of Events
July 1997–May 1998

Date	Event
	Economic Resilience", comprising members of the Monetary Board and other ministers, plus representatives of the private sector. President Soeharto and Managing Director Camdessus jointly appoint Mr. Prabhan Naverkar, a former deputy managing director of IMF, to liaise directly between them. President Soeharto issues a decree to give freedom to Bank Indonesia to determine the interest rate.
26 January	Indonesia introduces blanket guarantees for all liabilities and assets of banks incorporated in Indonesia and IBRA is set up.
27 January	Bank Indonesia uses its new independence to determine interest rates by raising the one and two day SBI rate from 14 per cent to 30 per cent.
January–February	President Soeharto toys with the idea of adopting a fixed exchange system with CBS.
6 February	President Soeharto appoints Prof. Steve H. Hanke adviser to the new economic council during the meeting of the council.
12 February	I learn about my dismissal through a leak that a decree on this matter was signed on 11 February.
13–15 February	SEACEN Governors meeting in Denpasar, Bali, attended by 11 central bank governors and three non-member governors or deputy governors as observers
17 February	(Last) meeting with President Soeharto to be informed about my dismissal.
19 February	Installation of new BI Governor Sabirin at the State Palace.
11 March	President Soeharto is re-elected.

TABLE 1 (*continued*)
Chronology of Events
July 1997–May 1998

Date	Event
31 March	*Three-year SBA for the Philippines was agreed with IMF*
8 April	IBRA liquidates 7 banks and takes over 7 other banks
8 April	New LOI, which includes programmes on social safety nets and a matrix containing 117 items of structural conditionality
14–16 May	Riots in Jakarta and several other cities that cause more than 1,000 deaths. A lot of burning, looting and raping in Jakarta.
21 May	President Soeharto steps down, replaced by President B.J. Habibie
23 May	President Habibie announces his new cabinet and the independent status of Bank Indonesia by not giving the governor a cabinet state minister status in departure from past practice (since 1983).

Sources: Bank Indonesia; Carl-Johan Lindgren et al., *Financial Sector Crisis and Restructuring, Lessons from Asia* (Washington, D.: IMF, 1999).

2

Origin of the Crisis and Early Responses

Home Grown but Not Home Alone

During the first year of the Asian crisis, discussions among experts and writings in the media and professional journals had not been clear in showing the origins or development of the crisis.

Only after more than a year of confusion did some kind of general consensus emerge on the causes of the crisis, policy responses by governments, as well as market reactions toward the crisis. The different views on these matters could be traced to the different perspectives on economics, which are more difficult to mediate.

The differences seem to arise from different schools of thought, which may be based on the conventional distinction between classical and Keynesian economics. Simply put, classical economists rest their arguments on the belief in market mechanisms and argue that any form of intervention in the market is to be avoided because it creates distortion. In contrast, Keynesian economists argue that the market is basically unstable and that government should intervene to create stability.

Analyses about the Asian crisis itself can be distinguished in two broad groups. The first group argues that the crisis was home grown and arose from practices of crony capitalism and weak financial structures plus inept macroeconomic policies (Krugman 1998). The second group saw the crisis as triggered by a shift of sentiment in the financial market that caused financial panic. The second view argues that the crisis was basically a financial panic in the Keynesian tradition, as succinctly explained by Charles P. Kindleberger in his seminal work two decades ago (Kindleberger 1978). Jeffrey Sachs has been the major proponent of this view (Radelet and Sachs 1998).

Stephan Haggard refers to the first group as the internationalists and the second, the fundamentalists. In addition, he also mentions the existence of the third group; these he refers to as the *new* fundamentalists, who specifically mention weak regulations and institutions in the financial sector as the cause of the crisis (Haggard 2000, p. 4).

With respect to the Indonesian crisis, similar questions could be asked. Was the Indonesian crisis a financial panic that spread contagiously to different aspects of peoples' lives? Or, was it a crisis that was caused by weak economic fundamentals?

At the outset, President Soeharto and people in general believed that the crisis was no more than a series of severe financial shocks. But there were others who had argued publicly prior to the crisis about the weakness of Indonesia's economic fundamentals. Indeed, the inefficiencies and loopholes of the national economy from rampant corruption and waste had been widely discussed in public prior to the crisis.

Thus, opinions on the crisis in Indonesia were also divided. Some, including most government officials, viewed the crisis as merely financial. And other groups saw that the rampant corruption, public waste, and cronyism had triggered some shock that developed into a crisis.

It is my contention that the Indonesian crisis was not determined by one single variable, whether external or domestic in origin. The Indonesian crisis and presumably crises in several Asian countries arose from a combination of the working of contagion forces from outside the national economy on the one hand and weak domestic economic and financial structures on the other. The contagion emanated from a sudden change in market sentiment in the region leading to a shock in its currency markets. This resulted in panic selling of local currencies, and of other assets denominated in local currencies, for dollars. Dae-Hwan Kim has argued similarly for the case of Korea, "Admitting these 'homegrown' causes of the (Korean) crisis, it should be noted that they have not been home alone" (Kim 2001).

In my opinion, the Indonesian crisis developed from a combination of external shock in the currency markets as part of regional financial panic and weaknesses of the national economy, both in the financial and the real sectors. The twin structural weaknesses made the national economy vulnerable to external shocks.

The Indonesian experience showed that if either an external shock or domestic problem alone was at work, no crisis would have evolved. Indonesia had experienced shocks of both types that had not developed into a crisis. On both occasions, Bank Indonesia successfully acted to fight the shock in the foreign exchange markets, and crisis was thwarted.

The first was in January 1995. As an impact of the Mexican crisis or the "tequila effect", Indonesia experienced a dramatic surge in demand for the dollar in the foreign exchange market and the rupiah was depreciated more than normal. Within several days, Bank Indonesia intervened by selling dollars to the amount of US$580 million, and the rupiah was stabilized. All ASEAN monetary authorities put up a fight for the stability of their national currencies by actively intervening in the foreign exchange markets.[1]

It should be added here that, in September 1994, a couple of months before the Mexican peso crisis, Bank Indonesia widened the rates for intervention bands from 0.5 percentage points to 1.0 percentage point, or from 10 rupiah to a dollar to 20 rupiah. And when the market rushed to buy dollars, Bank Indonesia stood ready to meet the demand, including opening its office on Saturday.

In short, the shock in the Indonesian foreign exchange market from the Mexican crisis did not develop into a financial crisis because the policy response was effective.

In 1996, the Indonesia foreign exchange market was again undergoing some shocks. This time, the shock was a combination of domestic problems and adverse external developments. The market was experiencing disturbances due to public concern over the possible weakening of the Soeharto regime with the demise of Madame Tien Soeharto and the deterioration of the President's health in April 1996. This disturbing news came together with public concern over the implications of the strengthening of the yen, also known as *yendaka*, on the health of the national economy. Finally, real alarm spread in July

1996 when riots erupted in Jakarta following the burning of the National Democratic Party headquarters, the nationalist party headed by Megawati Soekarnoputri.

In July 1996 demand for the dollar surged strongly and the rupiah was under pressure. However, the rupiah was stabilized within several days. Bank Indonesia intervened in the market by selling dollars to the amount of US$800 million. Bank Indonesia widened the intervention bands in June 1996 from 3 to 5 percentage points or from 118 rupiah to 192 rupiah to a dollar.[2]

The strengthening of the yen against the dollar caused market concern in Indonesia due to its implications for Indonesia's foreign debt. In 1996, 40 per cent of Indonesia's public debt was denominated in yen. However, 80 per cent of Indonesia's foreign exchange earnings from exports were in dollars. The strengthening of the yen implied that Indonesia's debt in dollar terms rose with the appreciation.

A statement by the Minister of National Planning commenting on the precariousness of the national economy due to the *yendaka* served only to heighten market concern. And market reaction was predictable, raising demand for the dollar, which in turn brought pressure on the rupiah.[3]

In terms of debt management the part that has to be watched carefully is not the stock of the debt, which fluctuates with exchange rates. Debt management concentrates on debt flows, especially how much has to be spent for periodic debt repayments. Bank Indonesia had taken some precautions for debt repayment by holding more yen reserves. I made a public announcement about yen holdings by Bank Indonesia as part of the policy to stabilize the rupiah. In fact Bank Indonesia's yen holdings had been high because of this. In 1993 when I began my term, Bank Indonesia held Indonesia's official reserves of US$11.5 billion, of which 27 per cent was denominated in yen. In 1996, out of US$18 billion in official reserves, 36 per cent was in yen. This was very high, even for Asian countries. But it was dictated by the high dependence on yen debts.

In neither of the above cases did shocks in the foreign exchange markets develop into a fully blown crisis. Why was the baht crisis in early July 1997 any different?

I would argue that the external shock that struck in early July 1997 was qualitatively different. The baht's rapid depreciation was immediately followed by the depreciation of the currencies of the whole region because of world market players who perceived all economies in ASEAN as basically one.

I depicted what seemed to be happening in July 1997 as follows,

> The rapid downgrading of the region's sovereign credit ratings by international rating agencies fuelled the shift in market sentiment, triggering panic selling of foreign-owned local assets. In the media, the term 'Asian miracle' disappeared suddenly, to be replaced by 'Asian crisis' or 'Asian meltdown'. But the most telling sign was the Institute of International Finance's publication on capital flows for Thailand, Malaysia, Indonesia, the Philippines and South Korea. The estimates showed a reversal in flows of capital of US$105 billion in these five countries in a single year, from inflows of US$93 billion in 1996 to outflows of US$12 billion in 1997. For Indonesia alone, the reversed capital flow was estimated at US$22 billion, from inflows of US$10 billion to outflows of US$12 billion. This was indeed a financial panic in the Keynesian tradition, as explained by Kindleberger (Djiwandono 2000, p. 49).

What happened then in ASEAN economies was clearly a contagion. A shift of market sentiment triggered panic selling of local currency-denominated assets for dollars. It started from market reaction of foreign hedge funds and corporations selling their local currency-denominated assets for dollars. This was immediately followed by "flights to safety" from *domestic* corporations and individuals with money.

However, it is also true that the external shock itself need not have caused crisis of the magnitude that these countries suffered, if their domestic economic, social and political structures had been robust. When Indonesia's currency market shook, the national economy that was ridden with structural problems wobbled, and the shock rapidly transformed itself into crisis.

In turn, the economic crisis induced social and political crises due to the fact that they were already suffering from structural problems. The combination of external factors and domestic problems, including inconsistent policy responses, created a downward spiral of development, which ultimately made Indonesia the worst hit country in ASEAN.

It is also not very convincing to argue that the Indonesian crisis was caused merely by the weakness of its economic fundamentals. If the crisis was caused by weaknesses in its economic structures due to crony capitalism (Backman 2001) the immediate question would be, why did it begin only in July 1997? It is difficult to accept that structural problems caused by rampant practices of monopoly and oligopoly coupled with corruption, collusion and nepotism of ersatz capitalism (Yoshihara 1988) emerged only this late. It is also difficult to believe that market players only learned about the weaknesses of the Indonesian banking system in 1997.

There was a rising current account deficit for sure. However, compared to the current account deficits of other crisis-affected countries in Asia, Indonesia's current account deficit was not alarming. It was closer to 2.5 per cent of GDP from 1991 to 1995, and rose to 3.2 per cent in 1996. Indonesia's 1996 current account deficit was smaller than Thailand's (8.9 per cent) or Korea's (4.4 per cent), or even Malaysia's (4.4 per cent).

The rupiah was indeed overvalued but the question of whether a currency is overvalued or otherwise depends so much on how one measures it. Some studies showed a high degree of rupiah overvaluation prior to the crisis. However, in general the overvaluation of the rupiah also did not justify the very drastic correction that took place. Indonesia also was similar to other Asian countries in terms of its high savings rate. Indonesia was also not known for having a problem of budget deficits, even if one argued correctly that the state budget was not effectively balanced. Corruption, cronyism and collusion were also nothing new.

What about problems in the banking sector? The general public may not have known the extent and the nature of banking problems due to the lack of transparency, but they were no secret. In fact, since the closing of Bank Summa in 1992, problem loans and bad debts had become a regular item in parliamentary hearings with the Governor of the Central Bank and reported prominently in the media.

In May 1993 there was a leak that appeared in some newspapers. It was actually part of my report to President Soeharto containing a list of names of Indonesian corporations and individuals that had debt problems with their respective banks. This list looked like a *Who's Who* of Jakarta. In fact, both the Minister of Finance and myself as Governor of Bank Indonesia were dubbed as "dish washers" in reference to our having to solve the problem of corporate debt early in our terms.

From the above observation the argument for structural problems as the sole cause of the Indonesian crisis does not seem to be convincing. During the crisis, colleagues in academic circles often reminded me about my mistaken arguments, prior to the crisis, that Indonesia's overall condition was strong and different from other countries in the face of external shocks. In a way this is almost implying that I misled the public about the condition of our economic fundamentals.

A question that I kept being asked was, if our fundamentals were strong how come Indonesia suffered so much? To shed some light on this issue, I like to think that there is a different perception about what constitutes the macro fundamentals of an economy. I would argue that at least until the Asian crisis, macroeconomists generally thought about growth of national products, exports, current accounts, inflation rates, unemployment rates and several other macro indicators every time they talked about economic fundamentals.

I would even argue that, in general, macroeconomists did not include the state of the banking sector as an important item in economic fundamentals. Banking issues have traditionally been treated as microeconomics. This was even true for most academic definitions of economics. In other words, in a macroeconomic analysis, the workings and soundness of the banking sector had been assumed to be present, or taken for granted.

Only after the Asian crisis did economists explicitly acknowledge that the soundness of the banking sector should be included in the analysis of a national economy. Richard N. Cooper was one of the few mentioning this issue in his discussion of Steve Radelet and Jeffrey Sachs' paper on the Asian crisis (1998, pp. 75–80). Likewise, Manuel Guitian of the IMF also stated that monetary management in particular and macroeconomic management in general cannot be effective without the support of a sound banking or financial system (Enoch 1997, pp. 41–63).

It should be noted that in my capacity as a Governor of Bank Indonesia, I never made any claims orally or in writing, let alone in public, that the Indonesian banking sector was strong. The banking sector in Indonesia expanded tremendously in terms of mobilizing funds, giving loans and in promoting the growth of the business sector. However, I was very much aware of its weaknesses, structurally and institutionally. Instead, I reiterated on different occasions, in particular in formal speeches given at the annual bankers' dinners in front of Indonesia's banking community, that Indonesian banking was still plagued with structural as well as micro problems. I repeated many times that the banking sector in Indonesia was still consolidating. This was also the message I presented at international conferences, such as the one organized by the IMF in January 1997 in Washington (Enoch and Green 1997, pp. 335–49).[4]

Furthermore, although studies identifying characteristics of banking crises and distress for different countries had been conducted in the early 1990s by the IMF (Sundararajan and Balino 1991), the link between soundness of a banking system and macroeconomic policy had not been identified. Analyses that showed the close link between a sound banking system and effective monetary policy were conducted by the Fund and the World Bank only after mid-1990s (Lindgren 1996, Sheng 1996). The argument became more prominent and started to receive a hearing from policy-makers on the eve of the Asian crisis (Alexander 1997; Enoch 1997).

Since the crisis, it has become commonplace to argue that a sound banking sector is a sine qua non for effective monetary policy. The point I am making here is that the awareness of the need for a national economy to have a sound banking system for effective macroeconomic policies came too late for countries caught up in the Asian crisis. Macroeconomists like myself should have the intellectual humility to acknowledge this flaw, in the manner that Richard N. Cooper and Manuel Guitian have.

Varying degrees of public knowledge about structural weaknesses of other sectors in the national economy had also been present for quite some time in Indonesia. Structural problems in the real sector, including production, consumption, and investment activities were routinely discussed long before the crisis. All these activities had been known to suffer from monopolies and oligopolies, corruption, and other leakages.

Furthermore, public complaints concerning stifling political lives, injustice and other social ills, even though in general expressed vaguely or indirectly, had been common long before 1997.

In short, I would argue that partial analyses, whether using internationalist or structuralist arguments would not convincingly explain how the Indonesian crisis unfolded.

More recent studies have shown the peculiarity of the Indonesian crisis. L. Kaminsky of George Washington University argued in her recent study that the Asian crisis was similar to crises in Latin American countries as well as Nordic countries in 1980s (Kaminsky 1999). All these arose following a period of economic distress. However, she also found that the Indonesian case differed from both those of Thailand and Malaysia. Thailand is shown as a clear case of financial crisis that was preceded by weak macroeconomic indicators. In other words, Thailand's crisis supports the argument that domestic structural problems had caused a shift in market perception and thus financial panic. Applying several indicators as an early-warning system to over 100 financial crises in 20 countries, she showed that some variables predict well the onset of a financial crisis. However, she noted that development of these variables could not properly account for Indonesia's. Other studies include ones by Andrew Berg of the IMF (Berg 1999) and Morris Goldstein of the Institute for International Economics (Goldstein, Kaminsky and Reinhart 2000).

From Financial Shock to Total Crisis

The Indonesian crisis began with the financial panic that hit the region in early July 1997. The Indonesian foreign exchange markets operated in a national economy that was riddled with structural problems, within a rather unstable context. Due to many years of high economic growth that to a certain degree went hand in hand with improvements in social indicators, economic, social and political ills had been swept under the carpet.

Within days after the sharp depreciation of the baht, the rupiah suffered similarly. The baht was floated on 2 July 1997. Bank Indonesia followed suit by widening its intervention bands, from 8 per cent to 12 per cent or from 192 to 304 rupiah to US$1. This was done on 11 July 1997, the same day the central bank of the Philippines floated the peso.

The initial shock and policy response followed by market reaction rapidly turned into a devastating crisis in Indonesia, involving and impacting almost all aspects of life.

Market and public reactions towards the financial shocks as well as the policy responses by the government and the ensuing panic basically demonstrated the loss of public confidence in the national economy and financial sector. Market and the public lost their trust in the banking sector and all the associated financial infrastructures, in particular banking supervision and the legal institutions. Ultimately, the government lost its credibility in being able to manage the national economy.

Change of market sentiment

For a long period there had been optimism in the way society viewed the economic performance of Indonesia as a part of the general boom of the Asian economies. High economic growth and improvement of social indicators, such as the declining percentage of people living below the poverty line, had caused the World Bank to coin the phrase "Asian economic miracle" (World Bank 1993).

The long period of high growth was accompanied by rapid expansion of the financial sector. In the changing world of finance characterized by the free movement of capital, the rapid development of the financial sector in the emerging economies of Asia facilitated the increasing volume of capital inflows, in particular short-term funds. This had fuelled the development of economic bubbles in the property as well as capital markets.

A similar phenomenon of increasing short-term capital inflows had developed elsewhere. The debt crises of the developing countries in 1980s and the Mexican crisis in 1994/95 were also preceded by influxes of short-term capital into these economies.

It became clear after the crisis struck that, aside from their short-term nature, these capital inflows were dominated by unhedged corporate debt. This was true for Indonesia, but to a certain degree other crisis-hit countries as well. The influx of capital was induced by high economic growth. In addition the high mobility of capital arose from the herd behaviour of financial market players and the widening practice of securitization in the financial markets.

It is unfortunate that the new mode of financial intermediation in a freer condition of capital mobility that eases capital availability for the emerging economies has come together with loosening prudential attitudes of both creditors and debtors (Adams 1998). Here, the ways banks push their rules to their clients do not bind debtors. Like-wise, creditors are also freed from prudential requirements by bank supervision. In fact, securitization replaces banks as financial inter-mediaries. Corporations issue debt instruments and sell them to whoever is willing to buy, and receive funds in return.

Moral hazards for both parties had also pushed further careless corporate investment in too many risky activities. In my observation, moral hazard arises due to market perceptions that are not supported by facts. There is a popular contention that foreign creditors thought that host country governments provided some sort of guarantees to national corporations that committed themselves to receiving loans or to selling debt instruments. Based on this perception, so the argument goes, foreign creditors were willing to loan funds to Indonesian corporations, for instance. In my recollection there was never any implicit, let alone explicit, guarantees on corporate debts promised or provided by the Indonesian government.

Similarly, there is another contention that the market perceived that the government of Indonesia had basically pegged the rupiah in the manner of a fixed exchange system. This being the case, corporations never felt the need to protect themselves against foreign exchange risks. Based on this, corporations in Indonesia, which were highly leveraged already, kept increasing their foreign exposure, investing in risky projects using cheaper funds from foreign borrowings.

With the sudden shift in market sentiment from optimism to pessimism, international hedge funds operating in the region wanted to get out of the market. Foreign investors sold their local currency-denominated assets for dollars, creditors stopped giving new loans, refusing to rollover the existing loans, and withdrawing them instead. Credit lines and trade financing that used to be common practice between foreign banks and their national counterparts were stopped.

The herd instinct that had characterized the influx of capital into the emerging economies was repeated in reverse. Everyone wanted to be above the curve to cut their losses. Capital reversal was the most convincing argument for the actual workings of the financial panic during the Asian crisis.

The shift in market sentiment that induced capital reversals from foreign hedge funds was followed by domestic corporations and individuals acting in similar fashion, either motivated by cutting losses or transferring their assets to safety.

The change of market sentiment that triggered capital reversal was fuelled by media reports that overnight changed the news about Asian economies from "miracle" into chaos, crisis and meltdown.[5] But the devastating blow that convinced the market to shift its sentiments came from international ratings agencies, like Moody's and Standard & Poor's. The ratings agencies seemed to outdo each other in repeatedly down-grading sovereign and corporate ratings, sending the crisis countries into a nightmarish downward spiral of economic distress.

The Institute of International Finance (IIF) of Washington recorded drastic capital reversals in most Asian economies. The IIF report showed that, for the five countries most affected by the crisis in Asia, i.e. Thailand, South Korea, Indonesia, Malaysia and the Philippines, capital reversals went from US$93 billion inflows in 1996 to US$12 billion outflows in 1997. This constitutes a flow of capital reversal of US$105 billion in a single year. For Indonesia, capital reversal in 1997 was estimated to amount to US$22 billion.[6]

This huge volume of capital reversals proceeded in a contagious manner, starting from Thailand and followed by other economies in Southeast Asia. Proponents of the financial panic argument of the crisis used the capital reversals to support claims that the crisis originated from a shift of market sentiment, which spread due to the herd instinct of market players.

It is curious that this argument does not actually explain the cause for the change of market sentiment itself.[7] There have been studies identifying vulnerability factors (Kaminsky 1998; Kaminsky and Reinhart 1998; and Goldstein, Kaminsky and Reinhart 2000) that could have led to a change of market sentiment. For sure the change of market sentiment could have arisen from the market players' realization of the financial vulnerabilities, whether of the weak banking sector, the presence of crony capitalism, or faulty macroeconomic policy. This argument has been used to explain how the financial crisis started in Thailand. However, it does not fully explain why it started in early July 1997. Furthermore, even based on observing vulnerability factors, some studies could not claim that this explained the Indonesian crisis (Kaminsky 1999).

Even if one accepts that the shift in market sentiment was critical, further analysis is still needed to explain why the financial panic spread. The question is even more pertinent for Indonesia where macroeconomic conditions and initial policy responses were generally timely and prudent.

Let us observe the World Bank and other assessments of the impacts of the crisis on people's lives in Indonesia, as follows:[8]

- Very drastic rupiah depreciation. The spot market for foreign exchange shows that the rate for the US$ was 2,456 rupiah in mid-July 1997 and went up as high as 16,538 rupiah in mid-June 1998. This is more than a 70 per cent depreciation of the rupiah, which was much deeper than any other depreciation of Asian currencies.

- A very drastic economic growth reversal of 22 per cent in one year, from 8 per cent growth before the crisis to 13.8 per cent in 1998. Income per capita in dollar terms went down to half of the pre-crisis level.
- The rate of inflation went up from single digit pre-crisis to 80 per cent in 1998.
- Reversal of private capital flows of US$22 billion in a single year, from capital inflows of US$12 billion in 1997 to outflows of US$10 billion in 1998.[9] This amount is equivalent to one decade of private capital inflows between mid-1980s to mid-1990s.
- This devastation occurred at the time of a severe drought caused by El Niño that produced low rice yields and forest fires in several areas.
- The drop in oil prices adversely affected Indonesian export earnings.

Furthermore, the socio-political impacts were also devastating, including:

- Increase of unemployment rates, especially in the urban areas of Java, coupled with a substantial increase of the population living below poverty line: one estimate showed an increase from 11 per cent of total population to 40 per cent.
- A drastic increase of school drop-outs and its social implications such as increasing incidence of crime and prostitution.
- Social disintegration as shown by unrest in Jakarta and several other cities in May 1998 that included burning of houses and other properties, killings, looting and raping. The violent May riots were one of the blackest moments in Indonesia, in particular because of the ethnic implications as the majority of the victims were Indonesian Chinese.
- Some statistics showed that in a period of one year in 1998, there were around 2,000 student demonstrations, 1,300 social protests, more than 500 strikes by workers and more than 50 riots in Indonesia.[10]
- The social unrest peaked in May, resulting in the ending of more than thirty years of authoritarian rule of President Soeharto, when he resigned in disgrace on 21 May 1998.

Combination of external and domestic factors

The crucial question remains: Why did the financial panic triggering panic buying of the dollar occur only in July 1997?

Even the argument that the rupiah's depreciation was a form of market correction, because the rupiah was overvalued, does not explain why the actual depreciation was much larger than expected.

Before the crisis there were those who felt that the rupiah was overvalued, and that it was detrimental to Indonesian exports. This was usually accompanied by a proposal to depreciate the currency more than the trend of annual rupiah depreciation of between 3–5 per cent. This view had in general enjoyed support amongst World Bank staff in Jakarta. However, for a while there was also the opposite argument for appreciating rupiah. In general this argument received support from IMF staff who wrote reports on the institution's usual Article IV consultation.

Both arguments had supporters in Indonesia, but the general pre-crisis view in Indonesia was that the rupiah should be depreciated more, or that it was overvalued. This was due to the tendency of the public to favour export-led economic development arguments. However, no one would have proposed a 70 per cent depreciation of the rupiah!

It should be noted that the two contradictory policy implications actually originated from the same concept of foreign exchange determination, i.e. purchasing power parity. Basically, in a free international trading environment, a country that adopts a free or flexible exchange system should let the exchange rate of its currency be determined by the inflation differential between its own rate of inflation and that of its trading partners. In this context, the argument for further depreciation of the rupiah prior to the crisis saw the difference between Indonesia's rate of inflation and that of other countries; the United States' in particular, was mostly more than the 3–5 per cent. To be consistent with the purchasing power parity analysis, the depreciation of the rupiah had to be larger than the actual depreciation managed by Bank Indonesia.

Of course there were also technical problems such as which countries were to be included as Indonesia's trading partners. There was also another issue that the government never formally revealed what were the exact features of the managed floating exchange rate arrangement adopted.

The argument for appreciating the rupiah also originated from the same analysis. The difference was that, after identifying the inflation rate differential, those arguing for the appreciation of the rupiah focused the policy on addressing the inflation problem. It was hoped that the rupiah's appreciation would dampen the inflation rate, thus reducing its difference with trading partners. The argument for further depreciation concentrated more on current account transactions, and hoping to improve the export competitiveness, while the argument for appreciation focused on the capital account and its impact on money supply and inflation. By depreciation it was hoped that export competitiveness would increase. But the argument for rupiah appreciation had a similar objective, i.e. by reducing the inflation rate export competitiveness would also improve. The difference actually originates in the Keynesian and classical analyses of the balance of payments.

Before the 1997 crisis Indonesia had indeed been facing a macro-economic dilemma. On the one hand, the current account was suffering from a widening deficit, although not as large as that of Thailand, for example. On the other hand, the economy was also facing a high rate of capital inflows with inflationary implications. The first issue caused pressure for depreciating the currency, while the second suggested the reverse.

At times, the opposing policy stands on foreign exchange manage-ment as described above were associated with the rivalry between two sister institutions, the IMF and World Bank, both advising the Indonesian government. The Fund has generally been associated with policies to fight inflation and a monetary approach to the balance of payments, hence its bias for using currency appreciation. The World Bank, which deals with financing projects in the real sector, is believed to be biased towards using foreign exchange to maintain export competitiveness.

The government of Indonesia has had to face the implications of this rivalry in the form of conflicting advice. On occasion, I remarked, half jokingly, in front of my guests from the two institutions, "Why didn't you discuss this issue with your sister institution in Washington, before coming here with that confusing advice?"

One of the lessons from the Asian and other crises of 1997 and beyond has been the weakening of this polarization. The Asian crisis, more than any other single event, convinced many about the interconnections between micro- and the macroeconomy, financial issues, and the real sector including institutional infrastructure. In such conditions, partial approaches to the problems and disregard of the interrelationships would never able to produce satisfactory solutions.

In the globalization of finance, where the distinction between one financial instrument and another melts, either transformed into a new instrument or effectively arbitraged, the dichotomy between the real sector and the financial sector in Peter Drucker's terms (Drucker 1986) really took shape. Currency no longer exclusively functions as a means of transaction. In fact, it becomes a traded commodity. As a consequence, exchange rates between currencies, or the price of one currency in terms of another is no longer merely a function of international trade, or exports and imports.

Thus, managing the exchange rate based exclusively on its function to clear market demand and supply arising from exports and imports would also be erroneous because it does not reflect the actual workings of different factors in the market. Before the 1997 crisis, the daily volume of dollar trading in Indonesia was US$8 billion. This was much bigger than the daily volume of exports and imports of around US$250 million. This also shows that the major part of the dollar transactions were not for serving the financing of exports and imports. The demand for the dollar is to satisfy the financing for import of goods and services, debt repayments, transfers and other needs, including currency speculation. Hence, whether or not the spot price of the dollar reflects the need to maintain export competitiveness becomes a very complicated problem for exchange rate management.

The Indonesian crisis does not seem to fit either the description of an external financial panic or the domestic structural weaknesses of a crisis. It started with a financial shock arising from regionally contagious panic in the foreign exchange market, which caused a drastic depreciation of the rupiah. The initial shock, the policy responses and market reactions that followed themselves intertwined closely resulting in a multi-dimensional crisis.

Early Policy Responses

Band widening

Confronted with the financial panic in July 1997, the government took adjustment steps promptly, relying on the current adopted monetary and fiscal policies. The initial policy response was to widen the central bank intervention band in the foreign exchange market from 8 per cent to 12 per cent, or from 192 rupiah to 304 rupiah, the same day the Philippines peso was floated, on 11 July 1997.

After the last devaluation of the rupiah in 1986, Indonesia had adopted a managed foreign exchange technique by setting up a band of exchange rates to guide Bank Indonesia when to intervene in the market. The band was managed with a view to allow creeping depreciation such that the rupiah was neither over- nor under-valued.

Within this mechanism, the intervention band had occasionally been widened by the central bank. From January 1994 to September 1996, the band was widened six times, from the initial narrow band of 0.5 per cent to 8 per cent (Table 2). Indonesia adopted a regime that was similar to a crawling band, as practiced then by Chile, Columbia and Israel (Williamson 1996). However, in Williamson's definition of a country formally practising a crawling band, the band had to be equal to or larger than 10 per cent, or plus and minus 5 per cent around the mid-rate.

The decision to widen Band Indonesia's intervention band in July 1997 was part of the eclecticism that I introduced in the central bank since joining in March 1993. It had been my contention that in the midst of the globalization of the Indonesian economy, there were so many uncertainties. And the challenge facing the central bank in monetary management was to minimize uncertainties that were sometimes embedded in the implementation of government policy.

TABLE 2
Bank Indonesia's Intervention Band (1992–97)

Dates of Widening	Before (Rupiah)	Per cent	After (Rupiah)	Per cent
16 Sep 1992	6	0.25	10	0.50
3 Jan 1994	10	0.50	20	1.00
5 Sep 1994	20	1.00	30	1.50
30 Jun 1994	30	1.50	44	2.00
29 Dec 1995	44	2.00	66	3.00
13 Jun 1996	66	3.00	118	5.00
11 Sep 1996	118	5.00	192	8.00
11 July 1997	192	8.00	304	12.00

Source: Bank Indonesia

In monetary management, it is important that the central bank avoids shock therapy, including avoiding currency devaluation. I felt that monetary management should be conducted with some flexibility and changes should be done in a measured way through small steps. I took the cue from observing what Alan Greenspan seemed to be doing with his brand of monetary management.[11]

An eclectic management of foreign exchange was designed around the creation of a realistic exchange rate for the rupiah through a managed floating with creeping depreciation, which in effect was the adoption of a crawling band technique. In fact, the managed floating principle was initially adopted in the late 1970s. However, the rupiah exchange rate was more managed than floated but since 1993, the rupiah had been more floated than managed, through discretionary band widening.

The implementation of a managed floating system with a crawling band actually indicates that the policy is allowing the currency exchange rate to fluctuate more freely over time. The wider the band, the bigger the spread between buying and selling before the central bank has an obligation to intervene. Every time a decision to widen the band was made, it was stated that the central bank was giving the market more freedom to determine the spot rate of the currency.[12] By widening the band the central bank clearly signalled the development of the foreign exchange inter-bank market. In turn, it signalled that the central bank wanted to withdraw from the spot market for foreign exchange. In fact, though no specific time frame was mentioned, the direction of the policy was towards a flexible exchange system (Henderson 1998, p. 130).[13]

In this manner, the rupiah rate was managed to make it stay at a realistic level. With a view to maintaining export competitiveness on the one hand, and the fact that there were a variety of motives that drive the demand for foreign exchange, a realistic exchange rate for the rupiah in terms of the dollar or other currencies was hard to gauge. Granted that the concept was not clear-cut, the aim of exchange rate management, then, was to guard the rupiah against overvaluation that could endanger export or under-valuation that could induce capital flight.

The demand for foreign exchange arises from the need to finance imports, debt repayments and other types of financing, while its supply comes from export activities as well as other sources of foreign exchange. The two parties meet in the foreign exchange market. The spread between the selling rate and the buying rate represents the transaction risk, which is usually small.

The intervention band represents the differential rates or the spread between the rate that the central bank has the obligation to buy and to sell foreign exchange in the market. The lower level of the band is the rate that the central bank would buy foreign exchange, while the upper level of the band is the rate that the central bank has to sell foreign exchange in the market.

In this mechanism, the decision to widen the band implies that the central bank would only have the obligation to buy and sell foreign exchange at a wider spread. Bank Indonesia was therefore consistently making the band wider between 1994–97 to give a signal to the market that the private sector should rely less and less on the central bank for their foreign exchange needs. The demand for foreign exchange should rely more on their counterparts in the market, and not on Bank Indonesia, in the form of rupiah liquidity in the inter-bank market. In other words, the policy was also in support of the creation of a foreign exchange market among businesses in the private sector.

Foreign exchange demand and supply had indeed been conducted among different market players of the private sector. This had also been the case with respect to the inter-bank money market, which efficiently clears the market demand for liquidity and its supply. The spread between the buying and selling rates of foreign exchange had been narrow, like the interest rate in the inter-bank money market. However, during the crisis, due to market uncertainties and a loss of confidence in the supply of foreign exchange in the spot market, banks refused to provide liquidity to other banks, even if they were able to do so.

Exchange rate management based on the technique of managed floating in practice was not only aimed at maintaining export competitiveness or controlling inflation. In fact, there were three areas of consideration. They included the condition of domestic and foreign money markets, interest rate and inflation rate differentials between Indonesia and her trading partners, and macro indicators of development, in particular the magnitude of capital flows.[14] However, insufficient relevant data made the implementation of a policy that properly incorporating consideration of all these factors very difficult.

The widening of the intervention band in 11 July 1997 was widely praised and positively received by the market. The policy was praised by delegates to the CGI (Consultative Group on Indonesia) meeting in Tokyo, which was convened in mid-July 1997.[15] The steps taken by the Indonesian government were considered to be timely in the face of financial panic in the region. The move was even considered to be preemptive, considering that the pressure on the foreign exchange market was not very strong yet.

However, widening the band very soon proved ineffectual in the face of the onslaught of dollar demand in the foreign exchange market throughout Southeast Asia. It was ironic that almost immediately after the CGI meeting that lauded its early moves, Bank Indonesia was forced to intervene in the market to defend the rupiah.

In fact, Bank Indonesia together with the Ministry of Finance were soon engrossed with efforts to fight the crisis At Bank Indonesia, I organized daily meetings with members of the Board, directors and staff in charge of the monetary sector, payments system and banking supervision. These Board meetings were conducted twice a day, in the morning prior to the opening of the foreign exchange market and in the evening, after its closing. The morning meeting was called "morning call", and the evening meeting "evening call".

The morning call was aimed at preparing the steps to be taken during the day, while the evening call was to monitor the current day's problems and developments. Morning and evening calls were conducted from late July 1997, and continued for several weeks after my departure from Bank Indonesia in mid-February 1998. On many occasions the meetings were also held on Saturdays and Sundays. During this period, except for emergency matters, I did not allow members of the Board and directors to leave Jakarta. I did not leave Jakarta, except for a bilateral meeting with Bank Negara Malaysia on the weekend of 8–10 August 1997, the annual meeting of the World Bank and IMF in Hong Kong, 19–23 September 1997, and a knee operation in Singapore, 2–8 January 1998. During the recuperation period I managed to have a meeting with the Board in Jakarta through a conference call.

On 2 July 1997 panic buying of dollars in Bangkok which had been going on for several days had forced the Thai government to abandon its fixed system of foreign exchange, and change it into a floating system. The Philippines followed suit on 11 July 1997, and Malaysia on 14 July 1997. By mid-July Indonesia became the only country that had not adopted a floating system.

The escalation of financial panic in Indonesia has not been studied carefully. However, it is most likely that foreign fund managers were the first to dump their rupiah assets for dollars. The domestic market players then followed their foreign counterparts by selling rupiah assets for dollars.

Several factors support the above argument. First, by this time Indonesia was the only country in the region to have a managed peg foreign exchange regime. The rupiah was an attractive currency for profit taking. The market players used Bank Indonesia's selling rate as their target for testing the central bank's next move.

Second, on the previous occasions of band widening, initially the rupiah had appreciated. In fact, before the 11 July 1997 decision, the spot rate was always close to Bank Indonesia's buying rate or the lower limit of the band. The tendency showed that the market generally did not make any moves that could be detected as defying central bank policy, and there were no market disturbances.

It was generally accepted that the herd behaviour of Indonesian market players was high. Domestic fund managers followed, sometime belatedly, the actions of their foreign colleagues. The domestic reaction towards the widening of the band on 11 July was following past patterns. Due to expectations that the rupiah would appreciate, they reacted to the policy by buying rupiah, not knowing that their foreign colleagues were reacting differently. The foreign players bought dollars immediately after the central bank widened the band instead. The foreign players made this decision because they were already well informed about what had been developing regionally. All regional currencies were already under attack at this time. The dollar was appreciated immediately as a result. With the dollar appreciation, the domestic players were forced to unload their rupiah to cut their losses. What happened afterwards is history.

So, contrary to the past, the dollar was appreciated right away after the band widening. In fact, the spot rate of the dollar went up so rapidly that within a few days the spot rate hit through Bank Indonesia's selling rate. The market did not believe any longer in the effectiveness of Bank Indonesia's current policy of managed floating. The policy that had effectively defended the rupiah's stability against financial shock in January 1995 and again in July 1996 proved hopeless in July 1997.

In accordance with the rule of the managed floating regime, Bank Indonesia had to intervene in the market when the market rate for foreign exchange hit the upper side of the band, or the selling rate. The central bank executed its intervention policy, initially by selling the dollar forward. However, when the rupiah kept depreciating, the central bank started to intervene in the spot market, either through brokers or state banks.

From the third week of July to mid-August the central bank spent US$1.5 billion on market intervention. The central bank's effort to halt the rupiah's drastic depreciation proved futile. Financial market developments in the region around this period clearly showed a similar pattern. The depreciation of the Singapore dollar, Malaysian ringgit, Philippine peso and the rupiah would immediately follow, i.e. a shock that caused baht depreciation. Any attack on a currency in the local market would immediately lead to an attack on other currencies regionally.

The regional nature of the financial crisis or the contagious process of the financial panic has now been generally recognized. However, due to the drastically declining credibility of the Soeharto government since mid-1997, the government's explanations about the regional nature of the currency depreciation were generally ignored.

Even basically sound national economies were affected. The fate of Singapore dollar was definitely influenced by the regional currency disturbances. The Hong Kong dollar was also under pressure in October 1997, when some hedge funds attacked the dollar via the equities market. However, since fundamentally the national economies in these two countries were sound, the regional contagion that did some damage to the stability of both currencies did not cause their collapse. Hong Kong successfully defending its fixed system through monetary tightening that briefly sent inter-bank rates sky-high.

Rupiah float that shocked the market

Pressure on the rupiah and other currencies in the region continued in late July and early August. Confronted with contagious pressure that made the rupiah vulnerable, the government decided to float the rupiah on 14 August 1997.

The term "free float" is of course meant to distinguish it from a managed float. At the announcement of the government's decision, the press asked me whether Bank Indonesia would abandon its intervention to stabilize the rupiah. I told the journalists that in practice there is no pure flexible exchange system. Of course, with the new system, theoretically the obligation of the central bank to intervene in the market was gone. There is no longer any legal level as a target that obligates the central bank to intervene in the market. I said that, since it was not a freely floating or flexible exchange system, if one wanted to be specific about terms, then we could call it a "managed floating without band". What was actually different in terms of Bank Indonesia operations was that the central bank no longer made daily announcements on the foreign exchange buying and selling rates after 14 August 1997.

However, Bank Indonesia has occasionally intervened in the market. This is actually just to describe the central bank action for selling foreign exchange in the market. Of course, there is no longer any obligation for Bank Indonesia to do so since there are no upper or lower ceilings that obligates the central bank to intervene in the market every time the band hits the spot rate. The selling of foreign exchange by Bank Indonesia after the rupiah float was not aimed at forcing the rate to a certain level, but to slow the rate of depreciation and to guard against adverse implication of a drastic depreciation. Furthermore, after the banking sector suffered from the drastic rupiah depreciation, banks were no longer willing to supply foreign exchange in the market. Bank Indonesia had to supply some foreign exchange for different purposes. The central bank's sale of foreign exchange was perceived as intervention.

I announced the new policy at the end of an address to an international conference on capital markets, organized by Security Commission (Bapepam) together with the Jakarta Security Exchange (BEJ) at the Jakarta Hilton on 14 August 1997. The conference was attended by over a thousand businesspersons, both domestic and foreign.

I stated that, by lifting the crawling band, the monetary authorities would leave foreign exchange trading in the hands of the market players. The market players had to bear the risks associated with foreign exchange trading, and not the central bank. Market players could trade and speculate, but do so at their own risk.

During the ensuing informal questions and answer session, there were businesspersons and journalists who wanted to press me with related questions. There was one instance that indicated the confusion and dismay of the Indonesian business community with the government decision to float the currency. A group of businesspersons posed a question that gave me a clear picture of a much bigger problem. "Mr. Governor, how could you do this (abolishing the intervention band)?" The question or complaint continued, "We were used to the band that Bank Indonesia managed nicely by a crawling depreciation of 4–5 per cent annually that all of us could work with in conducting our business". I could vaguely catch the tone of desperation, however, I tried to sound convincing by shooting back with another question, "Don't you cover (by hedging) your foreign exposures?" The implicit answer that was given was "of course not".

This discussion gave me real first hand information about market reaction to the floating of the rupiah. This issue would linger developing into one of the major factors that deepened and broadened the Indonesian crisis, i.e. the unsustainable amount of short-term corporate debt denominated in foreign currencies.

The fact that businesspeople accepted Bank Indonesia's policy of a crawling band had been based on market perception that, contrary to the basic tenet of managed floating, the business community perceived the system as a pegged or fixed system. Corporations were willing to work on a creeping depreciation with a creeping band widening. In their calculation accepting the risk from the widening spread of the managed floating was still better than paying the cost of hedging. This way of reasoning is good for the moral hazard argument.

The decision to float the currency freely should be looked at in its relation to the managed floating regime. Basically, by widening the intervention band in stages, the central bank signalled the market about its intention to gradually retreat from playing an active role in the foreign exchange market. Bank Indonesia was letting the market work to clear the demand and supply of foreign exchange, in a similar way as the inter-bank money market for the rupiah. Bank Indonesia stepped into the market only when imbalances arose.

This is not to say that the decision to float the rupiah in mid-August was made on the basis of a well-defined plan. However, the logical sequence of a crawling band with the band continuously being widened tends towards a flexible exchange rate regime.

But, then, how was the decision to abandon managed floating made? I would like to underline that a flexible exchange system or a free-floating exchange system implies that the monetary authority tolerates the rate to fluctuate without limit. The Monetary Board assessed that all the steps that had been taken to stabilize the rupiah thus far had not worked. Bank Indonesia's intervention in the market in support of the widening of the band, despite its impact on depleting the international reserves, had also proven ineffective. The depreciation of rupiah from mid-July to the second week of August was close to 20 per cent, despite Bank Indonesia's intervention in the market during the period which used up a little over US$1.5 billion worth of foreign reserves. The intervention was mostly in the form of forward sales of the dollar. Limited sales of the dollar in the spot market and swap transactions were also conducted.

During this period meetings in the Monetary Board were conducted more often than normal, twice or thrice, and sometimes more a week. The Monetary Board, which was officially chaired by the Minister of Finance, usually conducting the meeting in the office of the Minister Coordinator of Economic and Finance. The regulars at these meetings were the Ministers of Finance, Trade and Industry, State Secretariat, the government Economic Advisers and the Governor of Bank Indonesia. Usually, preparations for matters related to economics, fiscal, finance and banking were done through a series of meetings at this forum. Policy recommendations or decisions and their implementation supported by necessary documents, were at a later stage reported and discussed with the President. Decisions were made, generally, after going through him. Sometimes decisions were made for immediate implementation. Otherwise, they went through Cabinet meetings, which were conducted once a month.

Confronted with the drastic rupiah depreciation, the Monetary Board held discussions on whether to freely float the currency or to widen the band further. The idea of further widening the band was put forward as one alternative, with a view to the fact that the European exchange rate mechanism (ERM) had a very wide band of 30 per cent (Wlliamson 1996, p. 21).

The decision to float was ultimately taken by President Soeharto in a meeting at his residence, on 13 August 1997. Members of the Monetary Board went to see the President to report on the latest developments, including efforts taken by Bank Indonesia to defend the rupiah.

I presented the case that everything that had been done to defend the slide of our currency seemed to be futile. I also mentioned that we would not be able to defend the rupiah's slide with the current policy. The reserves that Bank Indonesia managed at the time, though at a comfortable level in a normal situation, would not be sufficient to confront market pressures. I reported that, from the discussions in the Monetary Board there were two alternatives, to widen the band further or to float freely altogether. I explained the different features and implications between the two alternatives. After some discussion between members of the Monetary Board and the President, he decided on going all the way to float the rupiah.

It had become a practice for the government to announce rate changes, etc. through Bank Indonesia's daily announcement in the Central Bank dealing room. Indeed, Bank Indonesia did not hold any special press conferences. Journalists protested this procedure, because they only learned about changes of the rate, including the intervention band, from the market. The simple reason was that if announcements about exchange rate changes were to be done through press conferences, the possibility of leaks were high, which could be detrimental to the market.

However, the public announcement about the government decision on floating the rupiah, as mentioned before, was done on the morning of 14 August 1997. Towards the end of my speech in a conference on capital markets, I broke the news that since that morning the government started to implement a new system of exchange, a free-floating one.

There was a little incident after I finished my speech. So many journalists wanted me to discuss the new policy that they practically blocked my exit from the room adjacent to the auditorium where the conference was held. I was only released from the blockade to go back to the office after making a promise to the journalists that I would hold a press conference sometime later that afternoon. Late that afternoon I answered questions and explained how the exchange rate policy had changed from a managed floating to a free floating one.

In terms of foreign exchange reserve management, the decision to adopt a free float was a prudent policy to save the reserves held by the central bank. The IMF and many analysts lauded the government's decision to adopt a free floating system. However, the decision in effect put the private sector in a precarious position.

The government's decision in effect revealed one of the weaknesses of the private sector, i.e. the unsustainable amount of corporate debt denominated in foreign exchange. The moral hazard arose from the private sector's perception that the government would always come to their rescue. The private sector's perception was that the exchange system was basically a pegged system. Thus, it expected that Bank Indonesia would intervene to rescue the falling rupiah.

In this respect, putting the blame on the foreign exchange regime as perceived by the market by way of a moral hazard argument could be inconsistent. The argument is that due to the moral hazard arising from the pegged or fixed exchange system, the private sector relied heavily on foreign exchange denominated debts in financing their businesses. The financial panic argument of the crisis stated that the reason for financial panic was the market view that the government would not be able to defend the pegged system.

I have difficulty in following the argument that, on the one hand the private sector or the market players are assumed to trust the government so much that they expect to be rescued in case they ran into currency problems. On the other hand, the same argument relying on moral hazard assumes that that the private sector has no confidence in the government's ability to defend the pegged system, and hence the financial panic. The loss of confidence in the government's ability to support the perceived fixed system implies the inability to rescue the private sector with respect to foreign exchange exposure.

Similarly, there is an assumption about market perception that the government guarantees, at least implicitly, the private sector's external debts. Some studies argue that the accumulation of private sector debts in foreign exchange prior to the crisis was due to the explicit or implicit guarantee provided by the government.

I have to admit that I do not know how this perception arose in the minds of Indonesian or foreign businesspersons or that one would assume that it existed. If there was any explicit guarantee from the government, I am sure this was not a policy that generally applied to the private sectors' debts. If there was any implicit government guarantee on corporate external debt I, for sure, cannot identify its source. I am amazed at the way Indonesian businesspersons appeared to have the perception that Indonesia's exchange system prior to the crisis was a fixed system. It is even more difficult for me to understand the claim that in Indonesia there was, at least implicitly, a guarantee on corporate external debt prior to the crisis.

Coming back to the issue of international reserves management, one reason for floating the rupiah was acknowledging the impossibility of neutralizing the pressure on the currency by intervention in the current policy set up. The decision was to safeguard the international reserves, which would have been wiped out by the onslaught in the market had the current system continued. The experience of Thailand clearly showed this.

A valid claim could be made that the steps taken by the government did indeed save the international reserves from rapid depletion. The international reserves held by Bank Indonesia, even if one uses the Bank's more prudent definition, never went lower than US$11.98 billion, the amount of the reserves at the start of my tenure as governor, in March 1993. The definition of official international reserves is very close to what the Fund terms Net International Reserves (NIR). If gross concept of reserve is used, the amount would be much bigger.

Indonesia's reserves early in the crisis, or at the time the government asked for a stand-by loan, was much better than Thailand's. Thailand entered into an agreement with the Fund for a stand-by arrangement (SBA) in August 1997, Indonesia in November 1997, and Korea in December 1997.

Thailand's reserves in August 1997 were reported at US$28.6 billion. However, this was excluding a forward sale of US$29.4 billion. Korea's reserves in December 1997 were US$9.1 billion.[16] Indonesia's reserves at the signing of the first letter of intent was US$19 billion (Table 3). Indonesia's reserve position at the time of its application for the Fund's support was much better than Thailand's as well as Korea's. This showed that the foreign reserve management that was entrusted to Bank Indonesia was more prudent than either Thailand or Korea.

By this time all the currencies of the neighbouring countries were already floated. In this situation, being the only country in the region that officially practiced managed floating left the rupiah exposed to profit-takers operating in the region. Efforts to defend the rupiah's stability became more difficult, especially due to the general assessment of the market players who put the regional economic conditions in a single basket at this time. With market perceptions that the regional economies were unstable, there was panic buying of the dollar. Even the Hong Kong

TABLE 3
Indonesia's Official Reserves

Date	Official Reserves (US$ billion)
Jan 93	11,77
Mar 93	11,98
Jan 94	12,42
Jan 95	12,97
Jan 96	14,79
Jan 97	19,83
July 97	21,10
Aug 97	20,40
Sep 97	20,05
Oct 97	19,10
Nov 97	18,95
Dec 97	17,42
Jan 98	14,03*
Feb 98	12,46*
Mar 98	13,18*

Note: * Net International Reserves (NIR)
Source: Bank Indonesia.

and Singapore dollars were hit. Confronted with this environment, maintaining a managed currency float with a band ran the risk of losing precious foreign reserves. Thus, saving international reserves was an important motivation for the decision to float the rupiah.

With hindsight, the decision to float the rupiah saved the government foreign exchange reserves from fast depletion. But, at the same time, the decision put the corporate sector in trouble. It revealed the weakness of the private sector caused by excessive risk-taking that resulted in property- and equity-cum-debt bubbles. These management and governance problems of the private sector may be argued as having been caused by debatable macroeconomic policy and public sector governance problems.

The floating system freed Bank Indonesia from its responsibility to intervene in the foreign exchange market. However, this did not free the central bank from its responsibility to maintain the stability of the rupiah. Efforts to defend the rupiah from drastic depreciation were also done from the demand side of the foreign exchange market. The monetary authorities tightened liquidity using three means: Bank Indonesia raised the rates of interest on its own certificates (SBIs) of different maturities by doubling the rates;[17] the Ministry of Finance joined the efforts by instructing state enterprises to transform their bank deposits into SBIs; it also instructed them to cut budgetary expenditures. These steps were taken starting several days after the floating of the rupiah. In mid-July 1997 Bank Indonesia already made a move to close one window that was normally used by commercial banks to raise liquidity when needed by stopping the practice of purchasing short-term certificates from commercial banks (SBPUs).

Toward the end of August 1997 Bank Indonesia also issued a new regulation to limit the size of forward sales of foreign exchange against the rupiah to a maximum of US$5 million for non-resident clients of national banks. Transactions for financing investments, exports and imports were excluded from the limit. Basically, the rule was to try limiting the availability of financing means for currency speculation.

I have been expressing my reservations about resorting to shock therapy in monetary management. I belong to those monetary economists who believe that the monetary sector has to serve the real sector so that it should limit additional uncertainty that could arise from the policies or their implementation. In this respect, the policy to transform bank deposits into SBIs was very effective in reducing liquidity. However, the forced reduction of liquidity from withdrawal of deposits adversely impacted banks, especially those that were already experiencing liquidity pressures. The decision was a repeat of what was done by the previous Minister of Finance, J.B. Sumarlin in 1991 (Binhadi 1995, p. 138). The policy had since been nicknamed "Sumarlin shock".

The liquidity squeeze through monetary, fiscal and banking measures a few weeks following the rupiah float might have been more than necessary. There have been studies on the ineffectiveness of a high rate of interest as a means for currency stabilization, amongst others, a study by Prof. I.J. Azis (Azis 2001). Furthermore, a heavy toll seemed to be clearly shown in its impact on the banking sector.

Banking in distress

The liquidity squeeze through different measures was meant to support other measures for defending the rupiah that was under attack together with other currencies in the region. However, the liquidity squeezes ultimately adversely impacted the banking sector as the major means of intermediation in the national payment system. The scarcity in liquidity as reflected in abnormally high interest rates began to complicate banking operations, especially those that were already not sound.

The Indonesian banking sector prior to the financial crisis was suffering from a variety of structural weaknesses, such as capital deficiency, a high percentage of non-performing loans (NPLs), and weak compliance of prudential regulation, especially on legal lending limits, and weak governance. Furthermore, Indonesia's banking sector was also characterized by weak financial institutions, especially banking supervision and regulation, a weak legal and judiciary system, and general lack of transparency and poor corporate governance.

All these weaknesses made the banking sector vulnerable in the face of the regional financial panic and in the face of the government's stringent policy to defend the currency. It is debatable whether the weak banking sector caused the Indonesian crisis or the whether the crisis made Indonesia's banking sector weak. Of course banking statistics and reports on banks' compliance to the prudential measures showed that the Indonesian banking sector was unsound on the eve of the financial crisis.[18]

Before the crisis, the Indonesian banking sector was characterized by the general tendency of liquidity imbalances among the commercial banks due to past policies and banking practices. State banks, seven altogether, in general experienced liquidity surpluses due to their privileged position that made them major recipients of deposits. Until the liberalization in the 1980s, there was government instruction that public sector funds — funds belonging to state enterprises and funds from the budget — had to be deposited with state banks. There was also a general perception that the state banks gave better protection to deposits and savings. The private national banks, foreign banks and joint-venture banks, on the contrary, had the tendency to experience liquidity deficits. The inter-bank money market was generally characterized by demand for liquidity arising from the privately-owned banks supply from the state banks.

From the early days of banking liberalization in 1983 to the eve of the financial crisis, Indonesian banking experienced remarkable development, characterized by rapid growth of fund mobilization in deposits and savings, banking credits and the development of other financing instruments. After the liberalization of rules for new banks in 1988, the number of main banks and their branches also rose rapidly, especially between 1988 to 1994 (Table 4).

TABLE 4
Number of Banks before Crisis

	1983	1988	1993	1997 (June)
State	7	7	7	7
Private national	72	66	161	160
Foreign and joint venture	11	11	39	44
Provincial govt.	27	27	27	27
Non-bank financial Institutions	13	13	0	0
Total	**130**	**124**	**234**	**238**

Source: Bank Indonesia.

The rapid increase in bank loans had been stimulated by the rapid growth in demand for financing for investment, trading, as well as consumption, resulting in respectable GDP growth for more than two decades. It was also pushed by government policy that was generally pro-growth. Banking policy was clearly supporting the rapid increase in bank loans.

In 1983 the government reduced the reserve requirement for banking from 30 per cent of total bank deposits to 15 per cent. And in 1988 the reserve requirement was further lowered to 2 per cent of total bank deposits (see Table 5).[19] Furthermore, banks did not have to deposit the funds allocated for reserve requirements with Bank Indonesia. They could put the funds in their own vaults. This rule was later changed in December 1995. The regulation clearly meant to push bank lending for financing economic activities and national development. To support monetary policy for stability, banks should invest their excess liability in Bank Indonesia certificates (SBI).

In general, funds that had been effectively mobilized by the banking sector had been mostly used for bank lending, which had been growing rapidly prior to the crisis. The inter-bank money market had also been working well. Partly due to government policy, a pattern seemed to be established whereby some banks usually had surplus liquidity while other groups were in deficit. This seemed to create an inter-bank money market that worked well in the pre-crisis period. However, the liquidity squeeze that the monetary authorities launched adversely impacted the

TABLE 5
Pre-Crisis Monetary and Banking Policy

Date of Issuance	Main Features
1983 (June 1)	• Abolishment of credit ceiling for banks • Reduction of central bank liquidity credits • **Liberalization of banks' lending rates** • **Reduction of reserve requirement from 30 per cent of total deposits to 15 per cent**
1988 (October 27)	• **Liberalization of bank licensing** • Liberalization of bank branching and freer activities for banks and non-banking institutions • Simplified foreign exchange licensing procedures • Liberalization of licensing for money changers • **Further reduction of reserve requirement for banks and non bank-banking financial institution, from 15 per cent of total deposits to 2 per cent** • Banks had to invest 80 per cent of their excess liquidity in Bank Indonesia certificates (SBI)
1990 (January 29)	• **Limitation of central bank liquidity credits for government programmes;** self-sufficiency in rice programme, development of cooperative movement at the village level and farmers' enterprises • Stipulation for banks to allocate 20 per cent of their credits for small-scale enterprises • The development of banks and non-banking financial institutions as means for supporting national payment system and the central bank as the guardian of monetary policy and banking supervision
1991 (February 28)	• **Improvement of banking supervision**, including more stringent requirements for bank owners, management and commissioners of banks, with a view to professionalism and moral integrity • **Adoption of BIS standard on prudential measures, with a view to using band yardstick on measuring bank soundness by monitoring the capital adequacy ratio, assets quality, management, efficiency and liquidity (CAMEL)**

TABLE 5 (*continued*)
Pre-Crisis Monetary and Banking Policy

Date of Issuance	Main Features
1992 (March)	• **The enactment of the new banking law, Law of the Republic of Indonesia No. 7 of 1992 concerning Banking:** Improvement of banking regulation over Law number 14/1967
1993 (May 29)	• **Incentive to raise bank lending** to fight economic sluggishness • Improvement of various prudential measures, like CAR calculation, provisions for bad debts, rules on credits to SMS, and on legal lending limit
1994 (March)	• **Special audit for banks with problem loans** • **Banks having large percentage of problem loans were required to set up their own team dealing with problem loans** • Bank Indonesia set up a forum dealing with problem loans and bad debts, comprising of the Chairman of the Supreme Court, the Attorney General, the Minister of Finance, the Minister for National Land, and the Governor of Bank Indonesia. One of the important decisions was to limit the court settlement of bad debts to 6 months. • BI issued rules on minimum standards that had to be followed by banks in their lending. BI also issued rules on internal audit for banks. • Bank Indonesia issued instruction for banks having sizeable problem loans to exercise bank restructuring, including the possibility for merger and sale to interested investors • **Rules for banks to submit their annual credit plan, including credit for property to the central bank** • Advancing concept of self-*regulatory* banking and the use of *moral suasion* • Combining on-*site* and *off-site supervision* • BI enforced its authority to determine the allowable amount for each bank to borrow internationally. The total amount of allowable foreign borrowing is determined with a view to the balance of payments position.

TABLE 5 (*continued*)
Pre-Crisis Monetary and Banking Policy

Date of Issuance	Main Features
1994 (September)	• Widening of intervention band, from Rp 20 to Rp 30 per US$1 • BI announcement of conversion rate was moved from morning daily to afternoon • Raising the percentage of *Net open position* (NOP) from 20 per cent of bank capital to 25 per cent
1995 (January)	• BI intervened in the foreign exchange market to defend the rupiah that was under pressure from the "tequila effect" by selling US$580 million
1995 (June)	• Widening of intervention band from Rp 30 to Rp 44 per US$1
1995 (December)	• **BI raised the reserve requirement from 2 per cent to 3 per cent of third party funds in the bank, with an obligation for banks to put the funds in their Bank Indonesia accounts. The calculation of bank's reserve requirement was changed from once a week to once a day.** • **Signing bilateral agreements of repurchase on securities**, with the central banks of Malaysia, Singapore, Thailand, Hong Kong, Australia and the Philippines, respectively. The objective of the arrangements was to build deterrents against speculation on foreign exchange trading • BI assisted the Ministry of Finance in supervising non-bank financial institutions • Widening intervention band from Rp 44 to Rp 66 per US$1 • BI issued instruction for banks to exclusively use their foreign loans for providing export credit
1996 (April)	• Improving the national payment system toward an integrated system that would be safe and credible.
1996 (June)	• Widening of intervention band from Rp 66 to Rp 118 per US$1

TABLE 5 (*continued*)
Pre-Crisis Monetary and Banking Policy

Date of Issuance	Main Features
1996 (July) 1996 (September)	• **The sale of US$400 million Yankee bonds in the US markets. The bonds bore coupons of 7.75 per cent, which was equivalent to 100 basis pints above T-notes.** The sale was aimed at providing a benchmark for sales of Indonesian corporate bonds. • Widening of intervention band from Rp 118 to Rp 192 per US$1. A spread between buying and selling rate that was widened from 5 per cent to 8 per cent
1996 (December)	• BI introduced a rediscount facility for banks with export documents of priority commodity exports • Introduction of rediscount facility for local L/Cs
	• **The issuance of Government Decree number 68, 1996 that provided rules on Bank Liquidation.**
1996 (December)	• There were two important rules that would better facilitate bank closure. First, in the process of liquidation, the liquidated bank could make a stipulation to prioritize payments to deposit holders. This was not possible under the general rule of corporate liquidation. Second, the bank owner is not allowed to initiate a liquidation process of his/her own bank
1997 (April)	• The implementation of the requirement for banks to raise their reserve requirement from 3 per cent of third party funds to 5 per cent

Source: Bank Indonesia, *Report for the Financial Year, 1993/94–1996/97*, and Binhadi, *Financial Deregulation, Banking Development and Monetary Policy: The Indonesian Experience*, (Jakarta: IBI, 1993).

inter-bank money market. The scarcity of liquidity became severe after the three-pronged monetary, fiscal and administrative actions undertaken by the Ministry of Finance and Bank Indonesia starting the third week of August 1997.

The scarcity of liquidity caused additional problems for the banking sector, which by this time had been facing market pressures for more than one month. Some banks that had a history of experiencing liquidity mismatches started to have problems borrowing from other banks in the inter-bank money market. The regular suppliers of liquidity started to stop supplying liquidity, even if they had excess liquidity, for fear of having problems later. The inter-bank money market also started to function poorly. In the meantime, some banks started to have difficulties in complying with prudential measures and other banking regulations. For example, the number of banks violating the rule of a 5 per cent reserve requirement began to increase.

The problem that so far was limited to depreciation began to spread to hit the banking sector. As mentioned before, the banking sector had structural problems even before the crisis. High economic growth for many years prior to 1997 had hidden all these weaknesses under the carpet. This time, confronted with a regional financial shock and stringent monetary and fiscal policy, the banking sector was cracking. The external financial shock basically uncovered the weaknesses of the banking sector.

Lack of transparency had definitely complicated matters. With minimal information, the public had fallen prey to incomplete or wrong information. In banking, the public easily panicked in the face of any bad news without checking the validity of the news or whether they understood the issue or not.

The bad news, which was not always true, that bank A or bank B was experiencing a liquidity mismatch or popularly called "loss in bank clearing". The lack of transparency coupled with weak banking governance creates misinformed and suspicious clients for banks. In August–September 1997 some banks experienced heavy losses on their deposits because of rumours that they experienced losses in bank clearing. Of course, a bank that routinely ran liquidity mismatches must have had a more serious problem than liquidity.

By late August and September 1997 the banking sector in Indonesia was in distress. Experts distinguish between banking in distress and a banking crisis. The former is used to describe a condition whereby some banks are already experiencing insolvency. But, the general public does not know yet, so there is no bank run. A banking crisis is when a number of banks experience negative net worth or insolvency, a number of banks experience bank runs, with the fall of banks requiring intervention by the supervisory authority (Sundararajan and Balino 1991, pp. 3–4).

During this period a number of banks were actually insolvent. Due to a high percentage of non-performing loans, their capital was eaten up by their obligation to form provisions for bad debts. However, since the public had not learned about their real conditions they kept relying on these banks. These banks kept their clients by offering higher rates of interest on their deposits.

How could distress in banking be tolerated? This is a valid question to be raised. Let me address the issue in the perspective that seemed be held then. First, as I alluded to before, the lack of transparency and weak governance in both the banking community as well as the authorities definitely explains how this could happen. Weak governance in the banking community made it possible for some banks to take advantage of their less informed clients as well as weak banking supervision. Second, the public was also not completely innocent. They were easily lured to unnaturally high deposit rates by a number of banks, even if they knew that the market rates were actually much lower. Moral hazard certainly worked well for both the banking community as well as their clients. Third, the central bank that was also the bank supervision authority had a variety of limitations due to its position as part of the government (lack of autonomy) and weak governance in the face of unprecedented challenge. The lack of understanding or misunderstanding of general banking practices by bankers and the general public arose partly from a lack of professionalism by the authorities. The government policy of not being willing to liquidate insolvent banks was putting Bank Indonesia in an impossible position.

For the central bank, the widening of the problem of exchange rate management to banking in distress posed a greater challenge indeed. As the guardian of the national payment system, and the fact that banking had been the backbone of the working of the payment system put Bank Indonesia, which held responsibility for all these interrelated matters, in a difficult position.

Confronted with banks having liquidity mismatches, Bank Indonesia was forced to give assistance to them in defence of the payment system. As lender of last resort, the central bank was left with no choice but to provide liquidity support to banks in trouble.

In normal conditions, the inter-bank money market clears liquidity problems experienced by banks. A bank experiencing loss in bank clearing could tap funds from banks experiencing surplus, and the problem is solved. The interest rate in the inter-bank money market fluctuates in accordance with supply and demand at any given time.

In pre-crisis Indonesia, banks having a liquidity shortage would seek funds in the inter-bank money market rather than go to Bank Indonesia to ask for liquidity facilities like a rediscount window. There were two reasons for this strange behaviour. First, the rediscount window or liquidity support provided by Bank Indonesia carries a higher interest rate than the interest rate in the inter-bank market. This was, of course by design, i.e. to avoid banks' misuse of the facility, the rate reflected a penalty rate. Second, a bank generally avoided asking for Bank Indonesia's facility for fear of being exposed among the banking community about its financial condition. The downside of this strange attitude was that there was a segment of the inter-bank money market that was actually unhealthy. A number of banks that had repeated liquidity shortages fell prey to some other banks, which became providers of funds at much higher than the normal rate.

After the government stepped in to tighten liquidity, the inter-bank money market experienced a severe crunch. Aside from the general shortage, the move changed the attitude of banks that usually provided liquidity. Even banks that still commanded excess liquidity were starting to be very selective for fear of accumulating non-performing loans. The inter-bank interest rate shot up. For example on the third week of August 1997, the inter-bank rate, which used to be 22 per cent per annum went up to 90 per cent. This was devastating for banks in trouble. A new problem arose, namely the tendency for inter-bank market to become segmented or compartmentalized.

A new problem came in the form of more cases of non-compliance in prudential measures by commercial banks, including fulfillment of the reserve requirement. By the end of August 1997, one-fourth of commercial banks had funds with Bank Indonesia that were less than the 5 per cent required by the regulation that was effective April 1997.

This indicated that banks had started using their own funds held by Bank Indonesia, to cover their liquidity mismatches.

These banks' prudential situation worsened — they were no longer simply violating reserve requirement obligations, but in a more precarious situation. Some banks started to experience negative balances with Bank Indonesia. The problem was not just non-compliance or violation of banking rules, but also the cost that went with it. Negative balances bear a very high rate of interest. As an example, on 19 August 1997 when the SBI rate was doubled from 10 per cent per annum to 20 per cent, the penalty rate for a negative balance with Bank Indonesia was 52 per cent.

Since the banking sector as the major pillar of the national payment system was in distress, the other financial institutions, and ultimately the real sectors, were in turn affected. The liquidity squeeze hit the capital market very hard. The Jakarta composite equity index went down from 612 in mid-August 1997 to 475 in early September 1997, a drop of close to 29 per cent in two weeks.

The impact of the financial disturbance on investment, trade and consumption was not immediately visible. However, all signals indicated that the real sectors were starting to feel the pinch. Lending rates were rising, and for many entities bank credits were just not available.

In a dynamic process of sequential developments and feedback effects, the problem was spreading and deepening. A contagion evolved from external shock in the currency market, through government policy responses, to the banking sector, and the real sectors of the economy. The bottom line was the rapid erosion of market and general public confidence in the working of the national economy and the government's credibility.

Confronted with the widening economic woes, the government made a special effort to come up with actions that involved not just monetary and fiscal, but adjustments in real sectors as well. President Soeharto in his address to the Parliament on the eve of Independence Day, 17 August 1997, had already indicated his intention to address the economic problems facing the nation. On 3 September 1997, after a Cabinet meeting, the government announced a ten-point policy to address the pressing economic problems. The policy that was announced touched, aside from monetary and fiscal measures, adjustment policy in the real sectors. Prominent among the steps that would be taken was the postponement of large government projects which had high import content. The government also asked for the private sector to sharpen their priorities with a view to the current problems that the national economy was facing.[20]

For the banking sector, the President instructed the Minister of Finance and Governor of Bank Indonesia to take steps as follows: first, healthy banks that faced liquidity problems should be helped temporarily. Second, banks that were clearly unsound should be consolidated through merger with or acquisition by sound banks. Third, should the rescue operations fail, these banks were to be liquidated in accordance with the existing regulation with every effort made to save depositor's funds, especially those of small deposit owners.[21]

Due to its comprehensiveness, within Bank Indonesia I described the policy package as a "self-imposed IMF Programme". In fact, the 3 September policy was like a precursor of the government exercise to prepare for the stand-by arrangement that was coming later.

The problems confronting the national economy snowballed rapidly. The rupiah was strengthened a bit but only for a very short period. The tightness of the monetary stand in the ensuing weeks was extremely harsh on the real sectors, prompting protests by the business community through the media and business lobby.

Business demand for easing the monetary stand and reducing lending rates from the banking sector received a favourable hearing from ministers who were legally responsible for the real sectors. In fact, this was also President Soeharto's stand.

Amidst the lobbying by the business secctor, pundits and the press for the lowering of interest rates, Bank Indonesia was forced to comply. The central bank began to ease SBI rates in stages in the second week of September 1997. Other steps to ease the monetary stand followed, which included providing repurchase of SBI, rediscount facility, and reopening the discount facility for commercial banks' certificates (SBPU), which was closed in July 1997.

Other actions that were taken included the pledge for the government to continue exercising a flexible exchange system as introduced in mid-August 1997, and to continue its efforts to defend the rupiah's stability. As a follow-up to the policy to address the crisis, the government also initiating some steps to sound out the multilateral agencies, the World Bank, the IMF, and the Asian Development Bank, in particular, for possible assistance.

In the real sectors, the government coordinated measures to secure the availability and distribution of basic needs. However, the most prominent policy in the real sectors was the government decision to reassess big projects, both exclusively government projects and joint public-private sector projects. From the study that was conducted by the National Planning and Development Board (Bappenas), out of 267 big projects, 81 projects were postponed, 75 projects had to be reevaluated, and 85 projects were continued. In terms of their rupiah value, the Minister of Finance reported in the Parliament that the first group amounted to 38.92 trillion rupiah and the second group 62.69 trillion rupiah. The total value of the total projects was 161.78 trillion rupiah.[22] At the current rate of around 3,500 rupiah to a dollar, this was equivalent to a postponement of more than 100 billion dollars worth of projects.

Despite the government's relentless efforts to find ways to cope with the crisis, the rupiah continued to weaken, and the banking sector suffered more distress. Bank Indonesia faced a dilemma between defending the rupiah and saving the payments system through helping the banking sector. The problem became more pressing due to the weakening of market and public confidence.

Seeking IMF help

Problems continued, the most apparent of which was the currency depreciation. However, for the monetary authorities the problem was getting more complicated because of the liquidity shortage and its implications for the banking sector as well as the real sector. There was also the declining public confidence in the government's economic management.

Against this background, at a Cabinet meeting on 8 October 1997, the government decided to ask for assistance from the IMF. The government appointed Professor Widjojo Nitisastro, the architect of the economic programme since the beginning of the Soeharto presidency and government's economic adviser, to head the economic team to make the necessary preparations to notify the IMF.

Public reaction as reported in the domestic and foreign press was that the government was reactivating Professor Widjojo together with his colleague, Professor Ali Wardhana, the former Minister of Finance in the 1970s and early 1980s, and also serving as government adviser, from their retirement. I think the public was correct in sensing the seriousness of the problems as signified by the government decision to appoint an old and steady hand, and veteran crisis manager, who had experience of dealing with the IMF. However, it was not correct to say that this was a reactivation of two famous economics professors. Both of them were expert members of the Monetary Board who were always present at the board meetings, including many held since the outbreak of the financial crisis. The appointments also took place when the current Minister Coordinator for Economics and Finance, Professor Saleh Affif was undergoing medical treatment abroad.

The possibility for the government to seek the Fund's help was in fact already being raised during a meeting between the monetary board and the Fund's First Deputy Managing Director. Dr. Stanley Fischer was invited by Minister of Finance Mar'ie Muhammad to visit Jakarta in mid-September 1997, on his way to Bangkok and Hong Kong for the World Bank-IMF annual meetings.

And during Monetary Board meetings, asking the Fund for assistance was being considered as one alternative open to Indonesia to restore market confidence. During these discussions, I brought up the idea for using a precautionary arrangement provided by the Fund, instead of the usual stand-by arrangement (SBA). It was my understanding that a precautionary arrangement was basically the same as a stand-by one. An SBA involved an arrangement between the government asking for the facility and fulfilling all the requirements in the conditionality, while the Fund promised to provide the government concerned the use of its facility, liquidity for balance of payments' support. However, in a precautionary arrangement, the fund is only withdrawn if it is needed.

My argument for using the precautionary arrangement was that, by committing to a programme that was supported by the Fund, the basic objective that we would like to get from inviting the Fund would already be achieved, i.e. market confidence. However, Indonesia did not have to commit to too stringent a conditionality, since no drawing of funds would be made. It was my contention then — of course I was proven wrong here — that Indonesia had sufficient reserves to defend its currency, provided that market confidence was restored. My instincts told me then that our government would not be able to fulfill the stringent conditionality that went with the stand-by arrangement.

Dr. Fischer promised to work on the issues with his staff to come up with some suggestions on how to proceed with the possible alternatives that could be taken by the Indonesian government.

The Minister of Finance and the Governor of Bank Indonesia took up the discussion on the possibility for Indonesia asking to utilize the Fund facility further during the annual meetings of the World Bank and IMF in Hong Kong from 19 to 22 September 1997. At the meeting in Hong Kong, the Fund was represented by Dr Hubert Neiss, the Director of Asia Pacific of the Fund and Dr Bijan B. Aghevli, the Deputy Director for Asia Pacific. During the meeting of the Indonesian delegation with Mr Michel Camdessus and Dr Stanley Fischer, the matter was also taken up.

After the government decided to go ahead and ask for the Fund's help, the Minister of Finance wrote a letter to the IMF's Managing Director Michel Camdessus to convey the government of Indonesia's intention to ask for a stand-by arrangement, and all the necessary preparations were made. In the letter, a broad outline of the adjustment programme for addressing the financial turmoil was mentioned, together with the government's intention to ask for utilizing the Fund's facility.

The Fund immediately made an announcement commending the government's steps that had been taken as well as positively responding to its intention. In the press release, Camdessus supported the government's actions, and viewed its intention to ask for support from the multilateral institutions, the IMF, the World Bank and the ADB as a good opportunity to strengthen these policies, while recognizing that the economic fundamentals were basically sound.[23] The announcement also mentioned IMF readiness to supply Indonesia with funds, and its intention to immediately send two missions to Indonesia to start discussing the programme.

Actually the IMF had already agreed to send two missions to Indonesia prior to the government's decision to ask for any help. One mission was originally scheduled to evaluate Indonesia's macroeconomic condition. And another one was intended to prepare for financial sector restructuring, which was an ongoing programme requested by Bank Indonesia. In the face of the urgent need to address Indonesia's problems, the missions were transformed to preparing for an SBA for two to three years. Originally, with all the preparations needed, an IMF-supported programme had been timed to commence in December 1997.

However, the rapidly changing conditions that Indonesia had to face, as signified by a 34 per cent rupiah depreciation between July and October 1997, and the government's announcement to seek the Fund's help, led to a different course of events. The IMF missions to Jakarta, originally scheduled on 15 and 20 October, were moved forward to 9 and 13 October. In this process, the IMF facility that was geared toward a precautionary facility was shifted to a stand-by facility.[24]

The IMF missions included World Bank and ADB staff. The team comprised of ten staff from the Asia and Pacific Department (APD) under the leadership of Dr Bijan B. Aghevli, the Deputy Director for Asia Pacific, and eight from the Monetary and Exchange Affairs (MAE), under the leadership of Mr Reza Vaez-Zadeh. The first team was preparing macroeconomics, fiscal and monetary programmes, including structural changes. The second team was working on banking restructuring. During the negotiations, Director for Asia Pacific Hubert Neiss came for a few days, meeting with the Indonesian team and paying a courtesy call to President Soeharto.

The Indonesian team comprised of members of the Monetary Board, Minister of Finance Mar'ie Muhammad, Minister of Trade and Industry Tungky Ariwibowo, Minister of State Secretary Moerdiono, Professors Widjojo Nitisastro and Ali Wardhana, and myself as Governor of Bank Indonesia, led by Professor Widjojo Nitisastro. A small team, who negotiated the programme in details, assisted this team. This team comprised of Bambang Subianto, the Director General of Financial Institutions; Boediono, the Managing Director, Bank Indonesia; and Djunaedi Hadisumarto, Assistant Minister Coordinator for Economic and Finance. On banking restructuring, the Indonesian team comprised of two Managing Directors of Bank Indonesia, Hendrobudiyanto and Heru Supraptomo, and several directors of Bank Indonesia in charge of banking supervision and directors of legal departments of Bank Indonesia and the MoF.

The programme that was discussed originated from all the steps that had been introduced before; such as those announced by the Cabinet on 3 September and 8 October. Altogether the programme comprised of steps in macroeconomic policy, real sector economic reforms and banking restructuring that were negotiated between the government of Indonesia's economic team and the IMF team from 13 to 30 October 1997.

During the negotiations, the IMF team was always in communication with the IMF management in Washington D.C., including Stanley Fischer and Michel Camdessus. Likewise, the Indonesian team communicated constantly with different Ministers responsible for the real sectors. The team also reported to the President several times during the negotiations.

After all items in the negotiations were agreed upon, they were put in a document which was entitled "Memorandum of Economic and Financial Policies" (MEFP).[25] The document was sent to Managing Director Camdessus with a letter conveying the government's intention to ask for a stand-by arrangement. Minister of Finance Mar'ie Muhammad and myself, as Bank Indonesia's Governor, signed the letter. It was sent on 31 October 1997 to the Managing Director for approval. The Managing Director presented the letter and the document to the Executive Board. The board, which had 24 members representing all the 180-plus member countries, approved the proposal on 5 November 1997. The right to determine whether a proposal is approved or not, and whether a review of member's programmes is acceptable or nor, which is a precondition of any withdrawal of an IMF loan, lies with the Executive Board.

After the board's approval the stand-by loan for Indonesia became valid. The IMF assistance was in the form of a stand-by arrangement for three years with a loan to the amount of SDR 7.3 billion, equivalent to around US$10 billion. This amount constituted 490 per cent of the Indonesian quota in the IMF.[26] The stand-by loan for Indonesia was under an emergency procedure or the Emergency Finance Mechanism (EFM). The emergency procedure implied faster negotiations and board decisions in comparison to other IMF facilities, to facilitate disbursement in emergencies.

From precautionary to stand-by arrangement

The government of Indonesia had not asked for IMF stand-by loans for more than two decades. The last time the government received an IMF stand-by loan was in 1970. However, Indonesia had received a variety of IMF technical assistance such as preliminary studies that led to the need for bank restructuring, improvement of the payment system and monetary management. In fact, when the crisis struck in July 1997 the IMF study on bank restructuring was still in progress.

Indonesia had also resorted to the IMF Compensatory Financing Facility (CFF), during difficult periods of depressed export commodity prices, in 1975, 1983 and 1987.[27] But this facility is different from a stand-by loan. CFF is an IMF facility accorded to its members to purchase foreign exchange in exchange for their own currencies to compensate for a sudden decrease of export earnings of member countries due to depressed export commodity prices that result in balance of payments disturbances (IMF 2000, Box 2).

The IMF stand-by loan is intended to strengthen the balance of payments of member countries. Balance of payment problems often reflect or go together with imbalances in the national economy, either in the real sector or the financial sector or both. Usually it is followed by pressure on the exchange rate. A long period of absence from engaging in an IMF stand-by loan implies that Indonesia's balance of payments had generally been sound over this period.

During this period, Indonesia's relations with the IMF had mostly been through the annual consultation in the framework of the IMF surveillance function towards its members — usually known as the Article IV consultation — technical assistance on a variety of monetary policy issues, and other consultations through the IMF representative office in Jakarta.[28]

However, the government had been receiving stand-by loans from international commercial banks. These were lines of credit from syndicated international commercial banks that were available to be drawn up to certain time limit. Since the mid-1980s the government of Indonesia had maintained around US$2 billion lines of credit that were readily available to be drawn from between 40–50 international commercial banks in Asia, Europe, as well as the United States. Bank Indonesia entered the market to get these lines of credit on behalf of the government. Lines of credit were available for drawing, usually for a two-year period. When the line of credit was drawn it became a debt for the government of Indonesia, otherwise it remained a line of credit until the time was up.

These loans were used to finance a variety of imports, the most common of which was financing some export credits from foreign export–import banks to Indonesia. Usually, import financing through a loan from an export–import bank from abroad was accompanied by a requirement that a certain percentage of the imports had to be paid in cash by the receiving country. It was the government's policy to use stand-by loans from commercial banks to make cash payments for export credit financing and other financing of emergency needs in the past. By so doing, the level of official reserves was not disturbed.

Since the government had not committed itself to any stand-by arrangement since 1970, the decision to ask for IMF help on 8 October 1970 surprised many. Some government critics commented that Indonesia was not in such a desperate condition that it needed to ask for the IMF help.[29]

Usually, receipient countries have a depreciated exchange rate and depleted foreign exchange reserves. Indonesia's macroeconomic conditions in September 1997 were not so bad that they warranted an IMF stand-by loan. The three macroeconomic indicators, notably export growth, current account deficit and the international reserves were not as bad as the other two Asian crisis countries at the time. In general, the pre-crisis indicators of vulnerability for Indonesia were either better than or as bad as Thailand and Korea.

The basic problem that confronted Indonesia since July 1997 was the drastic depreciation of rupiah. From July to early October, the rupiah was depreciated by 34 per cent. It was the biggest currency depreciation in the region. The drastic depreciation of the rupiah actually signalled the presence of more serious problems in the national economy. The problem that confronted the national economy were different from the currency shock from the Mexican crisis that struck Indonesia in January 1995 or the impact of *yendaka* and social unrest in Jakarta in July 1996.

It was the government's view that Indonesia was suffering from a loss of market and public confidence toward the resiliency of the national economy in the face of financial panic in the region. The government realized that market confidence was definitely slipping. Of course IMF support had always been in terms of some form of stand-by loan.[30] The IMF provides different facilities to help member countries experiencing balance of payment problems. The most popular one is the stand-by loan. This is a loan for a period of between three months to three years. And since balance of payments problems could imply structural imbalances, the stand-by facility could be extended to become a longer-term loan of four years, when it becomes an extended fund facility (EFF).

Since the IMF operates like a credit union whereby a member country takes a loan from pooled funds that originate from other member countries, a stand-by loan is not an ordinary loan. The legal relationship between the IMF and the member country receiving the loan is not a loan contract. It is technically called an *arrangement* and thus, SBA and extended arrangement (EA). In this arrangement, the withdrawal of the loan is through a *purchase* of foreign exchange from IMF and the repayment is a *repurchase*. The receiving country uses its own currency to finance the purchases of foreign exchange. And the repayment implies a repurchase of its own currency, using foreign exchange to finance the transaction. This is also why the stand-by loan is sometimes called a *facility* or *window* that is provided by the IMF for member countries to use.

All IMF facilities carry a number of requirements that technically are called *conditionality*. Since IMF facility is aimed at assisting member countries correct problems in their balance of payments, the basic requirements are that the receiving countries have to satisfy what is required to get rid off the problems that caused the balance of payments problem.

There are several technical terms of conditionality, such as *prior actions, performance criteria, structural benchmarks* and *reviews*. But, basically the aim of putting these requirements (conditionality) is to provide *safeguard* measures. IMF conditionality provides safeguards that the objective of the loan is achieved, i.e. the recovery of the balance of payments, and the repayment of the loan. For the receiving or borrowing country it is a guarantee that there will be an amount of funds available to be used for balance of payments support.

The problem is that IMF conditionality, aside from its complexity, is not well understood by government officials and the general public.

The stringent requirements that a country receiving an IMF loan has to comply with have drawn a lot of public attention and debate. The terms "IMF bitter pills", high interest policy, and fiscal discipline are usually associated with IMF-supported programmes that have to be executed by countries asking for help. After the Asian crisis, there was criticism as to whether stringent fiscal and high interest, and other IMF policies, had been the right answer or actually became part of the problem.

Conditionality is a set of requirements that the recipient country has to fulfil in order to be able to receive the stand-by loan. And since the loan is disbursed in stages, the fulfillment of conditionality is a requisite for both the initial disbursement as well as each subsequent phase of disbursement. As mentioned before, technically conditionality is a set of steps that have to be undertaken by the government, a maximum or minimum limit in quantitative terms of financial and fiscal measures, a set of quantitative and qualitative benchmarks to be followed, and many other things. They affect macroeconomic sectors as well as micro-economic factors in monetary, finance and fiscal and the real sectors. Conditionality also includes legal and institutional reform as well as transparency and governance. In total these factors and items constitute adjustment programmes that have to be undertaken to address the problems that on the surface are identified as balance of payments and exchange problems.

Thus, basically they are adjustment programmes that have to be undertaken by the recipient government, legally proposed by the recipient government but imposed by the IMF. In reality, they are discussed, negotiated and worked out jointly between the recipient government and the IMF. They are neither purely a government initiative nor an IMF initiative.

The programmes themselves are complicated and generally difficult to implement. However, the problem is also political. It appears as if the government is surrendering its sovereignty and allowing IMF to dictate the government in addressing the problems that the national economy is confronting. In the case of Indonesia, the fact that the government did not have transparent discussions with the Parliament, let alone publicly, about the IMF conditionality only underlines this.

Concerned about the implications, initially I was not in favour of the government asking the IMF for a loan. Aside from my conviction that Indonesia's problems did not warrant an IMF stand-by loan, I was aware that it would be difficult for the economic team to get approval from President Soeharto, who would have to swallow his pride to accept IMF conditionality and its implications, politically or otherwise.

I sensed that, given the current relations between President Soeharto and the Economic Team, it would actually be difficult to explain clearly what conditionality implied. It was generally understood that a loan was granted with certain conditions. However, the degree to which the public was willing to accept IMF intervention in the national economy could not be taken for granted. In particular, due to public perception that the superpowers had been exercising their leverage to influence IMF decisions, this was a very sensitive issue.[31]

I was aware that with these issues in the background it would be difficult for the Economic Team to make all the necessary preparations to involve IMF in the government efforts to deal with the crisis through a regular stand-by arrangement. And, this was the reason for my suggestion to seek a *precautionary arrangement* instead of a stand-by arrangement. In a precautionary arrangement the recipient country also has to commit to producing adjustment programmes that bear the usual conditionality. However, in a precautionary arrangement the fund that may be in store would only be used if the country actually needs it. So, this facility does not automatically involve the use of IMF funds. And consequently, the requirements would be less stringent. The conditionality would be more acceptable to the government, economically, socially as well as politically.

Paul Blustein, in *The Chastening* (Blustein 2001, p. 101), writes that President Soeharto accepted the stand-by arrangement because the Economic team assured him that the IMF facility was a precautionary arrangement. This does not accord with what actually happened. The President was well aware of the essence of the programme. He personally negotiated and signed the second letter of intent. However, in my recollection, the discussion whether the Indonesian programme should be a precautionary or stand-by one was never brought up in discussions between the Economic Team and the President. After the signing of the first letter of intent, I proposed that the Economic Team explain the details of the whole programme, including the meaning of first and second line of defence and the issue of conditionality, to the President. But the Chairman of the Team told me to wait for a better moment. In fact, this never happened.

With hindsight, we can see that on several occasions the postponement of loan withdrawals was due to the postponement of programme reviews. In turn, the rupiah was under additional pressure due to the delay. The withdrawal itself was not really crucial, since the international reserves position was comfortable. In other words, the rupiah was under unnecessary pressure. If the fund itself was not actually needed, a stand-by loan was not warranted.

But what was the rationale for committing the national economy to comply with IMF conditionality without receiving any loan? There were three considerations that I could think of to justify a move to seek a precautionary, but not necessarily stand-by, arrangement. First, since economic conditions were not so bad, the problems confronting Indonesia would be manageable. The economic conditions were indeed better for some indicators and similar to Thailand's for others. From the size of the current account deficit, the international reserves available and exchange rate management, Indonesia was better off than Thailand. But the market perceived that Indonesia was exactly in the same position as Thailand. Second, the main problem confronting Indonesia was that market and public confidence had been eroding. Third, since understanding about IMF conditionality associated with stand-by arrangements was lacking and politically sensitive, I was concerned about involving ourselves in a stand-by arrangement.

It was my conviction that what Indonesia needed then was support from the international community for our efforts to win back the confidence of the market and public. So what Indonesia needed was IMF support for national adjustment programmes to convince the market, not the Fund per se.

This was proven to be a weak argument. In fact, after the crisis, it has become conventional wisdom to argue, as have Steven Radelet and Jeffrey Sachs (1998), that an economy should hold enough foreign reserves to cover short-term debt.

However, prior to the crisis the generally accepted measure for safe international reserve holdings was still in terms of months of import coverage: since the 1960s, the rule of thumb was still three months of import financing. Most countries would feel safe with international reserves that would be enough to finance three months of import demand. It should be noted that in Indonesia's first letter of intent, one of the stated targets in foreign exchange reserve management was to maintain foreign reserves at least enough to finance four months of imports.[32]

After the crisis, it was obvious that countries that held ample reserves, like Taiwan, Singapore, and Hong Kong suffered much less pressure on their respective currencies. Professor Martin Feldstein (1999) also proposed a "self-help guide" for emerging markets in defence against financial panic in the form of accumulating as much as foreign reserves possible. China was spared from the crisis, possibly due to the fact that its government held a huge amount of reserves, in addition to the inconvertibility of the renmimbi.

Were there alternatives?

Was inviting the IMF a bad or wrong move? Despite the occasional reappearance of public criticism about the government's decision to invite the IMF, arguing for Indonesia to shift gear and pursue a different path by discarding the present IMF-supported programme does not seem to make much sense. This is in spite of many valid arguments for faulting the IMF's involvement in the Asian, Russian, Brazilian, and Argentinian crises.

In fact, even recently under President Megawati's administration, some groups were still arguing for Indonesia to ignore the IMF-supported programme, to end IMF intervention and start implementing the government's own programme.[33]

The strongest criticisms arose from some quarters who accused the team who made the decision to invite the IMF of waging a conspiracy to topple President Soeharto. In November 1997 writings circulated in Jakarta through the Internet, arguing that the decision to close 16 banks, including three banks owned by the Soeharto family, was actually a conspiracy to shame the president's family and bring Soeharto down. These writings were compiled in a booklet entitled *Konspirasi Menggoyang Soeharto* ("The Conspiracy to Shake/Overthrow Soeharto").[34] The arguments therein would have difficulty passing the test of internal consistency, let alone empirical scrutiny. However, they must have been good propaganda for Soeharto's cronies to pass the blame for the crisis to others.

Was asking the IMF for help the only available alternative? I would argue that under the circumstances the decision to invite IMF was the right decision to make. However, initially I had a strong sense for resorting to a precautionary arrangement instead of stand-by arrangement. I will also mention later about what should or could have been done differently by the IMF and the government.

In the beginning, communication between the government and IMF was still referring to Indonesia's intention to seek a precautionary arrangement.[35] However, the snowballing problems that confronted Indonesia rapidly transferred the preparation for a precautionary into a stand-by arrangement.

With hindsight, some argue that Indonesia might have fared better had the government not resorted to IMF stand-by loans. Questions still linger as to whether Indonesia would have been better off following

Malaysia, in terms of not relying on the IMF, including implementing capital controls. Would resorting to a pegged system with a currency board have been better? I will address some of these issues later.

I think the answers to the above questions will not be very clear-cut. They might only be good for the purpose of analysis. In general, once a policy has been chosen, it is difficult for any economy to retract it without risking worse.

Since then, Indonesia has experienced occasions when things seemed to improve, but then the improvements were either short-lived or did not materialize. The lack of consistency between policies and inconsistencies in implementation, or non-compliance, have all hindered Indonesia's recovery.

3

Stabilization and Reform Programmes

IMF — Supported Programmes

By formally receiving a stand-by loan from the IMF, the government's efforts to address the crisis entered a new phase. The programme was very comprehensive, and supported by the Fund. The government policy became a macroeconomic adjustment programme to deal with balance of payments disturbances, which reflected imbalances in the national economy.

The IMF functions like a credit union, whereby member countries borrow from it by using other member countries' funds. On the other hand, the IMF also simultaneously plays the role of lender of last resort, providing member countries with international liquidity in times of need.

The rest could only be drawn with conditions. This would be the part that has the characteristic of a loan, not a facility. The fund is taken from the general resource account (GRA) of IMF, and interest rates are not subsidized. This can only be drawn in stages, depending on the compliance of the borrowing country with respect to the conditionality. If the member country fails to fulfil part or the whole of the conditionality, the country will be denied from withdrawing the remaining amount of the loan. However, sometimes the stand-by loan is also called a facility. I will be using these terms interchangeably.

The phasing of the loan on top of the credit tranche can be in accordance with the needs of the receiving country. It could be initially large and subsequently smaller *front-loading*, or the reverse of it, with a large disbursement in the later period and less in the early part (*back-loading*).

Technically speaking, the actual IMF facilities are IMF loans not funded from the member countries' contributions. The funds are, for example, from the sale of IMF gold. These facilities usually bear subsidized interest rates. The single most important facility is the loan to assist highly indebted poor countries (HIPC) in the form of an enhanced structural adjustment facility (ESAF). In 1999 this facility was transformed into a new facility, called poverty reduction and growth facility (PRGF).

Stand-by arrangements were introduced in 1952 but only included in the articles of agreement in 1978. The period of repayment is between 3¼ to 5 years. In 1974 a new feature was introduced, the extended fund facility (EFF). In the extended fund facility the repayment of the stand-by loan can be made over a longer period of 4½ to 10 years. The major reason was that the member countries were longer-term or structural problems associated with balance of payments' disequilibrium.

Indonesia's IMF-supported adjustment programme for addressing the crisis was put forward in the letter of intent (LOI) to the Managing Director of IMF on 31 October 1997. The basic document entitled "Indonesia — Memorandum of Economic and Financial Policy" (MEFP) contains a comprehensive and detailed set of steps on financial restructuring and economic reform with the support of prudent fiscal and monetary policies.

The documents comprised of four letters addressed to the Managing Director of the IMF, which includes the following:

- The first letter explains the strategy of intervention in the foreign exchange market in the context of an agreed programme explained in the MEFP. This letter mentions the daily and monthly limits of foreign exchange that could be used to implement the policy. It also mentions that the plan will be implemented immediately.

- The second letter (attachment I) is a covering letter that explains the aim of the whole exercise. It states that the government of Indonesia intends to implement a three-year programme as explained in detail in the MEFP (attachment II) to address the fundamental causes of its current financial difficulties for the national economy to get back to a sustainable growth path. To support the programme the government requests a three-year stand-by arrangement from the Fund to the equivalent of SDR 7.3 billion or 490 per cent of the quota. The MEFP contains 48 paragraphs, explaining in detail all the steps that will be implemented in the programme. This document has annexes detailing quantitative and qualitative performance criteria as well as structural performance criteria and benchmarks.
- The next letters are two side letters. The first one explains the plan to close 16 insolvent banks on 1 November, a plan for state bank restructuring policy, and the restructuring of regional development banks. The second side letter explains the government plan of action regarding different groups of weak banks.[1]

It should be noted that, according to the IMF document explaining member countries publication (http://www.imf.org/external/np/loi/mempuba.html), the definitions of LOI and MEFP are identical. Both are defined as documents that "describe the policies that a country intends to implement in the context of its request for financial support from the IMF". The public understanding seems to be that all these documents are what one calls letters of intent. I will use these terms interchangeably.

The fact that the programme was both comprehensive and detailed reflects the nature of the problems confronting the national economy. Indeed, the monetary and financial problems were interrelated with problems of the real sectors. Some problems were short term in nature, while others were medium or even long term. Some problems were microeconomic; others were macroeconomic, social as well as political. However, putting all these issues in a single package of policies involving different institutions within the government as well as the private sector in a framework of an agreement with different multilateral institutions would prove to constrain its implementation.

Overview of the programme

The programme in detail is presented in the MEFP. There is a brief outline of Indonesia's past prudent macroeconomic management that had brought stability and growth for several decades, which went together with a substantial reduction of the numbers of people living in poverty.

In spite of a history of respectable macroeconomic management, structural weaknesses had made Indonesia vulnerable to external shocks. Rigidities arising from domestic regulations and import monopolies had impeded economic efficiency and competitiveness. Rapid expansion of the banking sector had left a number of banks with significant amounts of non-performing loans, straining liquidity and undermining their financial viability. At the same time the rupiah's stability, together with high rate of domestic investment, had both encouraged and facilitated a high level of overseas borrowing, a significant portion of which had been unhedged, private, short-term debt. By the end of June 1997, Indonesia's external debt had increased to US$140 billion (about 60 per cent of GDP), of which US$33 billion was short term, while its debt service had remained close to one-third of its exports of goods and services.

In the wake of the regional currency crisis, the rupiah depreciated by more than 30 per cent from mid-July to mid-October, while the Jakarta stock index fell by 35 per cent. Both constituted the largest declines in the region. The government had taken vigorous corrective action in its exchange management, monetary and fiscal policies in addition to deregulation measures in the form of tariff reductions and abolishment of the 49 per cent limit on foreign holdings of listed shares in the capital market. However, these steps had not been sufficient to restore confidence in the rupiah and the economy. Therefore, the government came up with a comprehensive adjustment programme and asked for an IMF stand-by loan.

The programme was built around three main pillars that includes:

- a strong macroeconomic framework designed to achieve an orderly adjustment in the external current account, and incorporating substantial fiscal adjustment as well as a tight monetary stance;
- a comprehensive strategy to restructure the financial sector, including early closing of insolvent institutions; and

- a broad range of structural measures that includes programmes for improving transparency and governance.

The macroeconomic objectives of the programme in the duration of the three-year stand-by arrangement include the following:

- to stabilize the rupiah while maintaining a safe level of foreign exchange reserve holdings
- to reduce the rates of economic decline for the current as well as the following years prior to bringing back economic growth to its potential by the termination of the programme
- to limit the increase of the inflation rate due to rupiah depreciation or other factors to a maximum of 10 per cent in the fiscal year of 1998/99, and to reduce it subsequently to 5 per cent
- to reduce the current account deficit to a maximum of 3 per cent of GDP, a level which would guarantee the decline of foreign indebtedness and debt repayment; and
- to produce a budget surplus of 1 per cent of GDP in the fiscal year 1998/99 in line with a fiscal discipline.

First, a set of steps in macroeconomic policy would be implemented to stabilize the rupiah, and to support adjustment policies in banking as well as in the real sectors. The macroeconomic policies have three broad areas: fiscal policy, monetary policy, and external financing policy. Different steps would be taken to address budget expenditure and well as revenue in order to produce a budget surplus of 1 per cent of GDP.

In the macroeconomic sector, different steps would be taken to tighten the monetary stance to support intervention in the foreign exchange market for strengthening the rupiah. On external financing, the estimated amount of short-term debt due for the remainder of the fiscal year 1997/98 was US$11 billion, and for the fiscal year 1998/99 was US$22 billion. An immediate drawing from the loan was necessary to boost market confidence for granting roll-over of upcoming due debts. Judicious intervention in the foreign exchange market would be executed with the support of prudent monetary policy. In the tradition of IMF policy for addressing balance of payment problems, the intervention strategy for the rupiah, with its limitations on how much was allowed for each period, was explained in the first letter to the Managing Director.

The second set of actions constituted a financial sector restructuring, which presented in detail a comprehensive restructuring of the banking sector. Basically, there were four parts of banking restructuring that would be implemented in the programme, with technical assistance from the IMF, the World Bank and the ADB. They are:

- First, to liquidate the 16 banks that were identified as insolvent. Bank Indonesia and the Ministry of Finance in cooperation with the IMF, came up with the list of insolvent banks. The closure was to be executed on 1 November 1997.

- Second, proper procedures and policies to deal promptly with weak but viable financial institutions, so that they could be placed quickly on the road to recovery. Some banks would be placed under conservatorship or intensified Bank Indonesia supervision with an obligation to submit to Bank Indonesia for its approval a rehabilitation plan. Bank Indonesia was to closely monitor the operation of a number of banks that had contractual agreements with Bank Indonesia to implement rehabilitation programmes.

- Third, to resolve specific problems of the state and regional development banks. The government's goal was to ensure that these banks were safe and sound while at the same time reducing the risk of incurring fiscal costs to maintain their capital adequacy. The government was to set up a plan for the merger of some of the state banks. The state banks would be privatized as soon as legislation for this purpose was enacted. For transparency and to avoid jeopardizing the financial position of Bank Indonesia, costs associated with bank closures and state bank rehabilitation would be financed by the budget or by the issuance of government-guaranteed bonds, the carrying costs of which would be fully covered by the budget.

- Fourth, to improve the legal and regulatory framework of banking operations with a view to establishing a robust financial system. The government intended to phase out Bank Indonesia's quasi-fiscal operations, and to show all subsidies transparently in the budget. Bank Indonesia was to streamline its lender of last resort function. Loans to illiquid but solvent banks would be provided in accordance with stringent access conditions. Any emergency assistance to banks to prevent systemic risks would be explicitly guaranteed by the government.

The third part of the programme contained steps to be taken in structural reforms. The government aimed to promote greater transparency in policy-making and competition to support the ongoing restructuring of the economy that is necessary to promote growth. The government intends to speed up its structural reform programme through further trade and investment reform, deregulation, and privatization, while continuing to implement measures to alleviate poverty.

Point 41 of the MEFP mentions that

> The government intends to phase out import and marketing monopolies and price controls on agricultural commodities, except for rice, sugar, and cloves over the next three years. As a first step, wheat and wheat flour, soybean and garlic will be made freely importable on 3 November 1997.

In the social safety net no specific action is mentioned, except for a note in point 45 of the MEFP that states "… it is imperative that the adjustment programme does not result in worsening of their economic and social condition".

The structural reforms generally continued steps that had been taken before. President Soeharto explained the programme in his speech at the Parliament the day before Independence Day, on 16 August 1997. It was also announced after the Cabinet meeting on 3 September 1997. Included in the programme were steps to discard monopoly of imports of wheat flour, soybeans, garlic, liberalization of cement prices, tariff reduction and liberalization of import and export licensing.

The last part of the programme addressed the issue of monitoring programme implementation through different sets of requirements. They are all IMF conditionalities that take the forms of quantitative and qualitative performance criteria, such as the ceiling on base money, floor on international reserves, and the like; structural performance criteria and benchmarks on financial restructuring, and other policy measures. Included in these are four requirements related to the financial sector, such as when a bank would be placed under conservatorship, five procurement procedures, and one of each in tariffs, government expenditures, and regulated prices.

The stipulations of the IMF-supported programme in the MEFP also contained the following:

1. To outline the programme that Indonesia intended to implement over the next three years to address the fundamental causes of

    its current financial difficulties, thereby ensuring that the economy
was placed on a path of strong and sustainable growth. In support
of the programme the government of Indonesia request a three-
year stand-by arrangement from the IMF in an amount equivalent
to SDR7.3 billion or 490 per cent of its quota.

2. In line with the emergency procedure, the programme would be
reviewed within 1–2 months of Board approval, and four
quarterly reviews were to be completed during the first year.
The first review was to be conducted on 15 March 1998.

3. The programme outlined in the memorandum was a
comprehensive programme to address insolvent and weak banks
and reforming structural weaknesses of the national economy,
supported by prudent monetary and fiscal policies.

4. The government stood ready to implement any additional
adjustment necessary, and that any change of government policy
would be in consultation with the IMF.

Minister Mar'ie Muhammad and myself as the Governor of Bank
Indonesia on behalf of the government signed the letter of intent to the
Fund on 31 October 1997. All these documents were sent to the Managing
Director of the IMF for his approval. The Board of Executives approved
the stand-by arrangement for Indonesia on 5 November 1997.

It should be noted that the letter of intent is a formal letter written
by the government, of Indonesia in this case, to the Managing Director
of the IMF. He would present the letter and all the documents to
the Executive Board, who have the power to decide whether to grant
the stand-by loan or not, based on periodic reviews of programme
implementation that includes the compliance of IMF conditionality.

The Executive Board has 24 executive directors that represent
members that currently number 182 countries or economies. The policy-
making authority of the IMF lies in the Board of Governors that comprise
finance ministers, governors of central banks or other cabinet ministers
representing member countries. The Board of Governors meets once a
year in September. An Interim Committee, which since September 1999
was named the International Monetary and Financial Committee, that
has 24 Governors representing all members, meets twice a year in April
and September. This committee reports to the Board of Governors on
the management and development of the international financial system
and any proposals for amendment of the IMF Articles of Agreement.

Indonesia belongs to the Southeast Asian Group, which has 11 member countries and 3.19 per cent of the quota.[2]

Officially the letter of intent is prepared, and thus owned by, the government requesting for the stand-by loan. However, in the formulation of the programme that is outlined in the letter, and the role of IMF staff is definitely important. In practice, the IMF staff always make their own list of things that should be put into the programme, based on past reports and assessments on the problems confronting the member country. During the negotiations, the IMF staff report to the management, including the Managing Director, on every aspect of the negotiated items in the programme, including conditionality.

Therefore, even though the formal ownership of the programme was with the government of Indonesia, it is also true that the programme is a result of negotiation between the government and the IMF. Since the programme is a product of a negotiation between the government and the IMF, it is not completely honest for the government to keep responding to its critics by stating that all these steps were designed by the IMF. Likewise, the IMF cannot deflect criticism of poor results by claiming that the policies are completely designed by the recipient government.

Structural conditionality and the ownership of IMF-supported programmes have become the subject of much debate after the Asian crisis because the impact of the crisis was much worse than expected.

The loan and its withdrawals

The maximum amount of stand-by loan for a member country is determined on the basis of the member's quota. Indonesia's quota in 1997 was 1.5 billion rupiah (approximately US$2.1 billion). Since the last quota amendment in January 1999, the quota for Indonesia was raised to 2.1 billion rupiah (US$2.75 billion).

The amount of stand-by loan for Indonesia approved by the Executive Board in 5 November, 997 was 7.3 billion rupiah or US$10 billion, which was equivalent to 490 per cent of Indonesia's quota. Point 21 of the LOI mentions that this loan would be put together with loans from the World Bank and the ADB that could be disbursed fast. In addition, the IMF also mobilized credit lines from several countries on a bilateral basis. The LOI states that these funds would be sufficient to reduce capital outflows to a minimum and to maintain international reserves to the amount enough for financing four months of imports of goods and services.

Upon announcing the government of Indonesia's request for a stand-by loan, the Managing Director issued the following statement:

On 5 November, under the Emergency Financing Procedures, and in view of the major improvements that this programme is designed to bring about in the longer-term prospects of the Indonesian economy, I will be asking the Executive Board to approve Indonesia's request for a three-year stand-by arrangement in the amount of SDR 7.3 billion (about US$10 billion). In addition to the IMF funding, the reform programme will be supported by substantial financing from the World Bank and the Asian Development Bank, which have made notable contributions to the design of the programme, particularly in the fields of financial sector rehabilitation and structural reform. These institutions intend to contribute to the programme through their technical assistance and financing amounting to US$4.5 billion and US$3.5 billion, respectively. Furthermore, the Indonesian authorities will stand ready to draw on an amount of about US$5 billion that is held in the Contingency Reserve Fund of Indonesia (This amount is in addition to official reserves of US$20 billion). Thus the resources committed to the support of this ambitious programme will be on the order of US$23 billion. At the same time, a number of countries (including at this stage Australia, Japan, Malaysia, Singapore and the United States) have indicated that in the event that unanticipated adverse external circumstances create the need for additional resources to supplement Indonesia's reserves and the resources made available to the IMF, they would be prepared to consider making available supplemental financing in support of Indonesia's programme with the IMF.[3]

There has been some confusion about the amount of funds available for drawing by Indonesia. The above quote states US$23 billion, but in other statements that were frequently quoted, the amount of the funds available for Indonesia's bail out was US$43 billion.

Some proper explanation is in order on the funds that were actually made available. It should be noted that the actual loan made available for Indonesia was the sum of the stand-by loan from the IMF plus fast disbursement loans from the World Bank and the ADB. The sum of these loans was US$ (10 + 4.5 + 3.5) billion or US$18 billion. So, to say that the total loan is US$23 billion is not correct.

In the announcement the total US$23 billion was derived from adding US$5 billion, which was actually Indonesia's own reserves. It is strange, to say the least, that Indonesia's own reserves were included in the total loans from the three multilateral institutions to Indonesia. The actual loans amounted to only US$18 billion.

What was this US$5 billion fund? This fund was the difference of reserve arising from the method that Bank Indonesia used over the years and the standard reserve calculation according to the IMF. Bank Indonesia calculated reserves using the concept of Official Reserves that was basically equal to the Gross Reserves — the standard method adopted by the IMF — corrected by different categories of contingency funds.

Based on a prudent method of calculating reserves, the official reserve is calculated by leaving out items in the international reserves, which fluctuate easily, and items that in practice are difficult to liquidate. Based on this reasoning, all assets that are very liquid, like reserves invested in very short-run instruments and short-term claims, such as export receipts, are excluded from the official reserves. In addition, assets that for practical purposes are almost impossible to liquidate, i.e. gold, are also excluded.[4] Due to the difference in the methods of calculating reserves, at the time the government made a request for a stand-by arrangement in October 1997, there was US$5 billion of reserves available for immediate use, in addition to the gross reserves that Bank Indonesia held. This was indeed available for use, but it belonged to the Indonesian government. In other words, it was not part of the IMF stand-by loan or loans from other multilateral institutions.

The international reserves that Bank Indonesia managed on behalf of the government was called the Official Reserves. These were the reserves that Bank Indonesia reported in the monthly Cabinet meetings in the Soeharto period. The amount that was calculated in this method generally would be close to that calculated using the concept of *Net International Reserves (NIR)*. In such a way, the size of the reserves would show a more stable path of development. This concept was used for many years until January 1998. By this time, in compliance with the IMF request, the gross reserve concept was used. The gross reserve concept was changed again in April 2000 to the concept of *International Reserve and Foreign Currency Liquidity (IRFCL)*.[5] This concept has been used to the present.

Using the concept of the Official Reserve, the amount of reserves that the central bank announced monthly has always been smaller than the standard calculation. In October 1997, the official reserve was US$19.1 billion, while actually the standard calculated reserve was US$24.1 billion. The US$5 billion was the very liquid part of the reserve that the IMF called reserves held in Indonesia's contingency fund.

During my period as governor of the central bank, 1993–98, the amount of reserves held by Bank Indonesia was calculated as official reserves and gross reserves showed an increasing difference that could be called a contingent fund as shown in Table 6 below.

Internally within Bank Indonesia as well as my presentations to the Monetary Board, I called these differences "our fat" that could be used in bad times. It seemed that the bad time came when the government had to ask for stand-by loan from the IMF in October 1997. During the negotiations, IMF staff raised the issue, and formally asked the government to report reserves using the gross concept. The presentation of the Indonesian reserves followed the Fund's recommendation starting January 1998, in gross and net reserves.

It should be noted that the government actually protested to the IMF upon learning that the US$5 billion was included in the package.

TABLE 6
Official Reserves, Gross Reserves and the Difference, 1993–98
(US$ billion)

End Period	Official Reserves	Gross Reserves	Differences
Jan 1993	11.73	16.74	5.01
Mar 1993	11.98	18.32	6.34
Jan 1994	12.42	19.48	7.06
Jan 1995	12.97	16.81	3.84
Jan 1996	14.79	18.25	3.46
Jan 1997	19.83	26.96	7.13
July 1997	21.10	28.57	7.47
Aug 1997	20.40	27.54	7.14
Sep 1997	20.05	27.56	7.51
Oct 1997	19.10	24.59	5.49
Nov 1997	18.95	24.07	5.12
Dec 1997	17.43	21.42	3.99
Jan 1998	14.03	19.03	5.00
Feb 1998	12.46	16.21	3.75
Mar 1998	13.18	16.51	3.33

Source: Bank Indonesia.

However, the IMF insisted that the aim of the announcement was to build market confidence by showing the amount of funds readily available for Indonesia to use. And thus, mentioning the total amount of funds available for immediate use was important in addition to the support of multilateral financial institutions as well as a number of rich countries and neighbouring countries.

What about Indonesia's bail out of US$43 billion? As was mentioned in the announcement, several countries made pledges to provide some funds that would be made available for Indonesia should the need arise. This was like a line of credit, which could be withdrawn if the funds available from the multilateral institutions had been used up while Indonesia still needed funds during the duration of the programme. Such pledges are also called a second line of defence when the stand-by loans have been used up.

In the terms of the IMF facility, the loan to Indonesia could only be drawn on in stages. Immediately after the Board approved the SBA, US$3 billion was made available to the government. Thereafter, the withdrawals were to be made in stages, subject to compliance of conditionality. Actually, due to the condition of Indonesia's external debt, the major part of the loan was supposed to be made available during the first year of the programme (point 21 of the LOI). However, the phasing of the withdrawals had not been orderly. In addition, any non-compliance of conditionality would trigger a delay of review or even rejection by the Board, which ultimately postponed further withdrawals. The only prompt withdrawal was that of US$3 billion early in November 1997. In the event, the emergency mechanism and the "front-loading" nature of the loan was not utilized.

The loans from the World Bank and ADB were also not as quickly disbursed as stated in the LOI (point 21). This differed from the loans that Thailand received from the World Bank and ADB as well as Japan. These loans were in the nature of matching loans to the IMF SBA, which seemed to imply that for every disbursement from the stand-by loan, a similar amount would be disbursed from these sources (Blustein 2001, p. 79).

The terms and conditions of bilateral lines of credit were not standardized. The common feature was that, as a second line of defence, these loans could only be drawn after the funds from the multilateral institutions were used up. Only Japan and Singapore provided a different facility that was used in a joint market intervention immediately after the approval of the stand-by loan. Thus, for practical purposes the second line of defence of US$20 billion was not materialized. Thus the US$43 billion bailout did not reflect real conditions at all.

The funds that were used immediately were in fact those that the Bank of Japan (BOJ) and the Monetary Authority of Singapore (MAS) spent for market intervention in a joint operation between these two central banks and Bank Indonesia. The operation was conducted jointly several days after the Board officially approved the stand-by loan on 5 November 1997. The fund from the MAS was from the Government of Singapore Investment Corporation (GIC). It was part of the bilateral loan. The rupiah that GIC accumulated from the operation was used to finance Singapore investment in Indonesian corporations of GIC's choosing. The fund that BOJ used in the intervention was also part of the bilateral loan.

Even though these funds were immediately used after the approval of the stand-by loan, the Indonesian government did not draw them. In fact, the funds were disbursed by the two central banks on their own. The joint intervention strengthened the rupiah from 3,700 per dollar to 3,200 rupiah. However, the intervention was stopped after the IMF saw that Indonesia did not implement the programme consistently. From my telephone conversations with officials from the two institutions, even though none of them admitted directly, I drew the conclusion that IMF had instructed them to stop.

So the immediate funds available were US$3 billion and, of course, the US$5 billion of Indonesia's own reserves. The funds for joint intervention by BOJ and MAS altogether were in the order of US$1.5 billion. In other words, the amount of funds actually available was small in comparison to the amount of the maturing short-term debts of the corporations. The maturing short-term debts and the demand for hedging put heavy pressure on the rupiah to keep depreciating.

Generally the market knew that the size of funds that were readily available was not big enough to face the maturing debts. For this reason, mention of the amount of funds available that was intentionally inflated by the IMF was not achieving its objective. The market was not convinced by the availability of the funds such that the tendency to liquidate the rupiah and to buy dollars continued. At the same time, the inflated amount of funds available to support the programme created unnecessary additional public anxiety.

The drawing of the loan from IMF from November 1997 to January 1999 reached US$8.8 billion, while that from the World Bank and ADB US dollar was 3.3 billion (Berg 1999, Table 4). The sum of these drawings (US$12.1 billion) constituted 28 per cent of the total provision. Indonesia experienced several cancellation of its withdrawals. Withdrawals from the IMF loan from November 1997 to May 2000 totalled US$11.6 billion, while those from World Bank, ADB and bilateral loans amounted to US$10.3 billion, so that the total amounted to US$21.9 billion.[6]

Bank restructuring

Despite its crucial place in the adjustment programme, Indonesian's bank restructuring was not much discussed in the early days of the crisis and remains incomplete. The initial programme of bank restructuring as explained in the first LOI might not even have been known to the general public. The news and analysis on the banking issues of the first programme was dominated by the closure of the 16 banks. The bank closures overshadowed bank restructuring on the whole.

The programme actually included liquidating insolvent banks, re-capitalization and restructuring solvent banks that were weak for a variety of reasons, improving institutional financial infrastructures that includes improvement of banking supervision, legal and regulatory infrastructures for sound and efficient banking.

The original programme was very clear that the closing of the 16 banks was only an initial part of a wider bank restructuring. The bank closures was a *prior action conditionality* to the stand-by arrangement. However, due to the poor implementation of the bank closures, public attention only concentrated on this debacle.

It is also true that the bank re-capitalization that attracted so much public attention due to its sizeable cost would only help banks' balance sheets, i.e. to comply with the rule of capital adequacy ratio (CAR). But in order for the bank to be able to operate normally, other things have to be attended to. In general this implies improvement of bank management and liquidity, as well as improvement in the quality and income of banks' assets and income. The major problem here were the non-performing loans (NPLs). The last one relates to a different type of restructuring, that of the corporations.

A report by Carl-Johan Lindgren et al. identified ten steps that were classified into three phases of bank restructuring in the face of systemic problems. The phases include: acute crisis, stabilization, and the recovery phase. Restructuring in the first phase comprises measures to stop the panic and stabilize the system that includes four steps of action. The stabilization phase comprises of four measures to restructure the system. The recovery phase consisted of measures to normalize the system (Lindgren 1999, Box 2).[7]

Bank restructuring is an involved and complex issue that partly explains why not much is understood publicly. Misunderstandings at times led to public expectations that were much bigger than any programme implementation could deliver. In Indonesia when details of bank re-capitalization were announced — part of the stabilization phase — there was already public pressure for banks to start lending activities. Even earlier, shortly after the announcement of the IMF-supported programme, when banks started to suffer due to the failed bank closures — the acute crisis phase — there was already public pressure for banks to lend and for the central bank to lower interest rates.

To give a more complete picture of bank restructuring that was addressed in the IMF-supported programme, it should be mentioned that prior to the crisis, the IMF had been assisting Bank Indonesia in efforts to set up a comprehensive rehabilitation programme of the Indonesian banking system. The study was reported in a set of documents entitled "Strengthening the Bank Rehabilitation Effort". The study was conducted by 11 staff members of the Monetary and Exchange Affairs Department (MAE) of the Fund in collaboration with staff from the World Bank staff, under the chairmanship of Mr Reza Vaez-Zadeg.[8] Some of IMF staff who worked in the study had previously worked on a preliminary study on bank restructuring problems for Bank Indonesia that wrote a report in 1994 entitled "Indonesia: Bank Liquidation and Resolution".[9]

The reports were based on their discussions and analyses of different reports and data that were previously prepared by Bank Indonesia. From these reports on problems that confronted the Indonesian banking sector, the strategy that ultimately was formulated in the bank restructuring programme together with the IMF staff in October 1997 was actually preceded by an ongoing study that aimed at assessing

Indonesia's overall banking problems. However, it was also true that the dynamic nature of the problems made data and variables change rapidly in the several months of the financial turmoil that started to put Indonesian banking in distress soon after the floating of the rupiah in mid-August 1997.

So, the programme of bank restructuring explained in the first LOI to the Fund was comprehensive indeed. The plan was to begin implementing the programme by liquidating the 16 banks identified by the Indonesian team and the IMF staff. The implementation of other programmes that involved many banks with different problems as itemized in the MEFP and side letters would follow after the approval of the stand-by arrangement by the Board. As mentioned, these steps included closer monitoring and supervision of a number of banks, placing some banks under conservatorship, requiring other banks to come up with a rehabilitation programme, and planning for the merger for some state banks and conducting a special audit for others. The implementations of specific plans for a number of banks were made part of the conditionality of the stand-by loan.

I will discuss the impact of and other issues related to bank closures later. In this section, I will describe how the decision to liquidate banks evolved.

The process of the assessment to come up with the list of insolvent banks was as follows. Technically, the most important factor for a bank to be classified as candidate for liquidation is its solvency. So Bank Indonesia analysed each bank's balance sheet to determine its net worth, whether its assets could cover liabilities, the size of non-performing loans, the decreasing capability of the bank to mobilize funds from the public, the negative capital of a bank, and the bank owners.[10]

First, from the total number of 239 commercial banks that existed in 1997, 91 banks were included for careful analysis. These banks constituted all the banks that in Bank Indonesia's prudential measures were classified as poor and unsound, plus all banks that had assets 1 per cent or higher of total banking assets.[11] Second, from the assessment 34 banks were found insolvent — 26 private banks, 2 state banks, and 6 regional development banks. Third, among the 19 insolvent banks, 7 banks were under restructuring, with potential investors to rescue them.[12] Fourth, after discussions and reassessment together with the IMF team, it was agreed that the 16 insolvent private banks should be liquidated immediately.

The restructuring programme that was explained in the MEFP and the side letters encompassed 50 problem banks altogether. Each group showed the list of banks with the problems that confronted them and the specific steps to take as measures for bank restructuring. The insolvent banks were made up of two groups. The first was a group of 10 banks that were currently under an ongoing bank restructuring programme of Bank Indonesia, what was known as "nursing bank". The second one was the group of 6 banks that were put under intensive supervision by Bank Indonesia.

The detailed programme of bank restructuring was formulated in points 23 to 37 of the MEFP, while specific steps that needed to be taken and the deadlines were explained in the two side letters.

The first part of the programme was the actual closing of the 16 insolvent banks in 1 November 1997. The closed banks were mostly small banks. The assets of the closed banks constituted not more than 3 per cent of assets of all Indonesian banks. As mentioned in the MEFP, a limited guarantee of deposits to an amount of 20 million rupiah for each deposit account was provided. The payment would be financed using an advanced fund provided by Bank Indonesia, which ultimately would be borne by the budget.

The second part of the programme dealt with weak but viable banks. First, three small banks were placed under conservatorship on 1 November 1997. Their solvency status was uncertain; their net worth was either very small or slightly negative. In fact these banks were borderline cases. The arrangement was basically for Bank Indonesia to take control of the banks while management and shareholders' rights were suspended. A rehabilitation plan for each bank in order to bring them back in full compliance with all prudential regulations was to be produced within two months, failing which, they would be liquidated.

Second, there were 10 banks that could be classified insolvent when their restructured non-performing assets were assessed on the basis of economic value. These banks were still under restructuring with Bank Indonesia assistance, under the conventional method of a rescue package or "nursing bank" that was based on the Banking Law of 1992. They were given six months to come up with a credible rehabilitation programme that would be fully implemented by end-December 1998. The IMF would provide technical assistance on the first review of the stand-by arrangement in mid-March 1998.

Third, there were seven banks that had problems of capital deficiency. They each had to sign a memorandum of understanding with Bank Indonesia on the compliance with a specific time-table of rehabilitation of a cease and desist order (CDO).

Fourth, six banks were placed under intensive supervision by Bank Indonesia. This would include regular and frequent meetings between the bank's representatives and Bank Indonesia to review in detail the bank's current condition and prospects and daily monitoring of liquidity, foreign exchange exposure and/or any other variable relevant to the bank's specific weaknesses. These banks were placed under intensive supervision due to their large reliance on Bank Indonesia liquidity support that they suffered shortly after the floating of the rupiah in mid-August 1997. Three of these banks were large: Bank Central Asia (BCA), Bank Danamon and Bank Dagang Nasional Indonesia (BDNI).

In addition, two out of the seven state banks were insolvent. At the time of requesting the SBA the programme for restructuring state banks comprised of the following: first, to merge two state banks, Bank Bumi Daya (BBD) and BAPINDO. Second, the government would: (i) conduct a full review of state bank portfolios by 31 January 1998 with a view to determining the "good" and "bad" assets, (ii) prepare a plan for segregating between "good" and "bad" assets, (iii) place good assets into other state banks and bad assets into a loan recovery agency. Third, to increase private ownership of state banks. The government would engage internationally recognized firms to conduct portfolio reviews as well as financial and system audits of the remaining state banks by 30 March 1998.

With respect to the regional development banks, Bank Indonesia would place six regional development banks under conservatorship by 30 December 1997. They were BPD Jawa Timur, BPD Kalimantan Barat, BPD Maluku, BPD Nusa Tenggara Timur, BPD Sulawesi Tengah, and BPD Sulawesi Utara. This would imply that Bank Indonesia took control of the bank while management and shareholders' (regional governments) rights are suspended, that is, no dividends will be paid and shareholders will have no decision-making power. Within 60 days a new rehabilitation plan would be prepared that indicates their compliance with Bank Indonesia's prudential requirements and identifying the source of new funds. If this objective was not achieved within one year the bank would be liquidated.

From the above it is very clear that at the outset the programme for bank restructuring was comprehensive, encompassing not just bank closures, but also a variety of means, including more stringent supervision, CDO and other methods, as well as building financial infrastructure.

It was stipulated for a different group of banks that non-compliance of the required actions would put the banks in a more stringent programme, including possible liquidation. It was stated that another round of bank closures could take place after 1 November 1997. It was also true that there were more than 16 insolvent banks, not to mention weak or problem banks. However, had the programme of arresting the rupiah's depreciation succeeded and other bank restructuring steps taken judiciously, it was also possible that no other bank closures would be necessary.

I would like to reiterate that from the beginning, the bank restructuring proposals were comprehensive. It included closing of insolvent banks, re-capitalization of banks with good prospects operating normally but having insufficient capital, CDO for a number of banks, more stringent supervision by the central bank, and other supporting steps to building sound banking. The policy to freeze or to take over banks that was implemented in March 1998 and thereafter was based on steps that were prepared in the first letter of intent.

It should also be noted that in the first letter of intent it was mentioned that with the assistance of the Fund, Bank Indonesia would endeavour to improve Bank Indonesia's operation as lender of last resort, in using liquidity support to help banks facing liquidity mismatches. The second letter of intent also specifically mentioned steps for the government to take to grant Bank Indonesia its autonomy, and improvement of financial infrastructures, including a judiciary system to support the working of a sound banking system.

Structural reform

The Government's Economics team was well aware of the nature of the problems that confronted Indonesia. Before the government's decision to invite the Fund, the policy responses that were implemented to address the problems confronting the national economy had been progressing from exchange rate and monetary policy up to August 1997 to more comprehensive macroeconomic management that included fiscal, trade and administrative steps to address problems of the real sector. The decision to postpone or cancel big government projects came even before it became part of the SBA. The government introduced a new scheme of tariff reductions and postponement of government and state enterprise projects. The government also introduced a new scheme to give incentives for exports through a pre-shipment facility in September and October 1997.[13]

The structural reforms itemized in the LOI were aimed at increasing economic efficiency and reducing leakages of the national economy. The programme comprised of steps for increasing transparency in the formulation and implementation of government policies, and enhancing market competition through reform of the real sectors. The government would endeavour further deregulation and privatization and trade activities as well as investment. The government would also continue its programme of poverty reduction.

The structural reforms in the first LOI were basically a continuation of the programme that had been launched previously in support of the monetary and fiscal policies to stabilize the rupiah.

Included in the economic reforms were liberalization of wheat and flour imports, soybean and garlic that previously were monopolized in the hands of companies owned by Soeharto cronies. The programme also included the lifting of local price determination of cement, enlargement in the coverage of export facilities, reduction of import tariffs for a group of commodities, and simplification of import and export licensing procedures.

The programme also included postponement of big government projects. This was part of the policy to implement a prudent budget through expenditure reduction that also included reduction of subsidies in domestic oil and food. The objective of this exercise was for the government to produce a budget surplus of 1 per cent of GDP. And this became a quantitative performance criterion for the government to fulfill.

The programme for implementing a prudent budget went together with the programme to increase transparency and governance in the public sector. This programme comprised of steps to abolish the government practice of having non-budgetary spending. Government activities that in the past were financed using sources outside the government budget had to be incorporated into the budget. Included in this step was interest rate subsidies that was usually financed through Bank Indonesia liquidity credit. The proposal was to transfer all these expenditures into the government budget.

As part of the enhancement of transparency, Bank Indonesia's liquidity support was used to help banks having a liquidity mismatch during the crisis and payment to deposit owners up to 20 million rupiah for liquidated banks. The basic reason for transferring the mode of financing from Bank Indonesia to the government budget was to make it more transparent and accountable.

Rupiah stabilization

All the above steps were aimed at providing a base for sustainable stability of the exchange rate. However, the destabilizing of the currency continued in spite of the concerted efforts by the monetary authorities. Therefore, new steps were designed as a part of the adjustment policy programme to stabilize the rupiah, both via direct intervention in the foreign exchange market and other steps to influence demand and supply of foreign exchange.

The government and IMF agreed that after the signing of the LOI a joint intervention in the market would be conducted to jack up the rupiah's exchange rate. Bank Indonesia together with the Monetary Authority of Singapore (MAS) and the Bank of Japan (BOJ) simultaneously conducted the intervention in the foreign exchange market. As a result of the intervention as well as an early positive response to the agreement between the government and the IMF, the rupiah strengthened. In the spot market, the price of the dollar went down from 3,640 rupiah in 31 October 1997 to 3,295 rupiah in 7 November 1997, or an appreciation of more than 10 per cent. It was definitely a successful joint operation by the three central banks. It was, I believe, a rare joint operation between central banks in Asia to actually intervene in the market to stabilize a currency.

However, it was unfortunate that the joint operation worked only briefly. The rupiah went back to experiencing a heavy pounding, such that by the end of November 1997, the rupiah rate went back to the rate prior to the historic joint intervention.

The negative domestic market reaction arose due to the rumour of further bank closures and actions by the owners of two of the liquidated banks, owned by Soeharto's son and brother respectively, to sue the Minister of Finance and the Governor of Bank Indonesia in court, in protest at the closures. The foreign market, which responded favourably in the beginning, turned sour due to negative perceptions on the deal for Soeharto's son to acquire a small bank, Bank Alfa.

It is curious to know how the decision was made to terminate the joint intervention of the three central banks, which worked well for that short period. Since the joint operation was done through a loose arrangement, even though the aim was clear, the termination of the operation was also unclear. In fact, I have since learned that, toward the third week of November 1997, both the BOJ and MAS stopped the intervention altogether.

I did make a few phone calls to the MAS and the BOJ to persuade them to resume the operation. However I did not receive any positive answers. The answers I received from the inquiries were polite, but not straight to the point as to why they were not willing to resume their intervention in the market when the rupiah started to slide again. Actually I had a strong feeling then that both central banks must have been receiving messages from Washington to not continue the operation. They must also have come to their own conclusion that they could no longer help Bank Indonesia in its futile efforts to stop the drastic depreciation of the rupiah. It has been my contention that, due to the government of Indonesia's poor performance in implementing the adjustment programme, the Fund in close cooperation with the US Treasury advised the two central banks to terminate the joint intervention.[14]

In the meantime, the execution of the bank closures turned out to have an adverse impact on market confidence. In fact, a number of banks started experiencing runs. The industry suffered from a flight to safety, whereby depositors and other fund owners transferred their funds from banks that were perceived weak to safe ones. Some also converted their funds from rupiahs to US dollars.

Bank Indonesia was confronted with a difficult dilemma. On the one hand, it had to deal with banks that suffered from bank runs. Bank Indonesia had to act as lender of last resort as well as be the guardian of the payment system, which was in danger of collapsing due to bank runs. On the other hand, adding liquidity into the banking sector could jeopardize the efforts to strengthen the rupiah, and possibly violate IMF conditionality. In its actual operations, Bank Indonesia had to deal with the opposing sides. On the one hand, President Soeharto mounted pressure for easing liquidity to help the weakening real sectors. On the other hand, the Fund kept reminding Bank Indonesia on the need to keep interest rates high to defend the rupiah as agreed upon in the LOI.

Bank Indonesia had to make special efforts to deal with the issue, both in terms of the substance as well as the explaining of what was actually transpiring. Bank Indonesia substituted direct intervention in the rupiah inter-bank money market for the decision to raise the rate of interest, demonstrating Bank Indonesia's lack of independence. In fact, President Soeharto did not allow Bank Indonesia to raise the SBI rates.

In effect, what Bank Indonesia did was just make immediate mopping-up operations every time the liquidity level was close to violating the IMF performance criteria. This was done via a direct presence in the inter-bank money market, buying the rupiah out from banks that had surplus liquidity. By doing this, the interest rate in the inter-bank money market would automatically rise. Thus, even though the SBI rate was unchanged, the market rates increased due to Bank Indonesia's active participation that raised total demand in the inter-bank money market. Actually, the SBI rate at the end of November 1997 was still close to twice the rate in early August 1997, just before the government made a move to squeeze liquidity.

But, Bank Indonesia action to assist banks having liquidity problems could cause unnecessary additional liquidity, which was not allowed under the binding conditionality. It was our contention that the action did not necessarily constitute an increase in total liquidity because it did not lead to increases in bank lending. In fact, during this period there was a substitution of rupiah notes for bank loans. The loss of confidence in the banking industry — expecially of banks that were perceived as "bad banks" — caused the public to hold rupiah notes that they took out from their banks, either to transfer it to banks that were per-ceived "good" or save them "under the mattress". For a couple of months, the increase in demand for bank notes was so strong that I made a decision to put into circulation the 50,000 rupiah note that was issued by my predecessor early in 1993.[15] They were commemorative notes, printed on plastic and legal tender. The notes were in 50,000 rupiah denomination, but they were sold for 100,000 rupiah. The problem was that more were printed than Bank Indonesia could sell. In my recollection the total value was five billion rupiah. Only a small fraction of the total was sold, while the major part was stored in the vault for years. This stock of rupiah notes turned out to be useful in December 1997 when there was a huge surge of demand for rupiah notes due to the loss of public confidence in the banking sector.

Furthermore, due to public loss of confidence in banks and the payment system, some transactions were conducted in cash. Even if there were increases in base money, the money multiplier was drastically reduced such that the effective additional liquidity was not substantial. In fact the increase in liquidity was not much higher over the limit as determined in the performance criteria, as confirmed by the IMF assessment on programme implementation.[16]

When the lack of confidence also spread to banks themselves, the inter-bank money market was disrupted. In fact, the inter-bank money market started to experience segmentation when some banks suffered runs. It became worse after the bank closures, reflected in more bank runs and flights to safety. In the process of flights to safety, large banks, which comprised of state banks, a few private national banks and foreign banks, were in the position of receiving funds.

The inter-bank money market worked only among banks that knew each other well. The Jakarta inter-bank offered rate (Jibor) recorded the interest rate results of 24 large banks, members of an exclusive group. During the flight to safety, these banks did not have any problem in liquidity, and thus the interest rate that was recorded in the Jibor was low. And since the official report to the Fund for monitoring purposes was based on this data, Fund management observed only these low interest rates. However, the rest of the banks were actually in a liquidity squeeze. The inter-bank rates of interest among these banks were much higher than the Jibor. For example, when the Jibor was around 30 per cent in late November, the rate for other banks was more than 100 per cent.

Still, for other banks, there was no liquidity available from other banks due to the loss of confidence among banks. During the banking crisis, banks supplied less and less liquidity to the inter-bank money market. Even those that held surpluses shied away from supplying liquidity. This was when Bank Indonesia, in defence of the banking sector and the national payment system, provided banks facing liquidity problems with liquidity support.

Thus, aside from the fact that a tight monetary stance was not consistently implemented, there were also some misunderstandings on the part of the Fund with respect to what was transpiring in the financial sector. To convince the IMF, I wrote a detailed explanation to Deputy MD Stanley Fischer about the matter. In addition I also asked Professor Ali Wardhana to write a similar letter to Under Secretary Larry Summers, since they knew each other well since the time Dr. Summers worked with the World Bank. We fully recognized the role of the US Treasury in this issue. Still on other front, on 5 December 1997, Mr. Zamani, the Fund Executive Director for Southeast Asia, wrote a similar letter to the Managing Director Camdessus, with copies distributed to all the executive directors. So, a concerted effort was made to deal with a tricky issue that Bank Indonesia confronted during the first few months of implementing the Fund-supported programme.

The above story might not make sense at all under normal circumstances. With a President who has a better understanding of the issues or an independent Bank Indonesia, the problem should have been less complicated. In fact, the requirement for the government to give autonomy to Bank Indonesia was only mentioned explicitly in the second LOI, 15 January 1998 (item 22). This requirement was implemented partially in 21 January 1998 with the issuing of Presidential Decree number 23, 1998. And I did not wait any longer, after the issuance of the decree. Bank Indonesia doubled the current the SBI rates: for one-day maturing SBI, the rate was raised from 14 per cent to 30 per cent.

In addition to the complications in the inter-bank money market and the conflicting intermediate policy objectives between the President and the Fund, there were other developments that made monetary management extremely difficult. I would like to mention two things that, at the very least, distracted our energies. The first was the sudden appearance of several investment banks offering Bank Indonesia funds. The second was President Soeharto's wish to tap dollar funds from the Singapore market to strengthen the national reserves.

First, let me discuss the concerns about the sudden appearance of several international banks offering US dollar loans to Bank Indonesia. Actually, their actions still puzzle me, except that they wished to profit from the rupiah's fluctuations. Around late September to mid-October 1997, several international banks, including UBS (Swiss bank) and ABN Amro (the Netherlands) approached Bank Indonesia to ask whether Indonesia was interested in taking loans in US dollars. The offers were similar in nature: the availability of dollar funds that could be drawn fast at a competitive interest rate. The loans were between US$2 to US$5 billion for two to three years. One of the stipulations was that the lenders wanted to hold an option for being repaid in rupiah or dollars.

As I mentioned before, Bank Indonesia had engaged in the international market to raise funds through stand-by loans from international banks, to cushion Indonesia's foreign reserves. So the fact that these banks made an offer to Bank Indonesia was not unusual. However it was curious that they did it at approximately the same time, and that they made offers with similar terms. Of course, if they expected that the rupiah would strengthen, they would ask to be paid back in rupiah and vice versa: These banks could profit a lot from this operation.

To get a better picture about these offers, I asked the IMF staff who came to Jakarta for the preparation of the stand-by arrangement to study the proposals. The IMF staff suggestion was, as expected, for Bank Indonesia to ignore them.

I did not pursue the matter further. However, I found it a little bit intriguing when I studied the terms of some bilateral loans that became part of the second-line of defence of the IMF stand-by loan. Some of the loans carried terms that were similar to the ones offered by the international banks. Interestingly, the terms that seemed to be attractive was the option for the lender to be repaid in rupiah or dollars. The fact that the IMF staff advised Bank Indonesia to ignore loans offered by some international banks, and almost simultaneously organized a package of loans that included bilateral loans with similar terms, puzzled me.

The second development was President Soeharto's wish to issue Indonesia bearer's notes (bonds) in dollars to be sold in Singapore. Like many other ideas from President Soeharto, this one must have come from his business associates. In a way, the President did not want to show his disregard for the market, so this plan resorted to a market instrument. It was argued that exporters did not want to bring back their dollars, and parked them abroad instead. Thus, the argument went, the government should attract these funds through the mechanism of issuing bearer's notes.

President Soeharto told Minister Mar'ie Muhammad and myself that he had discussed the matter with the Singapore government. So he wanted us to take up the matter for its implementation. I was flabbergasted. But I asked Bank Indonesia staff to communicate with our counterparts in Singapore to look into the matter. I had to admit that I felt so bad to have to ask my staff to do this. Maybe it was our luck that by this time Standard & Poor's and Moody's were announcing their new ratings, and that Indonesia's sovereign and corporate ratings were both lowered.

I successfully asked President Soeharto to abandon his wish to issue government bonds in the Singapore market, using a valid argument that the time was not right due to the recent downgrade of Indonesia's ratings, in addition to the Fund conditionality that put a limit on the government's foreign exposure.

I felt relieved about the cancellation of the bond idea. There were two reasons that had scared me with the plan. The first one was that due to unfavourable market perceptions, Indonesia would have to accept a very bad price for the bonds. Second, even more worrying to me, I did not exactly know what the President wished to do with the funds arising from the bond issuance.

With respect to the government's concern that Indonesian exporters did not hold their foreign exchange onshore, and parked them abroad instead, Bank Indonesia actually designed instruments, swaps and options. Basically, the instruments would enable exporters who sold their foreign exchange to Bank Indonesia to get back their foreign exchange when they needed them. However, the instruments were not much used by exporters. This would, in turn, create a lack of supply of foreign exchange in the market.

Crucial Issues Left Out from the Programme

A common criticism about Indonesia's first LOI to the IMF has been about the failure of the policy to liquidate banks in November 1997, and the high rates of interest that hindered economic recovery. I will discuss the first issue in detail in the next section.

Excessive focus on the implications of bank closures and the high rates of interest have distorted perceptions of the adjustment programme, which had many more features than just the bank closures. The adjustment programme as explained in the LOI was definitely a comprehensive policy of adjustment.

However, immediately after the introduction of the adjustment programme, people were already commenting on some of the missing items in the Fund-supported programme. Two important issues conspicuously left out from the first LOI were related to the social implications of the crisis and the measures to be taken, and the issue of corporate debt. These two were either left out for certain technical reasons or to the lack of recognition of their importance. Both issues were not foreign to the economic team. But it was obvious that the IMF staff who came to Jakarta for the preparation of the SBA were not enthusiastic about addressing these issues, which rather belatedly were acknowledged as important.

My early observation concerning this omission was that these issues were traditionally outside IMF's theatre of operations. For the Indonesian team, it was clear that all the adjustments steps in the real sectors that had to be supported by prudent fiscal and monetary policies, including lowering subsidies and raising interest rates, would have profound social implications. I would like to discuss the development of the issues as they unfolded then to provide a better background for further assessment.

With respect to the reduction of subsidies, it was true that for the IMF, the most crucial issues were the formulation of a clear plan of reduction, and the transparency in their financing. For example, on the reduction of the oil subsidy, there were no demands to put them into effect immediately, but there was a need to begin with a clear phasing. In addition, together with getting rid of financing government activities with extra-budgetary sources, the financing of subsidy reduction should be done transparently by incorporating the expenditure into the government budget. This method would give way to social control that could also support the enhancement of governance.

The introduction of social safety net programmes to cope with the adverse social impacts of the crisis and the measures to be taken was only mentioned summarily in the first letter of intent (item 45). The detailed programme was formally adopted in the second LOI. With respect to the social programme, the first LOI only mentioned that the government poverty reduction programme would be continued.

The IMF stand on the issue was indirectly reflected in the requirement for the 1998/99 budget to produce a surplus of 1 per cent of GDP as quantitative performance criteria for the budget. It should be obvious that a social safety net programme to cope with the social implications of the crisis that implied budgetary spending would not go together with the requirement that the budget had to be in surplus.

Another issue was the absence of any corporate debt restructuring in the first LOI. The Indonesian economic team understood well the potential problems that could arise from the corporate debts during the negotiations. The problems were not just limited to the inaccurate data and information about the corporate debts in foreign exchange. But, the market was not happy with the government initial attitude, which in a way was reflecting IMF stand on the matter, of hands-off policy concerning the problems of corporate debts.

It was true that initially Bank Indonesia had some problems in terms of the quality of data and information about the private sector's debts. For one thing, the data that Bank Indonesia carried were limited to private sector loans in foreign exchange that bore loan contracts. There was also some technical issues, due to the fact that debt information was grouped into short, medium and long runs, based on the terms of each loan at the time of closing the contract.

In other words, debt classification was done on the basis of the maturity of the loan at the time of contract signing. Whereas, debt management should be more oriented towards debt flows to know how much foreign funds the economy would need at each period to service the debts. Debt management should be concerned with the flow of debt, not just the total stock. For debt management, it is important to realize that even debts that were classified long term in accordance with the maturity at the time of its inception became short-term if they were maturing in a short period. So, the most important information for debt management would be the remaining maturity period of all the outstanding debts.

Another problem was Bank Indonesia's incomplete data on corporate debt in the form of short-term notes and other debt instruments. There was a government regulation that required corporations to report on debts incurred, but compliance was loose. Bank Indonesia's information on corporate debt originated from debt instruments mostly coming from secondary data and were not accurate.

However, I implemented a crash programme to improve statistics on corporate debt several months before the government decided to invite the IMF in October 1997. In the third week of August 1997 I started to invite large Indonesian companies to discuss the private sector's indebtedness in foreign currencies, including inaccurate debt statistics. The meetings were conducted in stages with Indonesian corporations. They were started with corporations with US$100 million foreign exposure and continued downward with corporations having smaller amount of debts. Since these were done in an uncertain market environment on the wake of regional financial panic, I asked the Minister of Trade and Industry Tungky Ariwibowo to host the meetings. Following these meetings most corporations complied with Bank Indonesia's inquiries concerning their exposures in foreign currencies.[17]

After completing the process of compilation, the total private foreign debts of June 1997 was recorded as amounting to US$80 billion. In fact, the first LOI used this data in formulating the Indonesian problem with respect to foreign debts. In the LOI it was reported that Indonesia's total debt was US$140 billion, with government debt at US$60 billion. Out of the US$80 billion of private foreign debts, US$33 billion was maturing in one year or less. Thus, in spite of complaints against Bank Indonesia's poor and inaccurate data on corporate debt, the first LOI was specific enough on these figures.

Due to IMF insistence, the government's official stance on corporate debt in the early part of the adjustment programme under the Fund's SBA was basically a hands-off policy. In his public statements in Tokyo, Washington D.C. and New York in mid-November 1997, Minister of Finance Mar'ie Muhammad could only say that the Indonesian government would not bail out corporations. This was curious in light of the fact that the size of corporate debt was identified as one of the major causes, if not factors that exacerbated the Asian crisis. It was even more surprising if one compared Indonesia's hands-off policy and the active role of the governments of Thailand and Korea early in the implementation of their IMF-supported programmes.

It is my conjecture that the Indonesian government would have been involved earlier in policies for addressing the social implications of the crisis and dealing with corporate debt had there not been objections by the IMF. The government's involvement in these areas only became part of the adjustment programme in the second and subsequent LOIs.

4

Poor Programme Implementation

Poor Implementation or Bad Programme?

The implementation of the IMF-supported programme started with the execution of the decision to close insolvent banks on 1 November 1997. In the jargon of IMF stand-by arrangements, this was a prior action, part of the conditionality. In fact it was a step that had to be taken by a recipient of a stand-by loan prior to the board deliberation to discuss the LOI sent by the member government to ask for a SBA.

The government announcement on the bank closures was made by The Minister of Finance, the Governor of Bank Indonesia and the Minister of Trade and Industry in the Ministry of State Secretariat, on 1 November 1997. Both the Minister of Finance and the Governor explained the background and the reasoning for the government's decision. Minister of Finance Mar'ie Muhammad explained in detail about the government policy of bank closures and the whole adjustment programme in the Parliament on 10 November 1997. In his explanation, he mentioned five criteria for a bank to be targeted for closure, which included: bank assets that could not cover liabilities; when a bank had insufficient income to meet its liabilities; caused by bad debts; a bank's inability to mobilize public funds, forcing it to rely on the inter-bank money market; negative net worth; and ignoring repeated warnings from the central bank.

The bank closures involved 16 banks with more than 400 offices all over Indonesia. A limited deposit guarantee was provided that was modelled on the liquidation of Bank Summa in 1992. At the liquidation of Bank Summa five years earlier, the government paid deposit owners a maximum of 10 million rupiah. This time, each deposit account was paid to the maximum of 20 million rupiah (approximately US$6,000). So, deposits equal to or less than 20 million rupiah would be paid the full amount, and those over it would be paid 20 million rupiah each. The number of deposit accounts equal to and less than 20 million rupiah of the closed banks numbered more than 660,000 accounts, which equalled to more than 94 per cent of the total number of deposit accounts of the closed banks.

The bank closures aimed at winning back market confidence in the banking sector, caused the reverse effect.

The fight to stabilize the rupiah was a very important part of the programme. Rupiah stability would help bank restructuring and structural reform as well. Efforts to stabilize the currency were conducted through steps to influence the supply of and demand for the dollar as well as implementing direct intervention in the foreign exchange market.

It was mentioned before that a joint intervention in the foreign exchange market between Bank of Japan, the Monetary Authority of Singapore and Bank Indonesia was conducted for a short period after the signing of the LOI. The two central banks must have used up substantial amount of funds to help Bank Indonesia prop up the rupiah that resulted in an appreciation of more than 11 per cent from 3,600 to 3,200 rupiah to a dollar. However, it was sad that the strengthening of the currency was short-lived. Towards the last week of November 1997 the exchange rate went back to the previous level.

The pressures on the rupiah reappeared partly due to the market reaction to the bank closures. The adverse market reactions came after an outburst of irrational reactions from owners of two of the closed banks who sued the Minister of Finance and the Governor of Bank Indonesia, and public suspicion about the purchase of Bank Alfa by a former owner of a closed bank. Both cases involved President Soeharto's family: Mr. Probosutedjo, Soeharto's stepbrother and major owner of Bank Jakarta, and Mr. Bambang Trihatmodjo, Soeharto's son and minor owner of Bank Andromeda, who acquired Bank Alfa.[1]

The implementation of the structural reform programme was also in disarray. A number of public enterprise projects, which had been originally postponed, were reinstated. In the IMF review it was stated the reinstatement of projects included a power plant that had been opposed before by the World Bank because it was economically unnecessary. The review stated further that for the first two months after the announcement of the IMF arrangement and the closure of the 16 banks, economic reform seemed to disappear from the government agenda.[2]

Furthermore, the implementation of the bank restructuring programme was not on schedule. Compliance of performance criteria in this area was very poor. Banks under conservatorship that had not submitted adequate rehabilitation plans had not been liquidated and there were no established performance targets for state banks. In fact, the bank restructuring programme, which was crucial, were complicated by the adverse effects of the bank closures.

Important quantitative targets like the growth of money supply and interest rates were not fulfilled. In fact, the IMF stated in the preliminary review that

> performance under the programme so far has been decidedly disappointing. As a result of this policy performance, hard-won market confidence, built up over three decades of rapid economic progress, and revived at the outset of the arrangement, has now vanished. To turn the situation around the authorities need to demonstrate a public and unequivocal commitment to their programme.[3]

Several developments seemed to be behind the disappointing performance of the Indonesian government in implementing the stand-by arrangement:

- Monetary policy was unevenly implemented. During the first few days of programme implementation, in particular due to the joint intervention in the foreign exchange markets and the following monetary tightness, the rupiah was strengthened. But once the exchange rate began to strengthen, Bank Indonesia could not stand the government pressure to start easing the monetary stance. In other words, the liquidity easing was done too rapidly.

- Public reaction to the banks closures was negative, in particular after legal actions that were taken by owners of liquidated banks close to President Soeharto, to sue the monetary authorities in court.
- The reinstatement of government projects due to intervention by President Soeharto and his cronies.
- The emergence of political uncertainty due to rumours about the state of President Soeharto's health as publicly noticed by cancellation of his public functions for almost two weeks.[4]
- Contagion effect from regional currencies' depreciation in early December 1997 that forced Korea to request for a stand-by arrangement.

In a way it was true as IMF staff pointed in their review that the monetary policy was uneven. During this period the execution of consistent monetary policy was close to impossible. As explained before, the monetary authorities already took a tight monetary stance since the rupiah floating in mid-August 1997. When the joint intervention to strengthen the rupiah was done after the approval of the stand-by arrangement in early November, the monetary stance was further tightened. In other words, the tight monetary policy with high inter-bank rates had been going on for several months.

The banking sector, which suffered from a liquidity squeeze, was already experiencing some casualties, whereby a number of banks started to experience severe liquidity mismatches by late August 1997. In fact, the banking sector was in distress already when the stand-by arrangement commenced. The poor execution of bank closures that led to bank runs ultimately drove the distressed banks into crisis.

The market had been experiencing the adverse effect of high interest rates and scarce liquidity. Pressure for Bank Indonesia to ease the monetary stance was strong: the Chamber of Commerce and Industry lobbied strongly for interest rate reduction and easing bank loans; some members of the Cabinet and pundits and the media voiced their support; and President Soeharto pressed the monetary authorities to deal with the liquidity problem and to ease the tightness of the monetary stance.[5]

The Monetary Board had to comply with the President's instructions. The three-pronged liquidity squeeze of August 1997, which was apparently overdone since it drove a number of banks into distress, had to be overturned.

I recognized that the ongoing liquidity squeeze had put the economy and the banking sector in trouble. However, I also realized that there was a performance criterion that Bank Indonesia had to comply with. The only thing that Bank Indonesia could do was to ease liquidity in stages to reduce its adverse effect on the exchange rate.

The dilemma facing us was twofold: on the one hand, the IMF kept asking Bank Indonesia to keep its promise to tighten the monetary stance in line with targets of monetary growth with high interest rates; on the other hand, President Soeharto kept asking Bank Indonesia to reduce the lending rate and to ease bank lending.

In the meantime, due to the unexpected market and public reactions to the bank closures, the banking industry faced flights to safety and bank runs that finally pushed it into crisis. With the government policy of not closing more banks and the previous presidential instruction in early September 1997, Bank Indonesia defended the banking sector and the payment system that were in danger of collapsing by providing liquidity support to banks. As with the bank closures, this policy ultimately became controversial.[6]

If the tightening of monetary stance had been drastic, the monetary easing was also so fast that it caused complications in the conduct of monetary management under stringent IMF conditionality. Domestic pressure for Bank Indonesia to ease monetary stance was so strong that efforts to do it in stages were swept under the rug. But, instead this action jeopardized the promise to uphold performance criteria under the stand-by arrangement. In a short period Bank Indonesia's window to allow banks to rediscount their papers (SBPUs) was reopened for banks to use. Bank Indonesia certificates (SBIs) that originated from deposits owned by state enterprises were liquidated.

On top of this, the President also instructed state banks to start lending to small and medium scale enterprises with subsidized rates of interest. And to make things worse, this scheme was designed by the President and some Cabinet ministers and senior officials of several ministries without consulting either the Governor of Bank Indonesia or the Ministry of Finance. So, even if there was some justification for easing the monetary stance, the timing and the pace were not right.

The decisions to start easing the monetary stance and to rescue the banking sector and payment system from collapsing put Bank Indonesia in an impossible position. President Soeharto took out the one instrument available for Bank Indonesia to use for sterilization of the additional liquidity that was pumped into the system through liquidity support. Bank Indonesia had to ask permission from the President through the Monetary Board to change the interest rate. I asked for the permission by the President to raise the interest rate in compliance with the government's promise in the LOI but permission was never granted. He wanted to do the opposite, of course.

Inconsistencies were not the monopoly of the government either. The IMF and its inflexibility had certainly contributed to the problems. I mentioned before that the hands-off policies of the government in dealing with the corporate debt issue and social implications of the programme had to do with the inflexible attitude of the IMF. In terms of technicality, it was mentioned before that in the so called "bailout" programme, the IMF had place US$5 billion Indonesia's own reserves as part of the facility.

It should also be noted that there had been differences in the design of the facility available for Indonesia compared to that for Thailand and Korea, in a way that was less advantageous for Indonesia. Loan withdrawals by Indonesia were not running as smoothly as those by Thailand and Korea. Aside from inconsistent programme implementation, which implied government mistakes, the different experiences in loan withdrawals originated in the different nature of the loans themselves.

Observing statistics of withdrawals of the loans under stand-by arrangements in the three countries in their first two years, the relative positions of each country appeared as follows (Berg 1999, Table 4, p. 22):

- Of Thailand's loan of US$17.2 billion, the total withdrawal in the first two years, up to August 1999, amounted to US$14.1 billion or closed to 82 per cent of the total package. From this amount, withdrawals from IMF were US$3.4 billion, ADB and the World Bank US$4.4 billion and from bilateral countries US$8.7 billion.
- Of Korea's package of US$54.4 billion in loans, total withdrawals up to January 1999 or the first 13 months amounted to US$29.7

billion, or 13 per cent of the total package. From this amount, withdrawals from the IMF loan were US$19 billion out of US$21.1 facility, and withdrawals from the ADB and the World Bank loans were US$9.7 billion.

- Of Indonesia's loans of US$42.3 billion, up till January 1999 or 15 months into the programme, total withdrawals were US$12.1 billion or 29 per cent of the total loan. From the IMF loan, withdrawals were US$8.8 billion, from the ADB and the World Bank, US$3.3 billion. No withdrawals were made from the bilateral loans.

There were some differences in the details of the loans. In the case of Thailand, it was specifically mentioned in terms of the World Bank loan, and perhaps also part of the bilateral loans, that they were co-financing the IMF loan. This implied that for each withdrawal of the IMF loan, there was an equal amount of withdrawal from these loans. This explained the disbursements of bilateral loans in the case of Thailand. There was no such stipulation in Indonesia's package. Was this the government of Indonesia's fault? It must be so. But, certainly it was more curious that the IMF had not suggested that Indonesia be given similar terms.

The loan to Korea was, of course, different from the one to Indonesia. In fact, this was the first case of the new IMF facility that was called Supplementary Reserve Facility (SRF). This facility was only introduced in early December 1997, and basically it was a facility to provide balance of payments' support to member countries that could be drawn much faster in much bigger amounts than a regular stand-by arrangement and SBA with emergency procedures. This facility could be larger than the SBA with faster disbursement to help member countries coping with the contagion problem. But, it also carried more stringent conditionality. It carried a higher rate of interest and a shorter period of repayment. Korea was lucky indeed to enter into an agreement with the IMF for the new facility. It was almost as if the facility was designed for resolving Korea's problem.

Korea was in a better position in dealing with its short-term corporate debt. I do not know how much the IMF played a role in the matter. However, it is possible that the IMF had learnt its lesson from the sloppy handling of corporate debt problems in Indonesia, and decided to deal with the issues very early. There have been claims that the U.S. Treasury also intervened strongly to push the Korean government to accept steps to reform the economy in its LOI to the IMF. In other words, they became part of the conditionality of the stand-by arrangement. It is actually irrelevant whether the push for corporate debt restructuring originated from the IMF or the U.S. Treasury. But, for sure the Korean government dealt with the corporate debt issues very early in the crisis.[8] Joon-Ho Hahm also mentioned that Korea launched a financial restructuring programme before inviting the IMF in late November 1997.[9]

Thus, even though the three countries basically faced similar problems at the outset of the crisis, ultimately asking for IMF stand-by arrangements, Indonesia had experienced its implementation differently. Indonesia, which started with similar or even better macroeconomic fundamentals at the outset, and put up better policy responses at the initial stage, ultimately became the worst case.

Pre-crisis magnitudes of some selected macroeconomic variables were either similar or better for Indonesia. The reserves of both Thailand and Korea were in a much more precarious condition at the time of the inception of the stand-by arrangements. Paul Blustein quotes the Korean Minister of Finance: "He (Mr. Camdessus) said that when — the IMF negotiated its programme with Thailand — the Thais had almost no reserves. But, Korea has at least one month and a half to go" (Blustein 2001, pp. 29–30).

However, after the turmoil ran for sometime, the Indonesian condition worsened relative to the other two countries. The depth and length of the crisis, the social as well as economic implications, all had been worse for Indonesia compared to the two countries. The table below shows some of those statistics.

Several studies on the Asian crisis confirm the idiosyncrasies of the Indonesian case. Hussain and Wihlborg (1999) showed that the depth and length of the recession in the crisis was determined, among others, by bankruptcy regulations and procedures. Countries adhering to bankruptcy law, which gives strong protection to debtors and weak protection to creditors, tend to experience a longer recession. This happened due to the tendency for these countries to not liquidate distressed corporations or insolvent banks prior to the crisis. This is none other than the popular argument of "too big to fail" in banking. In Indonesia this condition, in combination with political intervention

TABLE 7
Impacts of the Crisis: Indonesia, Thailand and Korea
(per cent)

	Indonesia	Thailand	Korea
Currency depreciation	74.8	37.6	40.9
Inflation rate	54.4	10.8	8.3
Economic growth	−13.7	−9.4	−5.8
Loan withdrawals	28	82	49

Notes: depreciation rate: nominal, June '97–March '99
　　　Inflation: CPI, annual, June '97–May '98
　　　GDP growth: 1998
　　　Loan withdrawals: withdrawals of loan in the IMF package up to January '99 (for Korea and Indonesia) and August '99 for Thailand.
Source: taken from tables in Andrew Berg, "The Asia Crisis: Causes, Policy Responses and Outcomes", IMF Working Paper (Washington D.C.: IMF, October 1999).

in bank lending to groups closely related to the centres of power within a concentration of corporate ownership, led to high growth of bank lending and a high percentage of non-performing loans. The low index of law enforcement and high index of corruption put Indonesia in a worse situation than either Korea and Thailand (also Pomelearno 1998; Claessens 1999).

Kaminsky has argued that the Asian crisis had seemed similar to the Latin American one. It was preceded by economic distress that was shown in different variables, like currency appreciation, current account deficits, large size of short term external debt relative to reserves, and the weakness of the financial sector. However, she stated that the Indonesian crisis could not be classified as belonging to this group (Kaminsky 1999, p. 33). Berg also showed differences between the Korean and Thai crises on the one hand and the Indonesian and Malaysian experience on the other. The crisis in the first two countries had originated from deteriorating economic fundamentals, while the last two resulted from regional contagion (Berg 1999, p. 18). All these studies basically showed that the Indonesian case was different from others. In spite of Indonesia's claims for having better conditions at the outset, it was Indonesia that became a basket case.

The Infamous Bank Closures

The most controversial implementation of the Fund-supported programme was the government's decision to revoke the licences of 16 banks as a prior action of the stand-by arrangement. In popular terms, it was bank liquidation as a part of a comprehensive bank restructuring programme. I use the terms bank closure and liquidation interchangeably here.

After the closures in April 1999, Indonesia had 170 commercial banks in operation. This implies that since the implementation of bank restructuring under the Fund-supported programme, and up to April 1999, 68 commercial banks had been liquidated. However, the much talked about bank closures had undoubtedly been those in November 1997. People have even argued that the Indonesian crisis became so deep and its impact so widespread because of the closures.

The government's decision to liquidate banks during the crisis was heavily criticized. However, the subsequent liquidation of close to 50 banks did not encounter criticism, as if the society had gotten used to bank closures.

The criticisms included:

- the bank closures were a failure because Indonesia did not have a deposit guarantee scheme. People panicked after the government decision to liquidate banks, which triggered bank runs;
- that more insolvent banks should have been closed;
- the lack of transparency in the criteria that the government used for the decision on which banks to close, with bank owners arguing that some banks in worse condition were not closed; and
- the bank closure seemed politically motivated to hurt the pribumi group or that it was a conspiracy against the Soeharto family.

The deposit insurance issue

I do not agree with those who argue that the bank closures failed because of the absence of a deposit insurance scheme (for instance by Jeffrey Sachs of Harvard University, Radelet and Sachs 1998).

A deposit insurance scheme usually covers a limited amount of deposits. In other words, it covers small depositors only. The present scheme under the US federal deposit insurance corporation (FDIC) for instance, covers deposits of up to US$200,000. So, when a bank is liquidated, depositors would get back their funds up to this amount. For deposits larger than the maximum amount guaranteed, settlement would have to wait the completion of the liquidation process.

Due to unfinished preparations for the implementation of a deposit insurance scheme, the Indonesian government decided to guarantee payment for small deposit holders. This was done in the case of the liquidation of Bank Summa in 1992, with a provision that the government would pay the deposit holders up to 10 million rupiah (a little less than US$5,000). For deposits larger than the maximum guaranteed, payment would be done through the liquidation process. The government reiterated the same policy for guaranteeing small depositors at a Cabinet meeting on 3 September 1997. In other words, the public was informed about the ruling through the widely publicized liquidation of Bank Summa in 1992, as well as the government announcement of the similar policy in September 1997 and repeated at the announcement of the bank closures in November 1997: the government guaranteed to pay depositors up to a maximum of 20 million rupiah (US$5,500).[10]

Bank Indonesia staff, working together with the association of private bankers (Perbanas) and government bankers, tried to reduce the shock of the announcement. Through a variety of channels, including formal announcements, advertisements, talk shows on television, free telephone lines, and the Internet, detailed information on the payment of the deposits up to a maximum amounts and how to get the payment and other relevant information was widely publicized.

At the execution of the closure and deposit repayment Bank Indonesia was assisted by the police and the association of bankers, such that there was no single obstruction. The payments to deposit owners also went well as such; most people did not realize that the operation for making payment to small depositors actually involved more than 400 bank offices all over Indonesia with more than 800,000 deposit accounts altogether. It was a very neat operation considering that it covered the whole nation during a distress period. It was unfortunate that not many people noticed the scope of the operation involved, let alone showed any appreciation.

The IMF evaluation on this matter, that the bank closures were not explained well publicly, is definitely not well founded.[11] But, then, what was the difference between these bank closures and any others that involved a deposit guarantee scheme? Despite the absence of a scheme, what happened was exactly the same. There was no meaningful protest by small deposit holders. Had the deposit guarantee scheme been instituted, would the bank runs have been avoided? I doubt this very much.

That there was a run on banks after the closures and that Indonesia did not have any deposit insurance scheme then were true. But one did not happen due to the absence of the other.

What actually did happen was that almost immediately after the closures, the banking industry lost the public's confidence completely. Banks suffered because of the withdrawal of funds from their big clients, not small depositors. Although the small deposit accounts (i.e. those up to 20 million rupiah) constituted more than 80 per cent of the accounts, they represented less than 20 per cent of deposits in value. The situation may have been different if there had been a blanket guarantee — I will come back to this point later.

Of course I did not foresee that bank runs would ensue after the bank closures. I was a believer then, as now, in liquidating insolvent banks as part of bank restructuring. My only concern at the time of announcing the bank closures was how to deal with the more than 800,000 depositors who would flock to all these banks to withdraw their money. To my surprise, there was no problem whatsoever from this aspect. But I was not aware initially of the more devastating impact, the flight to safety of the largest clients and the run on the banks.

The IMF staff were not helpful either; when I was wavering they argued that I should not worry about the impact on the banking industry, since the closures involved only three per cent of the total banking assets. I am sure that the IMF staff themselves did not foresee how disastrous the bank closures would be.

The loss of confidence in the banking sector by major depositors was signalled by moving funds from banks that were perceived as weak and risky to ones that were perceived strong and safe, including the inter-bank money market, and between national banks and their counterparts abroad. With business confidence in the banking sector gone, some transactions were conducted in cash.

The loss of confidence amongst banks themselves created segmentation in the inter-bank money market. Banks were grouped in at least three categories. Those in the first group were considered to be safe banks, and comprised of state-owned banks and foreign banks plus some large private banks. The second group comprised of medium-sized private banks and joint venture banks. And the last group comprised of small private banks that suffered badly from the segmentation. The inter-bank money market among members of each group seemed to be working, but not between groups. Among members of the "safe" group, there was no problem of liquidity. In fact, they became recipients in the process. But among the small and medium-sized banks there was extreme scarcity of liquidity, constraining IMF conditionality.

With the segmentation of the interbank money market, these banks could not borrow from the money market. In turn, Bank Indonesia's moves to defend the banking industry and the payment system by providing liquidity ultimately became controversial due to allegations of corruption.

The deterioration continued. In December 1997, Standard & Poor's and Moody's announced a lowering of the sovereign rating of a number of Indonesian banks, which fuelled negative reactions by the national banks' counterparts. Early in January 1998 many national banks had their letters of credit refused by foreign banks. Foreign banks joined bank clients in stopping credit lines to Indonesian banks in addition to immediately withdrawing maturing loans and refusing to roll over their loans.

It should be noted that financial experts and multilateral institutions, especially the IMF, had been campaigning on the importance of a sound banking sector for supporting monetary policy sometime before the Asian crisis erupted. Since the beginning of the 1990s, different studies by the Fund had shown the proliferation of problems in banking within the member countries that constrained monetary policy.

However, it is also true that it was only after the mid-1990s that these studies became more specific on the requirements of a sound banking sector for effective macroeconomic policies (Sundararajan and Balino 1991, Hausman and Suarez 1997, Lindgren 1996). Analysis of Asian cases only appeared approximately one year prior to the crisis (Enoch and Green 1997). And yet, Indonesia's macroeconomic management, which I reported on in the seminar organized by the Fund, was still receiving a very positive response.[12]

World leaders started to pay more attention to the close link between a sound banking system and macroeconomic management during the G-7 Summit in Lyon, in June 1996. Even the Fund, whose mandate includes assisting its member countries in their policies addressing macroeconomic imbalances, only began recognizing this issue in 1996. At the annual meeting in September 1996 the Interim Committee of the Fund issued a declaration entitled "Partnership for Sustainable Global Growth", which explicitly mentioned the importance of the soundness of the banking system in the conduct of monetary policy. The declaration in fact showed the requirement of micro–macro consistency, transparency and governance, which became a new paradigm of global economics and finance:

> Ensuring the soundness of banking systems through prudential regulation and supervision, improved coordination, better assessment of credit risk, stringent capital requirements, timely disclosure of banks' financial condition, action to prevent money laundering, and improved management of banks.

I was one of the signatories of the declaration, on behalf of the Southeast Asian group.[13]

Thus, even if there was understanding about the magnitude of the problems that the Asian countries confronted, it was far too late. Nevertheless, one of the lessons from the crisis is that in dealing with contagious problems, the sooner the better (Sheng 1998).

Would a blanket guarantee have made a difference?

It is unclear whether the argument for a deposit insurance scheme referred to by the critics was about an ordinary deposit guarantee scheme or a blanket guarantee. I would assume that they were talking about the normal deposit insurance scheme. But in one evaluation on the Asian experience, the IMF used the terminology "full guarantee on depositors". Referring to the Indonesian case it stated, "This news (about bank closures) in conjunction with the lack of a full guarantee on depositors, led to a flight to safety because depositors expected to incur further loss" (Lindgren 1999, Box 8).

It is important to note what actually unfolded during the negotiations between the Indonesian team and the IMF during the drafting of the programme. During the discussions that led to the decision to liquidate the banks, IMF staff never brought up a *blanket* guarantee. The IMF staff only mentioned the *limited* guarantee for small depositors, which was in fact formulated by the Indonesian team. The agreement was documented in point 26 of the first LOI.

It was only after the devastating effects of the bank closures became apparent that the IMF came up with the proposal for Indonesia to adopt a blanket guarantee. In fact, this discussion was only conducted after the signing of the second LOI of 15 January 1998 and implemented on 26 January 1998.

As in the case of private debt, the adoption of a blanket guarantee, if one accepts it as a proper policy, came definitely too late, at least in comparison to Thailand and Korea. In Thailand, when the government decided to freeze 66 finance companies in June 1997, a scheme that provided full guarantee for bank depositors and loans was also introduced. The programme was even strengthened in October 1997. Korea offered a blanket guarantee for banks' external liabilities in August 1997. Even Malaysia adopted a blanket guarantee one week before Indonesia (Lindgren 1999, Box 1).

The fact that blanket guarantees were adopted by practically all countries severely affected by the Asian crisis has made me wonder why the IMF did not suggest that Indonesia adopt the scheme prior to, or together with, the bank closures in November 1997. This issue is relevant because Thailand and Korea had done so prior to the time Indonesia liquidate the 16 banks. For both countries the blanket guarantee was adopted in relation with the decision to freeze financial companies (Thailand) or merchant banks (Korea), which seemed to appear as prior actions for their SBAs.

It is even more puzzling when one observes the conceptual difference between what Thailand and Indonesia did in bank restructuring. On this issue Cole and Slade (1999) correctly showed the substantial differences between the closing of 16 banks in Indonesia and the suspension of 58 finance companies in Thailand and 14 merchant banks in Korea. The 16 banks in Indonesia were part of the national payment system and their closure, which led to public concern that other bank closures would follow, was bound to have a substantial impact on it. In addition, the bank closures were permanent and settlement was immediate, while the suspension of finance companies and merchant banks in Thailand and Korea was not permanent and the settlement was carried out without immediately affecting the payment system. The total impact of bank closures was more significant than the suspension of finance companies. And yet, the guarantee that the government provided was more limited compared to a blanket guarantee.

Why did Indonesia not adopt a blanket guarantee scheme? I myself was not familiar with a blanket guarantee scheme, which was why I never suggested it. In fact, I first learnt of it when Dr. Bijan B. Aghevli wrote a memo on 18 January 1998 and another one in 23 January 1998, both about the banking sector crisis and proposed measures to deal with it. In the first memo he mentioned the need to introduce a generalized guarantee for depositors and creditors of banks, which later became known as a blanket guarantee.

I have to admit that my initial reaction on the proposal for adopting a blanket guarantee was to reject it. I said in one of the many meetings between the Indonesian team and the Fund staff that I had never heard before about guaranteeing all the liabilities of banks. Providing a full guarantee to depositors, even though I was not aware of any precedents, was still alright in my opinion. But giving a full guarantee to both the assets and liabilities of a bank was something I could not visualize. However, the Fund argued that the crisis was becoming systemic and without immediate drastic action the banking sector as a whole could be technically bankrupt. Ultimately, the Monetary Board agreed to adopt the scheme, and after getting approval from the President, the blanket guarantee was officially introduced on 26 January 1998.

The first memorandum described the grievous problems in Indonesia financial sector that led to the decision to adopt a blanket guarantee scheme as follows: problems (the flight to safety, bank runs, the demand for bank notes and the central bank liquidity support) had been mounting at an increasing rate, and seemed to be approaching a crisis. The gravity of the situation was apparent from the following developments.

- About 42 private banks, representing 73 per cent of total assets of private national banks, had risk-adjusted capital below regulatory norms.
- Currency holdings, which were programmed to increase by about 7 per cent during the fourth quarter, had increased by 17 per cent over this period, and a further 18 per cent just in the previous

two weeks. Bank Indonesia was having difficulties in supplying bank notes — there was even a risk that it could run out of fresh notes.

- As demand for currency increased and deposits withdrawn from the banking system, liquidity support from Bank Indonesia had expanded dramatically from 2 per cent of GDP at end-October, to 7.5 per cent at end-December. Alarmingly, it grew by another 2 per cent of GDP during the first two weeks of January.

- Despite this sharp increase in liquidity support, broad money (at constant exchange rates) had remained essentially unchanged since 2nd-October, while credit had actually declined (2 per cent).

- The three largest private banks in the country were all in trouble: two had borrowed about 2 per cent of GDP (apiece) from Bank Indonesia, while the third had a CAR of just 3.5 per cent.

- Commercial banks were increasingly unable to fulfill their normal functions, forcing Bank Indonesia to assume a greater and greater role in financial intermediation. Since November, the inter-bank market had become highly segmented, requiring Bank Indonesia to intervene to recycle liquidity from surplus to deficit banks. More recently, the currency swap market had also began to breakdown, as local banks were defaulting on their obligations to deliver dollars, forcing Bank Indonesia to consider active intervention in this market as well.

- Since early January, foreign banks had cut their credit lines to Indonesian banks (even state banks), and the letters' of credit were no longer acceptable. To open LCs, importers had to provide margins of 100 per cent.

In brief, the problem of the banking system was no longer one of individual banks. Rather, the problem was that the banking system as a whole was no longer functioning properly — and Indonesia was approaching a systemic crisis. Based on this, two steps were proposed and ultimately adopted by Indonesia, namely the creation of the Indonesian Bank Restructuring Agency (IBRA) and the introduction of a blanket guarantee.

In conclusion, it is indeed curious that the IMF only suggested the adoption of a blanket guarantee in January 1998. Even if Thailand and Korea adopted the scheme on their own initiative, both countries did that prior to Indonesia's decision to liquidate the 16 banks.

A related issue that should be raised here is whether executing the decision to liquidate banks in stages, as was done in Thailand and Korea, would have prevented the Indonesian bank runs. Would earlier adoption of a blanket guarantee have made a difference? Would liquidation in stages have helped? It is not possible to argue with certainty whether Indonesia's banking crisis could have been avoided if these steps had been taken.

Indonesia also made use of bank freezing the way it was done in Thailand. It was safely done in April 1998, after the adoption of a blanket guarantee.

But, Korea and Thailand did have blanket guarantees in place prior to the decision to freeze their respective merchant banks and finance companies. The decision to liquidate these financial institutions was only done sometime later, after they were frozen. Both Thailand and Korea fared much better than Indonesia.

Should more banks have been liquidated?

Criticisms about the bank closures also arose from those who argued that there were more than 16 insolvent banks. In other words more banks should have been closed.

There were indeed more than 16 insolvent banks but I do not agree that there were some banks in worse condition than the ones liquidated. However, it was indeed true that due to non-compliance in disclosure requirements for banks and a lack of transparency in general, plus a rigid interpretation of bank secrecy, the number of problem banks was never made public.

The lack of transparency clouded assessments about the condition of the banking industry. As an example, a report in *Warta Ekonomi* about the Indonesian banking sector mentioned that there were 31 problem banks.[14] During this period the media also quoted experts who made similar assessments. In addition, tables of troubled banks were circulated anonymously.

The lack of official information about banking conditions and the proliferation of inaccurate analyses and reports added to public anxiety. The public reacted by trying to save their assets. People moved their funds from banks that they perceived as unsound to ones that were perceived sound, or kept the funds at home, or transferred their rupiah assets into dollar assets, including abroad.

The panic sometimes exhibited strange characteristics. For example, there was a report that since the government seemed to have a habit of announcing major moves (such as the closing of the 16 banks) on Saturdays, some people tried to "hedge" their bank deposits from this risk. This was done by taking their money out from the bank every Friday, and if nothing changed during the weekend, the money was put back into the bank by Monday. According to this story quite a number of people did this, repeatedly.

A bank that was rumoured to have a negative balance with Bank Indonesia from its daily clearing, or having its branch office closed, could became a victim of a run easily. In mid-November 1997, a rumour was reported in several newspapers that Mr. Sudono Salim or Liem Sioe Liong, the head of the biggest conglomerate in Indonesia, was dead and that the BCA branch in Singapore was closed. The rumour caused a run on many of the BCA branches in Indonesia.[15] Aside from wrongfully reporting a death, the BCA branch in Singapore did not even exist. However, this was the environment that ultimately led to panicking among bank clients and the flights to safety that ensued. Even large sound banks like Bank Dannamon and BCA experienced runs.

Bank Indonesia's policy for nursing problem banks initially was on a case-by-case, as stipulated in Banking Act No. 7, 1992. Article 37 of the Act stated that, where the central bank thinks that a bank is encountering problems that endangers the viability of its operations, Bank Indonesia could take several actions. The actions could range from instructing the bank to increase its capital, change its management or merge with another bank, to issuing a letter to recommend the Minister of Finance to revoke its licence.

In the case-by-case approach, Bank Indonesia could actively mediate negotiations between prospective investors and bank owners. After studying the financial and other conditions of the bank, a workable plan was drawn that usually included a calculation of how much new investment was needed in order for the bank to meet the CAR requirement. The plan also included the requirements for the bank to be able to resume its operation, which might include additional liquidity as well as a necessary change in management.

In the programme Bank Indonesia provided a facility for supporting the restructuring. The support was in the form of subordinated loans for the bank to meet the CAR requirement. The concept was basically the same as bank restructuring under IBRA in March 1998 and after. Under both schemes, the bank owner had to provide 20 per cent of the total amount of bank funds to become solvent, which was a CAR of 4 per cent. The government would provide support, in the form of government bonds, of the remaining 80 per cent.

However, because of the lack of transparency in the past, the case-by-case approach that Bank Indonesia employed in bank restructuring was misconstrued or misunderstood. Bank Indonesia was criticized for practicing discrimination. During the crisis, when more banks experienced distress, Bank Indonesia had to deal with a new problem, namely the danger of compromising its function as bank supervisor and lender of last resort, and at the same time as monetary policy manager defending the rupiah.

Included in the case-by-case method of bank restructuring was also asking banks to merge. I started as early as 1995 to ask owners of small and weak banks to make concerted efforts to merge their banks as a part of a drive to create a competitive and sound banking industry. But bank mergers were very difficult to execute.

In the meantime, the number of problem banks grew after a few months of financial turmoil and the case-by-case technique could no longer be relied upon. A more systemic approach was adopted. This approach started with an overall assessment of the problem banks. Problem banks were grouped into those that could be rescued and those that could not. For those that had the prospect of being rescued Bank Indonesia tried to find interested investors and designed a rescue programme.

Preparations for a more systemic approach actually began earlier. Bank Indonesia had asked for help from the Fund for resolving these problem banks systematically. In June 1994, a team from the Monetary and Exchange Affairs Department (MAE) studied materials and reports by the Department of Banking Supervision of Bank Indonesia. The IMF team wrote a report in August 1994, "Indonesia: Bank Liquidation and Resolution" (Mehran 1994), with a strategy for solving problem banks. Even though it was very general, this was basically the strategy that was used in setting up the comprehensive bank restructuring programme, which included liquidation of insolvent banks as a first step.

To implement the systematic approach to bank restructuring, Bank Indonesia came up with a proposal to liquidate a number of banks prior to the crisis. In December 1996, I went to President Soeharto to propose closing seven small commercial banks as a first step.

The President did not approve Bank Indonesia's proposal for bank closures. Instead, I was instructed to finalize a government decree to regulate bank closure. It was true that at that time there was no specific regulation governing bank liquidation, only a general regulation on company bankruptcy. The most important stipulation was that a bankrupt company had to treat all its creditors equally. This implied that a liquidated bank could not treat depositors differently from any other creditors. In other words, the bank could not make payments to depositors prior to making payments to other creditors. The obligation to depositors could not be treated as more important than that to other creditors.

The government issued a government decree on liquidating banks at the end of 1996 (Government Decree No. 68, 1996) that among other things, allowed a liquidated bank to pay bank depositors prior to the settlement of other liabilities.

In April 1997 I went back to the President with the proposal to close the seven banks. This time actually he gave his approval. However, he asked me to postpone execution until after the general election and the general assembly of the People's Consultative Assembly in March 1998. Unfortunately, by July 1997 the financial crisis began in Indonesia.

The actual implementation of the closures was planned by the Banking Supervision and Legal Department staff of Bank Indonesia, who had been dealing with banking restructuring, the Ministry of Finance, and the IMF.

The major determinant for a problem bank to be liquidated was its solvency. A bank is classified as insolvent if it has a zero or negative net worth, usually this condition is associated with violations of prudential measures. The decision to liquidate a bank is also based on other considerations, which include the attitudes of the bank's owners and its management, the prospects for its bailout and the impact of its closure on the banking system.

The bank closures in November 1997 were based on a careful study on the condition of the banking industry in Indonesia. Of the 239 banks in operation, Bank Indonesia carefully studied the reports of all classified banks plus all banks that individually had assets of one per cent or more of the total banking assets. Ninety-one banks were found to fulfill the criteria. The study found that of the 91 banks, 34 banks were insolvent, i.e. having zero or negative net worth. They comprised of 26 private banks, 6 provincial development banks and 2 state-owned banks.

Out of the 26 private banks, 19 were insolvent, while 7 were under a Bank Indonesia restructuring programme (nursed banks). And after many days of continuous discussions with the IMF, it was decided that 16 had to be liquidated immediately. Three banks were excluded because of their borderline position. They were put under Bank Indonesia conservatorship, instead.

In the meantime, the general perception was that the government decision to put a bank into liquidation was based on its condition as judged by its compliance to prudential measures. In particular, it was a general perception that a bank was liquidated either due to its violation of the legal lending limit (LLL), the size of its bad debts, and its negative balance, popularly known as "loss in bank clearing". Public perception was reflected in comments by owners of some liquidated banks that appeared after the government announcement. For example, some bank owners were shocked by the government's decision to close their banks, protesting that their banks never experienced any loss in bank-clearing, or because their banks never received any liquidity support from the central bank. Other bank owners claimed that their banks were healthier than some banks that were not liquidated. And others agreed with the government decision, because these banks had large problem loans or gave too many loans to their own shareholders.

Nevertheless, it is true that bank restructuring by Bank Indonesia in the past, and the criteria for bank closures in November 1997, were never explained clearly in public although regular public hearings of the Governor and Bank Indonesia Board with the Parliament had almost always discussed problem loans and problem banks long before the crisis. There had also been periodic discussions between Bank Indonesia officials and the banking community about problem banks and bad debts.

Let me come back to the issue of the number of insolvent banks and the number of banks being liquidated. What was actually the reason for the failure of the bank closures of November 1997? Did the policy fail because too many banks were liquidated? Or did it fail because the government did not close enough banks?

There are different views on the number of banks closed. Banking experts such as Morris Goldstein who knew or learnt about the state of banks in Indonesia, argued that the closures should apply to *all* problem banks. In other words, they believed that more than 16 banks should have been liquidated (see for eg., Goldstein 1998, p. 36). Others argued that even closing 16 banks had caused damaging bank runs, so closing more banks would certainly make things worse for a fragile economy. But, irrespective of whether too many or too few banks were liquidated, what seemed to happen was that with the lack of transparency, the public itself was influenced by reports in the media that there were more than 16 unhealthy banks and that more closures would follow.

I myself was comfortable about liquidating the seven banks with the president's approval. However, I had to admit that liquidating more than twice the number of banks really scared me. I was scared to think about the implications, social and economic, of closing such a large number of banks. I realized that Indonesia had never experienced this before, except in early 1970s. I had also observed how difficult it was to complete the liquidation of Bank Summa, which took many years.

However, every time I explained the above, I was immediately reminded by the leader of the Fund team in the negotiation, the Deputy Director for Asia-Pacific, that I should not worry. He kept reminding me that the total assets of the sixteen banks constituted less than three per cent of the total assets of the banking sector in Indonesian.

With hindsight, those arguments definitely did not take into consideration the psychological impact of the closures. To those who argued that more banks should have been closed, the obvious counter argument would be that even merely 16 banks had the banking sector close to collapsing. Had more banks been liquidated, a total collapse may have resulted.

Public reaction to the subsequent bank closures was much less dramatic. Certainly conditions had changed. Bank closures in 1998 and thereafter were executed with the blanket guarantee already in place.

In Indonesia, even though the ratio of assets of the liquidated banks to the total assets of banking industry was small, they were part of the implementing agents of the national payment system, so the impact of the closures was more substantial. This, plus the fear of other bank closures and the absence of a blanket guarantee, seemed to contribute to the immediate loss of confidence.

It is curious that Indonesia did not imitate Thailand to freeze banks, at least to have a breathing space. I actually raised questions in both meetings with the Fund as well as within Bank Indonesia on what was actually involved in freezing a bank. Our understanding within Bank Indonesia was that it was in effect terminating a bank's participation in our daily clearing. However, at that time, even just the rumour on a bank a loss in bank clearing, could cause a run. But I never received any clear answer to my query concerning the freezing of banks until after I lost my job.

I only learned about what might have happened then, more than one year after returning to the academy. It came from my discussion with an Economics professor from Hitotsubashi University, who worked on the Asian crisis, when he visited me in Cambridge, MA, sometime in the Spring of 1999. He told me that during their SBA discussions with the Fund, the Monetary Authorities of Thailand had adamantly refused to accept the Fund's suggestion to close the problematic financial companies and came up with a formula of freezing them instead. Shortly after, he met with the Fund official who dealt with Thailand and Indonesia, and congratulated the official for succeeding in pushing the Indonesian officials to liquidate banks.

The other questions concerned why all the insolvent banks were not liquidated at once. Was the government intentionally misleading the public when announcing that no more banks would be liquidated?

It was true that the Governor of Bank Indonesia and the Minister of Finance announced after a meeting with the President on 3 November 1997, that there would not be another round of bank closures.[16] And in January 1998, at the signing ceremony of the second LOI, the President made an even stronger statement that the government would not close more banks.[17]

With the benefit of hindsight, I can say that the government should have been more forthcoming in explaining to the public and the Parliament about the overall Fund-supported programme of adjustments, including the bank closures. However, it is wrong to assume that the government had a secret plan to make bank closures that would be executed in stages. It is definitely incorrect to accuse the government of intentionally lying to the public. If the implementation of bank restructuring, including the closing of the 16 banks and other adjustment policies went well, further bank closures might not have had to be carried out.

Ultimately, the basic problem was that the government had lost its credibility. The loss of government credibility, including in the monetary and supervision authorities, led to market and public reactions that resulted in a banking crisis.

Confronted with an ongoing financial crisis and a loss of public confidence, Bank Indonesia had difficulty trying to implementing the adjustment programme. Members of a special committee to investigate Bank Indonesia correctly stated that the government handling of the crisis was inconsistent.[18] These back and forth shifts of policy were not intentional but due to the extraordinary circumstances. Looking back, it was true that there were inconsistencies in the implementation of the adjustment programmes.

Hypothetically, if only there were no bank runs, there would not have been an increase in the number of problem banks. Banks would be in some process of improvement or negotiating mergers with other banks to avoid closure. Even if some banks failed to be saved, an orderly liquidation would not have created a negative impact on other banks in a systemic way. In other words, this would not have adversely affected the whole banking sector and the payment system. If this happened the liquidity support to banks would not have increased sky-high, and the total cost of bank restructuring would have been smaller. Could this scenario have worked? Well, to a certain degree that was what happened in the cases of Korea and Thailand. Malaysia definitely performed better, which means that their bank restructuring programmes worked.

Public reactions to bank closures

It is interesting to note here that initial reactions to the bank closures in the domestic and foreign markets were very different.

The Indonesian public was in disbelief when it learned that among banks that were closed, three were owned at least partly by President

Soeharto's family. Those who had been suspicious of the general condition of the banking system, partly due to long-standing debates on the size of problem loans and problem banks, saw the government decision as confirmation of the unsound condition of the banking sector. If even banks close to the centre of power were liquidated, it was only logical that another round of bank closures was imminent.

Abroad, the market reaction was initially the reverse. Initially, the foreign market reaction towards the bank closures was very favourable. The successful liquidation of well connected but insolvent banks was lauded as a healthy decision that showed the seriousness of the government's resolve to address banking problems.

Unfortunately, positive reactions from the foreign market were short-lived. Very quickly, the government's actions were tainted when the former owner of Bank Andromeda, one of the 16, who happened to be a son of President Soeharto, was allowed to acquire a small bank, Bank Alfa. Bank Alfa was perceived as the reincarnation of the Bank Andromeda.

It should be noted that, aside from the fact that the President's son, Bambang Trihatmodjo, was only a minor owner of the liquidated bank Andromeda, there was no formal connection between him and the bank's insolvency. In other words, legally Bank Indonesia could not deny his wish to acquire Bank Alfa, a very small bank. But, of course the decision was perceived by foreign markets as showing the softening of the monetary authorities' stance and the foreign market immediately shifted its perceptions on the bank closures.

Market reaction further worsened because of the legal actions of both a brother and a son of President Soeharto, part owners of the liquidated Bank Jakarta and Bank Andromeda, to sue the Governor of Bank Indonesia and the Minister of Finance for closing their banks. With these, the prestige of the monetary authorities was tarnished, and the foreign market joined the domestic market in distrusting the Indonesian banking system.

The public misunderstood the real meaning of banking operations and prudential measures. Immediately after the government announcement of the bank closures, the owners of Bank Andromeda and Bank Jakarta campaigned through the media to protest the government's decision to close their banks. Only bank owners that happened to be members of the President's family launched formal protests.

More astonishing was what they were protesting about. Both bank owners argued that their banks were in better shape than other banks that were not liquidated by the monetary authorities. Mr. Probosutedjo (Bank Jakarta) argued that his bank never experienced any loss in bank clearing, and never received any liquidity support from Bank Indonesia. With respect to violation of the legal lending limit, he challenged the monetary authorities by stating that most banks committed the violation.

Bambang Trihatmodjo (Bank Andromeda) admitted that his bank violated the rules on the legal lending limit. However, he argued that the loan was to finance a national project, the Chandra Asri, a petrochemical project, which was one of President Soeharto's pet projects. He further argued that Bank Indonesia was treating the management of his bank unfairly, because the day before the announcement he went to the central bank with a check of several hundred billion rupiah to pay for the needed capital to keep the bank afloat. Furthermore, he argued that the bank closures were politically motivated to shame the family of President Soeharto and stop his re-election. Both appeared on television over a few days to launch their protests.

The rumour that the central bank governor did not inform the President about the ownership of banks had also been circulating in public for sometime. Many, including members of the Cabinet, questioned me on this issue on many occasions. This story, even though it was easily understood in the current environment, nevertheless was strange, even absurd. Was this to mean that even if these banks were insolvent and to be liquidated, they would not had been closed had the President knew that three of them were owned by members of his family? Or was it their argument that Bank Indonesia's assessment about their banks was wrong?

Due to the public protestations by members of the President family, and questions raised by many, I wanted to check this with the President. The occasion arose when I was summoned by him.

I refreshed his memory about my report to him on the preparations to liquidate 16 insolvent banks. I told him that the meeting had been in the same room, after a meeting with Hubert Neiss, who came to Jakarta before the finalization of the negotiations with the Fund's team for the stand-by arrangement in late October 1997. Ministers Mar'ie

Muhammad and Moerdiono were present. From his remarks and subsequent exchanges on the issue, it became crystal clear to that he had known that the affected banks included Andromeda, Jakarta and Industri.

As stated, the major determinant for a bank closure is its solvency. But the above problems could indeed lead a bank to become insolvent and thus be liquidated. A bank was not closed solely due to its violation of the legal lending limit; on the other hand, banks could not be allowed to violate the legal lending limit just because the loans had been made to finance a government project.

The soundness of a bank was determined by the total scores that the bank earned from each of the whole range of prudential measures, which included the condition of its capital, assets quality, management, earnings and liquidity (CAMEL). In addition, there were several other prudential measures and administrative requirements that determined the relative soundness of a bank. They included a stipulation on the limit of loans to its own group or the legal lending limit, the net open position, and a minimum ratio of loans to the small-scale sector to total bank lending. The comparison of one bank's relative position to another was determined from the total scores that each bank assigned periodically by Bank Indonesia. The report containing the list of banks with their scores in the rating was not publicly available. Thus, it was impossible for anyone to claim to know that Bank A was better than B.

The bottom line was that there was a problem of governance that was embedded with bank owners and management. After the liberalization of bank entry in 1988, many owners of established corporations, both in manufacturing and trading, established new banks or acquired existing banks with the objective, aside from expanding their business, of having banks inside their business groups. In other words, many new banks after 1988 were established, not primarily as financial institutions that mediated surplus and deficit sectors of the economy, but institutions that would provide cheap funds for the groups which owned them. Corporate governance is still one of the major problems facing Indonesia. For example, in a survey conducted by McKinsey & Company on foreign investors' views on six Asian countries, Malaysia, Thailand, Korea, Taiwan, Japan and Indonesia, Indonesia's corporate governance was placed at the bottom.[20]

There is a phrase in Bahasa Indonesia that fittingly described many banks that were born after 1988, namely *bank dengan mental pedagang* or banks with a trader mentality. When the prudential measures in the Basle code of banking principles was adopted in 1991, one of the most difficult items to comply with was the rule on limiting the rampant practice of group lending.

It is interesting to note the behaviour of bank commissioners in the state-owned versus the private banking sectors. Commissioners of state-owned banks largely comprised of retired or active government bureaucrats or generals who were appointed so they could earn additional income. Many of them did not do their job of supervising the management; in general they did not know what was going on in the banks. In the private banks, members of the board of commissioners were usually bank owners and held authority over the bank management. In both the two extremes, the role of internal supervision was not effectively executed. Bank management was run in accordance with the wishes and whims of bank management in the case of state-owned banks or the commissioners in the case of the private banks.

In 1996 Bank Indonesia issued a new rule that enhanced the role of bank commissioners in internal bank supervision. This policy was further strengthened by introducing the concept of an audit council in each bank to enhance internal banking supervision in line with a self-regulatory banking system.

In any case, the extreme reactions from the President's family with public campaigns through the media (their group also owned the two television stations used in this campaign) and the lawsuit against the monetary authorities had damaged the banking system.

I would argue that, had they acted like responsible bankers to accept the bank closures, bank runs may not have followed and banking restructuring could have proceeded as planned. Likewise, had the foreign market not reacted adversely to the acquisition of Bank Alfa, bank runs may not have happened. Instead, these actions almost spurred further adverse reactions by fund owners and bank clients to join the flight to safety. What followed was a self-fulfilling prophecy.

A lesson from the crisis was that bank closures could backfire if they were implemented in the midst of fragile public confidence. It is one thing to say that insolvent banks have to be liquidated. It is another thing to decide when and how to implement bank closures as part of bank restructuring. But when would be a good time to close banks? This is a difficult question to answer correctly.

It was difficult to persuade bank owners to improve their performance and adhere to the prudential measures even in normal circumstances. I had problems in persuading bank owners to strengthen their banks by mergers and reducing their exposures to risky sectors, like property lending.

Bank closures and the alleged conspiracy

One of the accusations from the owners of the two closed banks was that the policy was the result of a conspiracy to discredit President Soeharto in his bid for his re-election in March 1998. Similarly, there were writings spread through the Internet around mid-November 1997, alleging that the decision was politically motivated. These articles were numerous, and included "Scandals on the Monetary Authorities", "Conspiracy Theory of Bank Liquidation", "Conspiracy among Extremist Jesuits, Catholics and Chinese in the Indonesian Politics" and "Economy towards the Succession". These papers were collected in a small book entitled *Conspiracy to Rock Soeharto*, and circulated in Jakarta in November 1997.[21]

One of the arguments put forward was that Bank Indonesia provided liquidity support only to banks owned by Chinese. It was also argued that only "indigenous banks" were liquidated. Both of these arguments were, of course, counterfactual. Liquidity support were provided to banks having liquidity mismatch problem during the crisis, due to the government policy of not liquidating banks for fear of creating social and political instability prior to the general election in October 1997 and General Sessions of the People's Consultative Assembly in March 1998.[22] And of the 16 banks liquidated, the majority of owners were Chinese.

In compliance with government policy, Bank Indonesia as lender of last resort provided liquidity support to banks in need.[23] The support was provided to all banks in need of the liquidity support irrespective of who the owners were, or the size of their assets. Ultimately 164 banks altogether received Bank Indonesia support (Djiwandono 2004).

The accusations were definitely unfounded and to a certain degree based on a wrong concept about bank ownership. It is actually incorrect for a minor shareholder of a bank to claim that the bank is his or hers, even though legally it is correct that any shareholder is a legitimate owner. In the case of Bank Andromeda, Bambang Tri Hatmodjo only owned 12.5 per cent of the total shares, while two other businessmen owned 75 per cent of the shares.

I can only speculate on the reasons behind the accusation that there was a conspiracy to close banks belonging to President Soeharto's family. It could only be conjectured that in a society that does not have any tradition of transparency and has problems of governance in its public and private sectors, one would have difficulties in finding out the truth about anything.

In general the public was also less motivated to conduct careful analysis to find the truth. On the other hand, objective analysis was also be difficult due to the lack of accurate information and data. Weak and corrupt law enforcement did not help. Even freedom of the press in the post-Soeharto era has not lent support to the efforts to find the truth or fairness.

Borrowing Arief Budiman's use of the term, there was a tendency for people to resort to "tribalism" (Budiman 1999). By tribal here I mean family, ethnicity, race, religion, region, alma mater, profession, institution or any other groupings. In a tribal community, the assessment of truth is determined by the position, whether the object belongs to the same tribe of the subject or not. In a tribal relationship the non-tribal member could be treated as enemy. Everyone outside the tribe would be treated as unfriendly. They could be under suspicion or even denied their human rights. Thus, anything about or related to someone belonging to your own tribe was right while conversely, anything about or related to the "enemy" had to be wrong.

In the months and years that followed, bankers and bank supervisors have become easy targets for criticism and accusations by the public, who feel victimized by the crisis. They are easy targets of critics because they have the tendency to be silent. Of course, criticisms have not been without validity. Indeed, there are problem banks and problem bankers, both in the private and state-owned sectors. But, misunderstandings about bank operations and central bank operations in particular, coupled with stereotyping, have facilitated the public's tendency to place all the blame on them. Only transparency and good governance will straighten these out.

Very Expensive Lessons

Several points listed below could be noted as lessons from the bank closures in November 1997.

- The last time I mentioned publicly on the possibility of bank closure prior to the actual decision was in an interview with Indonesian journalists during the annual meetings of the World Bank and the Fund in Hong Kong in early October 1997.[24]

- Bank Indonesia's policy was initially based on a case-by-case approach, which turned out to be long and winding, creating suspicions of corruption, costly, and not very effective. Observing these tendencies, and confronted with an increasing number of problem banks, in 1994 preparations for a more systemic approach to bank restructuring was initiated. Bank Indonesia under my direction asked for help from the Fund, which came up with a detailed programme for bank restructuring, including liquidation. Towards the end of 1996 and in April 1997 I presented a plan to liquidate seven private banks to President Soeharto, stating that it was crucial that the problem was addressed as rapidly as possible.

- The huge cost of the bank closures in terms of both financial expenditure as well as the loss of market and public confidence in the banking sector definitely underlined the need to address the issue as quickly as possible. However, with the benefit of hindsight, it has to be said that the preparation and the execution should have been done more carefully. It could be argued that it was unwise to execute bank closures during a time of fragile public confidence.

- Bank restructuring is always costly. A study by the Fund showed that since 1980, 130 countries or approximately three-fourths of Fund members had experienced bank problems, many of them severe (Lindgren et al. 1999). The cost of bank restructuring, which in most cases was borne by state budgets, had been substantial. In the neighbouring countries that suffered from the Asian crisis in 1997/98, the cost of bank restructuring were 17–18 per cent in Malaysia, 28 per cent in Korea and 35 per cent in Thailand, all respective to their GDP. Other countries that spent huge amount for bank restructuring included Uruguay in 1981 with 33 per cent, Mexico in 1994 (22 per cent), Chile in 1981 (43 per cent), Japan in 1992 (22 per cent), Finland in 1991 (12 per cent), Brazil in 1994 (14 per cent), respectively of their GDP.[25] Similar things happened in Nordic countries in the early 1980s and the United States in the 1980s. Bank restructuring in Indonesia is ongoing. However, even up till 2001 the cost to the budget had already reached 60 per cent of GDP. The cost of Bank Indonesia liquidity support alone constituted 17 per cent of GDP in 1998 (Lindgren et al. 1999, Table 3). Aside from the staggering cost, the more sensitive issue has been the question of who should bear the cost. In other countries, ultimately the cost of bank restructuring is usually borne by the state budget, i.e. the taxpayers. And this has been the case in Indonesia too, which has been a thorny issue. The popular argument is as follows, the banks (bankers) and their clients plus bank supervisors should be accountable for all the mess, why should the average taxpayers bear the cost of their mistakes? Of course bank owners should bear the cost, and they do. This has become a socio-political problem. But the lack of understanding about issues, coupled with the negative image of central bankers, bankers and conglomerates, the issue of who should bear the cost of bank restructuring has become murky.

- Within the public sector, there are issues that have not been dealt with successfully, namely accountability and the burden of responsibility between the Ministry of Finance, the budget authority and the central bank, at least on the issue of Bank Indonesia liquidity support to the banking sector during the crisis. The issue of accountability arises in relation to questions like, were there clear mistakes? If so, were they the policy decisions or in the implementation? Was there any breach of law? Totally disregarding the value of assets of banks, the Supreme Audit Board (Badan Pemeriksa Keuangan/BPK) came up with a figure for the potential loss to the state to the amount of over 95 per cent of the total liquidity provided to banks of 144 trillion rupiah. Without a clear legal basis on how it should be done, the government under President Abdulrachman Wahid and Bank Indonesia produced an agreement for sharing the burden of the potential loss from Bank Indonesia liquidity support to banks during the crisis, based on the findings of the Supreme Audit Board, in November 2000. In the agreement, Bank Indonesia's share of the burden was 24.5 trillion rupiah (Bank Indonesia 2002, pp. 91–100). The issue was still pending settlement in June 2002. With governance and accountability still in their infancy, it is difficult to get a clear-cut resolution on the issue. In the meantime, the liquidity has been spent, and the burden of the financing as well as losses incurred must be settled one way or another.

5

Stronger Programme with Weak Commitment

First Review

Confronted with deteriorating economic, financial and banking conditions towards the end of 1997 and beginning of 1998, the government undertook a variety of adjustment steps. But since the programme was part of the agreement with the Fund in a stand-by arrangement, a review to evaluate the implementation of the programme, including compliance to performance criteria and other conditionality as stipulated in the first letter of intent, had to be conducted.

The evaluation of programme implementation would determine whether a drawing from the loan could be made. The evaluation was also needed to determine any other changes or additional steps that should be included in the adjustment programme.

The second LOI was negotiated directly by President Soeharto with the Fund team. The new programme of financial restructuring and economic reform was basically an enhanced and improved programme of the one contained in the first LOI. President Soeharto himself signed the second LOI on 15 January 1998. The President's direct involvement was an extraordinary step.

In the IMF's review of 7 January 1998 it was stated that "performance under the programme so far has been decidedly disappointing". It was further stated that "although some progress has been made, there have also been policy slippages in every area of the programme". In particular, it was noted that the interest rates finally being raised would not be sustainable due to pressures from government officials who demanded the lowering of rates. The promise to produce a budget surplus also seemed to be remote. Most troubling, in the Fund's evaluation, was that the authorities had taken a number of structural steps backward, especially in governance.[1]

The review noted further that as a result of the policy performance, hard-won market confidence, built up over three decades of rapid economic progress, and revived at the outset of the arrangement, had vanished. The development had prompted the collapse of the exchange rate. By this time the US dollar rate to the rupiah was over 9,000 from 3,200 in the first week of the arrangement.

The Fund asked the government to demonstrate a public and unequivocal commitment to the adjustment programme that had been agreed upon. The review stated that:

> The envisaged measures need to be implemented, in full and according to schedule, as part of a steady drumbeat of policy announcements, designed to reassure the public that the programme is, in fact, being implemented. At the same time, the government needs to eschew measures that are contrary to the spirit of the arrangement, especially those which suggest that some groups will be favoured and shielded from the need to take painful adjustment measures, as this only undermines confidence and fans discontent.

The government was asked to face the severe crisis by strengthening policy reforms through an accelerated implementation of measures already agreed, as well as adopting further measures. In particular, the Fund asked the government to strengthen structural reforms, to accelerate financial sector restructuring, and to bring budget prospects back on track.

It was obvious that the adjustment programme as stipulated in the first LOI was not implemented in a consistent or timely manner. However, there were different opinions as to why this was so.

Prior to the second LOI negotiations, the Fund's Board of Executive Directors indicated their concern about the drastic rupiah depreciation. In their evaluation the currency plunge reflected the poor implementation of the adjustment programme and gave confusing signals to the market. The confusion resulted from statements by government officials demanding that the central bank lower the interest rate and increase liquidity. Both were considered to contradict what the government was expected to do under the circumstances. In addition, they were also concerned about the inconsistencies in the implementation of structural reforms.[2]

The Fund asked the government to implement the programme consistently as agreed upon in the first LOI. To make the programme more transparent, the Fund asked the government to announce the LOI, so that the public could follow the details of the programme. As a follow up, the Fund sent their team back to Indonesia. The team later also joined the discussions to prepare for the second LOI, taking into consideration the review and the Board discussion. To underscore the Fund's concerns about Indonesia, First Deputy Stanley Fischer, and later Managing Director Camdessus, came to Jakarta to hold discussions with President Soeharto on the new programme that became the second LOI.

Unfavourable Conditions

Before discussing the second LOI and its implementation, I would like to spend some time analysing the poor implementation of the first programme, which led to the second and others that followed. In a chain of revised and improved programmes as documented in the letters of intent to the Fund (of which there were 17 by the end of 2001), Indonesia's efforts to cope with the crisis seemed to demonstrate the true character of muddling through. It may be instructive to analyse the early inconsistencies, struggles, and debates on the policy formulation and their implementation.

The implementation of the Fund-supported programme on financial restructuring, which started with the closure of insolvent banks, did not achieve the desired effect of regaining public confidence in the banking sector and payment system, nor in the government's credibility in managing the national economy. What evolved was even further loss of that precious market and public confidence.

The execution of the programme for restructuring other banks, and of structural reform in the real sectors as stipulated in the document was constrained. The agreements, stipulations and objectives of the IMF-supported programme itself seemed to be misunderstood among different sectors in the government. These could possibly have arisen from a deeper problem, i.e. different perceptions about the problems the nation was facing and how to address them. In addition, the market was so uncertain in the face of the regional crisis.

The period from the start of the Fund-supported programme in November 1997 to my dismissal from Bank Indonesia in mid-February 1998, had arguably been the most uncertain and confusing in the history of Indonesian economic management. It may also be true that what happened during this period was the least understood or accepted publicly, due to the complexity of the problems, the dissolution of Soeharto's power, coupled with people's perceptions of what was unfolding.

It is important to reiterate that the adjustment programme to cope with the crisis since November 1997 was undertaken by the Indonesian government. However, because of the stand-by arrangements, the programme contained policies and steps to be taken that were discussed with the Fund. Since the Fund's help has been in the form of a stand-by loan, it was provided with conditionality that is binding. The conditionality in different forms that goes with the stand-by arrangement was designed by the Fund.

These obvious things were sometimes debated in the polemics about who should be held responsible for the adverse impacts of the programme or the crisis. The design of the programme or binding requirements as part of the conditionality have become easy targets for critics who protested the Fund's role as an encroachment on Indonesian sovereignty. However, there was also a tendency for the Fund staff to quickly make public disclaimers about the programme. Ownership of the programme, in particular steps on structural reform that had adverse social impact, became an important issue. Misunderstandings and pre-conceptions that were sometimes coupled with political arguments tended to blur the actual issues. These had been adding to the constraints for smooth implementation of the programme, and in the short run jeopardizing the stabilization of the currency.

It has already been noted that public information or education about the nature and characteristics as well as implications of the Fund-supported programme were inadequate. Of course government in Indonesia at the time was centralized in the person of President Soeharto, such that there was almost no effort to explain the measures taken even to the Parliament, as was the case for Thailand and Korea. And even within the government, explanations were inadequate.

A clear example was the emergence of a debate in the media on the use of credit lines from the Singapore government. The government of Singapore made a commitment to provide a line of credits, together with similar facilities from a number of countries supporting the Fund stand-by arrangement for Indonesia. These commitments were offered in the form of a second line of defence, which basically meant that they could be drawn after the IMF funds were exhausted. Of course, the governments of Singapore and Japan also provided funds for a joint intervention to boost the rupiah in the market in early November 1997.

The debate in the Indonesian media was on the usage of the Singapore loan. The Chairman of the Indonesian Chambers of Commerce and Industry, Aburizal Bakrie, who accompanied President Soeharto on his state visit to South Africa in early December 1997, made a statement that the loan from the Singapore government would be used for financing the development of small and medium-scale enterprises (SMEs). It was also reported that the government of Singapore raised the issue with President Soeharto on whether it was the Indonesian intention to use the line of credit for helping SMEs.

The above "incident" would not have happened if the Indonesian public, including the business community, had proper understanding about the nature of a stand-by loan, including a second line of defence. Curiously, this issue appeared also in Singapore during the campaign period for the November 2001 parliamentary election. At issue was whether there was some loan by the Singapore government to President Soeharto during the crisis.

What had been developing in and around November 1997 did not support a well-organized implementation of the programme for the stabilization and recovery of the national economy.

- First, (1) immediately after the signing of the first LOI on 31 October 1997, the President left for Kuala Lumpur for a bilateral meeting with Prime Minister Mahathir Muhammad. Professor Widjojo Nitisastro and Minister Moerdiono accompanied the President. It was a short visit during a weekend. However, this was the time when the announcement of the bank closures was made. This was also when the owners of Banks Jakarta and Andromeda used the media to campaign against the closures, including their announcement to sue the Governor of Bank Indonesia and the Minister of Finance in court. (2) After the President, Minister Moerdiono and Professor Widjojo came back from Kuala Lumpur, Minister Mar'ie Muhammad went to Tokyo to meet with Japanese officials and the creditors to explain the bank closures and the adjustment programme.[3] (3) At the end of November 1997 President Soeharto accompanied by several cabinet ministers, including Minister Moerdiono and Professor Widjojo went out of country again for two weeks. This time it was visits to Namibia and South Africa, attending the APEC Summit in Vancouver and a pilgrimage to Mecca. During this time the Minister of Finance also went to Washington DC and New York to explain the programme to different parties.[4] (4) Upon his return from the two-week trip, President Soeharto fell ill. It was not officially announced that he was ill; instead the public announcement was that he needed rest. However, there was strong speculation that he had suffered a stroke. All these developments showed that the key players in the decision-making on the Fund-supported programme were out of Indonesia such that, physically, it was impossible to conduct coordinated efforts to brief the nation and the Parliament. There was also no time spent on consolidating and coordinating the necessary steps of programme implementation. In other words, crucial steps that should have been done at the launch of the programme were not properly followed.

- Second, the working relations between the President and the central bank Governor and the Minister of Finance started to turn sour, which hindered the day-to day decisions that needed to be made rapidly. As an example, it was impossible to tighten liquidity through an interest rate hike because the President would not grant Bank Indonesia approval and I was not given a chance to discuss it with him. Bank Indonesia tried to make a compromise between the Fund's demand and the President's refusal by designing a step to intervene in the rupiah market. This was done through buying rupiah from banks that held excess liquidity. The inter-bank interest rate was pushed upwards through this operation even though the SBI rates were kept constant. Another example happened in late November 1997: the President made a move to instruct state banks to provide low interest loans to small and medium-scale enterprises. In preparing the policy, the President summoned several ministers and some officials from the ministry of finance. But neither the Central Bank Governor nor the Minister of Finance were invited to the meeting.

- Third, the priority of the President was basically contrary to the policy that was pursued by the monetary authorities to strengthen the currency. By this time, the President was in favour of reducing monetary tightness due to the pressures that the business community and several government officials kept advancing in public debates. Actually, this was a classic case whereby short-term and long-term objectives were debated. There were also empirical studies showing the ineffectiveness of high interest rates for strengthening the exchange rate. But be that as it may, the apparent clash between members of the government further eroded the government credibility in its control over the event.

- Fourth, the rumour about President Soeharto's worsening health and the poor management of the news about it created further uncertainty in the market. For about two weeks from early December 1997 the President cancelled several engagements, including an ASEAN summit in Kuala Lumpur, which added to the suspicion that he was seriously ill. The rumour, which seemed to be credible later, was that he suffered from a stroke. The handling of the news by the government added to the problem.

- Fifth, there were two incidents in Bank Indonesia. On 8 December 1997, Bank Indonesia's not completely finished new building was on fire and it was not clear as to how the fire originated. And on 19 December 1997, the President summarily dismissed four of the seven managing directors of Bank Indonesia. These two events further weakened Bank Indonesia's role in monetary and banking management.

Thus, the factors that in effect constrained programme implementation included the lack of clarity about the details and their implications, time constraints in discussions to iron out differences, the worsening working relationship between monetary authorities, and a lack of government credibility in general.

The Mysterious Fire and the Dismissals

I have to admit that up to the time of this writing I have not been informed of what actually happened in the mysterious fire in late 1997. At the time of my dismissal from Bank Indonesia, I was told that the investigation was not complete. During the Supreme Audit Board's investigation on Bank Indonesia in relation to the issues concerning the central bank liquidity support, Police Colonel Dudon Setia P, the Deputy Director to the Center of Forensic Laboratory reportedly stated that "there was a high probability that the building was intentionally put on fire, which burned 23rd, 24th and 25th floors of Bank Indonesia Tower A on 8 December 1997."[5]

It was also rumoured that the fire was related to efforts by a group to burn down documents that recorded transfers of funds belonging to the Cendana family to foreign countries. It was not clear whether the transfer was made by the central bank or that the latter was just holding the records of the transfers. During the investigative audit on Bank Indonesia by the Supreme Audit Board there was another rumour that some documents containing bank reports were burnt during the 1997 fire.

The rumours on the loss of documents due to the fire have puzzled me. When the tower was on fire the construction was not complete. Yet, due to urgent need for space, all floors from first up to the fourteenth of the building were already in use. But, since the fire only destroyed 23rd floor and up, there should have been no destroyed documents. And I do not recall anyone reporting the loss of any document up till my departure from Bank Indonesia.

Several things have not been brought into the open on the fire that caused the death of one staff and two security guards of Bank Indonesia, and twelve construction workers working in the tower at the time.

More shocking for me personally was that President Soeharto decided on Bank Indonesia's leadership less than two weeks after the fire. On 19 December 1997 the President summarily dismissed four of Bank Indonesia's managing directors. The highest decision-making body in the central bank management in the current system was the board of directors, which comprised seven managing directors and the governor as the head. By replacing four of the board members with people of his own choice, he basically dissolved my board.

The decision shocked me personally because I was not consulted at all. It was indirectly signalled to me a couple of months before December that the President wanted me to dismiss a managing director. However, I did not response positively since it was not a direct instruction: perhaps because I did not response positively to his indirect instruction, the President dismissed four of my managing directors. The four were Hendrobudiyanto, Heru Supraptomo, Paul Sutopo and Mansyurdin Nurdin. Syahril Sabirin, Iwan Prawiranata, Miranda Gultom and Aulia Pohan were installed to replace the dismissed managing directors. In a little over a month, Syahril Sabirin was installed as a new Governor to replace me.

It was all the more distressing because only one day after the installation of the three new managing directors, the dismissed directors, except Mansyurdin Nurdin, was summoned by the Jakarta police for questioning on alleged corruption charges.[6] This was curious because in the President's statement about the dismissals, it was clearly stated that all of them were discharged with honour.

Both the mysterious fire that killed fifteen people and the sudden dismissal of my colleagues from the management of Bank Indonesia had definitely shaken my effectiveness in managing Bank Indonesia's part in the implementation of the adjustment programme.

I was devastated. In a normal situation I should have tendered my resignation. Indeed, I was pondering quitting. But obviously I was not courageous enough to doing it in the face of the risk of being publicly seen as overtly fighting against or in confrontation with President Soeharto.

The dismissal of all Bank Indonesia management of my own choosing continued. I myself was summarily dismissed about six weeks after the December purge. Dr. Boediono was dismissed one week after me, and the other two were replaced at the time of the installation of the new Cabinet, which lasted only 70 days, before they went down together with the fall of Soeharto on 20 May 1998.

Collapsing Banking System

The most damaging impact of all this was on the banking sector. The uncertainties and confusions during the period from early November to end-December 1997 could be described as resulting from the following.

- Monetary policy was confronted a dilemma involving two opposing objectives, i.e. monetary tightening for the defence of exchange rate and liquidity support to help banks facing runs. due to the flights to safety. The problem became untenable for the central bank when the President exercised his authority to press for monetary easing to prevent the real sectors from collapsing. The Fund's review correctly pointed out that the change from monetary tightness to easing it was too fast due to domestic considerations. However, given that the central bank had no autonomy, and had a strained working relationship with the President, it was extremely difficult to deal with the dilemma.

- Market reaction was to transfer funds from banks that were perceived as weak to ones perceived as safe, and from rupiahs to dollars. Bank Indonesia was helpless in observing the movement of funds from private banks to government banks or foreign banks. The number of banks that were net recipients of deposits was less than the ones that were net losers of deposits. In addition, the banking sector suffered a net loss of approximately US$7 billion between August and December 1997. In addition to capital outflows, the adverse impact was the near collapse of the banking sector.

- The inter-bank money market was not working normally because banks started to distrust each other. As a result the inter-bank market suffered from segmentation, and banks were less willing to provide liquidity to other banks, even those able to do so.

- Bank Indonesia had to provide liquidity to prevent the banking sector and the payment system from collapsing. By end-October 1997 the rediscount facility that was suspended in late August 1997 was revived. In a single month since the reopening of the rediscount facility, a total of 123 banks had used it. By the end of November 1997, 131 banks had been using a variety of facilities basically bearing the characteristic of liquidity support.

By this time the nominal value of Bank Indonesia liquidity support had amounted to 21.5 trillion rupiah. The volume of Bank Indonesia liquidity support kept rising during the crisis. When the Supreme Audit Board conducted a general audit to Bank Indonesia, the total liquidity support the central bank provided to the banking sector up to January 1999 was 144.5 trillion rupiah. The policy for Bank Indonesia to provide liquidity to the banking sector became controversial due to alleged corruption and misuse of the funds.

- Cash drawings by the public in December doubled from the previous month, amounting to 4.5 trillion rupiah. This also signalled the loss of public confidence in the banking sector. The use of cash transactions was rising such that in the first week of January 1998 the total cash drawings from the banking sector amounted to 7.4 trillion rupiah.

- By the end of November, two-thirds of the banks, representing over one-half of banking assets, had experienced runs on their deposits. Moreover, 39 banks (accounting for one-fourth of banking system assets) were running growing debit balances with Bank Indonesia. This amounted to about one-third of base money.[7] In addition, by the last week of December 1997, more than 51 banks violated the rule on reserve requirements.

- The depletion of international reserves for market interventions had also been substantial. The total depletion of foreign reserves since the break of the crisis in July to December was US$6.8 billion. The gross foreign reserves went down from US$28.9 billion to US$22.1 billion, while the total reserves used for market interventions, both spot, forward and swap during the period was US$10.35 billion. The amount of dollars used by both the Monetary Authority of Singapore and the Bank of Japan, reportedly US$1.5 billion altogether, was not included in the total reserves spent by Bank Indonesia.

- Rupiah depreciation, which was approximately 1 per cent in November 1997 — from 3,641 to 3,654 rupiah to each dollar — became 48 per cent in the month of December, from 3,654 to 5,395 rupiah to a dollar.

The banking system was collapsing and rapidly impacting adversely on the national economy.

A more careful study has to be conducted to determine conclusively what actually caused the Indonesian crisis. In the meantime, I would argue that the factors below, either individually or in conjunction with the others, had caused the economic crisis, which lingered on and adversely affected almost all aspects of Indonesian life.

1. The most likely causes seem to be inconsistency and a lack of political commitment in programme implementation. In the first two months of the IMF-supported programme, the government decision to revive 15 big projects that were previously postponed seemed to be the most damaging. This decision was perceived by the market as a blatant intervention by the President on behalf of the interests of his family and cronies.

2. The President's family's reactions to the bank closures by mounting legal suits against the Minister of Finance and the Governor of Bank Indonesia in the court, and the acquisition of Bank Alfa dealt a further blow to the credibility of the monetary authorities.

3. The monetary easing in November 1997 after a brief tightening had confused the market, or given a signal that monetary policy was erratic. It also demonstrated government intervention in the central bank's operations in the conduct of monetary policy.

4. The worsening of the working relationship between the President and the Governor of Bank Indonesia and the Minister of Finance that constrained programme implementation.

5. The rumour about the President's ill health that caused political uncertainty, which ultimately also constrained programme implementation.

6. The Korean financial crisis in late November 1997 that sparked a regional contagion, which renewed external pressure on Indonesia's foreign exchange market.

Budget Debacle

Another unfortunate incident that damaged the implementation of the adjustment programme occurred during the otherwise normal budget exercise for the fiscal year 1998/99. As was the custom during the New Order era, the government presented a budget for the incoming fiscal year that ran from April to March. The President submitted the budget for the fiscal year 1998/99 to the Parliament on 6 January 1998. It was not a great budget, but certainly it was not too unrealistic either. However, market reaction to the budget was so negative that it contributed to the collapse of the currency and the banking system, which ultimately put the adjustment programme in real disarray.

It should be noted at the outset that the budget itself had some problems due to several unrealistic assumptions. The first was the target of 4 per cent economic growth. Actually the monetary authorities were arguing for a target of one to 2 per cent. But the final decision was to adopt the growth target proposed by the Minister of National Development Planning. Of course even a growth of one per cent was still way too optimistic. The second one was on the assumption of an exchange rate of 4,000 rupiah to the dollar.

Besides, the budget was submitted to the Parliament in the form of a "balanced budget" as defined by the government.[8] If the budget were to be presented in a standard presentation, the budget of 1998/99 had a deficit of more than one per cent of GDP.

The budget was not realistic. Nevertheless, I would argue that it was not as bad as the market perceived. The market perception was that the budget was so unrealistic that it was defying the Fund's advice, and that the Fund-supported programme was doomed to fail.

The banking industry suffered the most from this negative reaction. Almost immediately after the budget announcement many national banks reported that they could no longer write letters of credit on behalf of their clients. Foreign banks denied letters of credits issued by many national banks. At the same time, many national banks also reported that their foreign counterparts started to withdraw their extended loans or stopped rolling over their advances, and stopped providing trade financing. This was almost the final blow to an already weak and wounded banking industry.

However, the market's negative reaction was perhaps excessive. The lack of understanding of foreign market players about the Indonesian budgetary process must have played an important role here. Many of them did not understand the Indonesian concept of a balanced budget. They did not want to accept that all these years the government had always come up with a balanced budget, even though the realized budget did not necessarily balance. Most of them did not realize that in the two years prior to the crisis, the government had produced surpluses in the budgets, even though all of them were balanced at the time of presentation to the Parliament.

The main concern of this group was that they learnt from the first LOI that the Fund required that the government produce a surplus budget for the fiscal year of 1998/99. So, when they learned that the budget was balanced, they must have decided that it would be a disaster, and they reacted accordingly.

I would argue that the Fund's requirement for a budget that produced one per cent of GDP surplus as a performance criteria was unrealistic. The requirement for the budget surplus was a guide for the market, such that when the proposed budget was balanced, the market decided to punish Indonesia.

At about this time a Fund staff member was quoted anonymously in the media as saying that the government had just proposed an unrealistic budget. Another anonymous Fund staffer was also quoted by the *Washington Post* as saying

> We would like to see the senior leadership in Indonesia stand up and be counted in the reform... I think the markets are asking themselves the question of just how much the senior Indonesian leadership is committed to this programme, and particularly to the reform measures that affect the family.[9]

The question arises as to why the government accepted the Fund's requirement if it was unrealistic. I do not know for sure. However, like the GDP figure, the figures here were a result of a compromise. With the benefit of hindsight, the budget surplus and its size became problematic due to the lack of thorough analysis and detailed calculations on about the risk of their non-compliance or possible social implications.

The extremely negative public reactions to the budget followed the devastating response to the bank closures. The rupiah took a beating. The currency depreciated 55 per cent in about a week, from 5,395 rupiah at end-December to 8,394 rupiah to the dollar on 7 January. The pounding on the currency further worsened when President Soeharto announced that he would take on B.J. Habibie as his running mate in the forthcoming election. The market perceived Dr. Habibie as someone with an obsession with grandiose projects rather than prudent macroeconomic management. As a result the currency plummetted to its lowest to over 16,000 rupiah to a dollar for a couple of hours, even though it rebounded to 14,000 rupiah in the last week of January 1998.

The onslaught on the currency created grave concern in the government as well as among the Fund staff. In the meantime the Fund itself started to face mounting criticisms on the way it was handling the Asian crisis. The deepening problems of the Indonesian crisis as well as the criticisms of the Fund must have influenced the apparent change in the Fund's attitude to be more accommodating and less rigid.

With respect to the 1998/99 budget, the Fund at a later date, after the signing of the second LOI, allowed the government to come up with a revised one, which in a standard presentation bore a deficit of one per cent of GDP. When the exercise was finalized in 23 January, the budget was actually carrying a deficit of close to 2 per cent of GDP. This budget was, further revised in July 1998 with a deficit of 8.5 per cent of GDP, even though at the end of the year the budget was reported to have a deficit of 2.6 per cent of GDP.[10]

When the Fund initially insisted on a surplus budget in October 1997, the social impacts of the crisis were yet to be considered. In the first LOI it was argued very mechanistically that the different subsidies that the government provided in the past had to be reduced in stages, and that all subsidies had to be made transparent by putting them in the budget. To finance the subsidies and to strengthen the rupiah, the budget had to be contractionary, thus a surplus of one per cent of GDP. The change from a surplus to a deficit budget was definitely a drastic one for the Fund to advocate.

I would argue that a combination of an unrealistic budget with extremely negative market reaction that originated from inept assessments by market players on Indonesia's budgetary practice caused the budget debacle in January 1998.

In addition, the budget failed to convince partly due to an unrealistic requirement in the stand-by arrangement that insisted on a budget surplus under conditions that, on the contrary, needed an expansionary budget. Had the Fund restrained itself from putting a surplus budget as a performance criterion, market reaction to the budget may not have been so devastating.

Stronger Programme with Weak Commitment

Based on the review of the programme implementation and further discussions and negotiations between the government and the Fund, a new strengthened and reinforced programme was formulated in the second LOI. The comprehensive policy package included bold reforms to sweep away structural rigidities, improve fiscal transparency, and restore the banking system back to financial health. As for the first one, these reforms would be supported by a prudent fiscal and monetary policy.

The document was formally negotiated and signed personally by President Soeharto. As far as I knew there was no other precedent for a Head of State signing an LOI to the Fund.

The programme comprised 50 points, and like the first one, formulated in an MEFP. The major items included were as follows:

1. With respect to macroeconomic policies, the programme was designed to prevent the economy from having a negative growth and an inflation rate of less than 20 per cent, and single digit the following year. The programme was simultaneously aimed at creating a surplus in the balance of payments for financing the national debts. The programme in fiscal policy was aimed at increasing transparency. The programme in monetary policy was aimed at maintaining a firm monetary stance for exchange rate stability of the rupiah and controlling inflation.

2. The 1998/99 budget would be revised in accordance with the agreement on the macroeconomic framework, taking into consideration the usual practice of the government of presenting a balanced budget. In terms of the standard concept of government budget this was equivalent to a budget deficit of one per cent of GDP. To reduce distortions, and strengthen the fiscal position the government intended to adjust administered prices with the aim of gradually eliminating subsidies of fuel and electricity. The government was committed to eliminating subsidies in stages, starting with initial adjustment in April 1998 in fuel and electricity prices, except for prices of kerosene and diesel fuel, where increases would be kept to a minimum to protect the poor. To increase transparency, starting in the fiscal year 1998/99, the reforestation and investment funds would be incorporated in the government budget. The government would postpone the implementation of 12 infrastructure projects that were recently revived or under review. Budgetary and

non-budgetary allocations of funds as well as special loans for the aircraft industry would be immediately terminated. Special tax treatment for the national car project would also cease.

3. A tight monetary policy would be continued to stabilize the rupiah and to control inflation. Bank Indonesia would conduct intervention in the foreign exchange market in defence of the rupiah judiciously. The central bank would also provide liquidity support to banks suffering from liquidity problems due to the bank runs. Bank Indonesia would be granted autonomy in exercising monetary policy that would begin with interest rate determination of Bank Indonesia certificates.

4. While some banks were already under restructuring in the previous programme, other banks had to face similar treatment due to the worsening conditions. Bank Indonesia would be working with the ADB, IMF and World Bank staffs to establish and expeditiously implement uniform, transparent and equitable rules for resolving liquidity and solvency problems of private banks.

5. The government was committed to improving the supervision of the banking system and to further strengthen the policy and institutional infrastructure for banking. The government also made commitments to improve the legal framework for banking operations, transparency and disclosure.

6. With respect to structural reform, the government made stronger commitments to remove various restrictions and monopoly practices including:

- To limit Bulog's monopoly on imports of rice starting in February 1998;
- To dissolve the Cloves Marketing Board in June 1998;
- To abolish marketing arrangements in cement, paper and plywood; and
- To set up a special credit scheme for small and medium-scale enterprises with assistance from the ADB.

To increase transparency, the government decided to make the second LOI and all subsequent ones publicly accessible. Since then, all documents concerning Fund-supported programmes for Indonesia have been posted on the IMF website.

It should be noted that the environment after the signing of the second LOI was better than the first one. As I alluded to before, after the signing of the first LOI, the government did not make concerted efforts to implement the programme well.

It was also noticeable that there were at least covert changes in the attitudes of the Fund staff in their dealing with the issues. It would not be surprising if this was due to a combination of the unpleasant surprise of the market reactions to the bank closures and their aftermath and strong criticisms from many parties about the way the Fund had handled the Asian crisis. Whether intentional or not, the atmosphere in the aftermath of the signing of the second LOI was better than the first one.

Two major issues that were not touched by the Fund in November 1997, corporate debt and the social implications of the crisis, were taken into consideration in the new programme. It is my contention that on these two issues, discussions between the Indonesian team and First Deputy MD Stanley Fischer during his visit to Jakarta were instrumental.

In contrast to the absence of immediate follow-up steps in November, by the second LOI, the government was more organized. Immediately after the signing, different discussions were conducted for steps to be taken in bank restructuring as well as initial actions on corporate debt restructuring. Again in contrast to November 1997 when the Fund officials left Jakarta immediately after the signing, this time they stayed on in Jakarta.

With respect to bank restructuring, the most drastic step was the imposition of the blanket guarantee by the government. The move was made in the face of a possible risk of Indonesia experiencing bankruptcy of its banking sector and collapse of its payment system. Simultaneously, the government also set up the Indonesian Bank Restructuring Agency (IBRA). The decision to adopt a blanket guarantee for banks and the setting up of IBRA were formalized in the President's decrees on 26 January 1998.

In addition to the proposals on the blanket guarantee and the formation of IBRA, which were adopted by the government after days of heated negotiations and discussions, there were a number of steps that indicated some change of attitudes of the Fund:[11]

- The insistence for Indonesia to have a surplus budget was changed to its willingness to accept a deficit budget for 1998/99

- The proposal for Indonesia to adopt a blanket guarantee in contrast to acceptance of the government scheme to pay only small deposit holders in November 1997
- The willingness of the Fund to assist the government to mediate between creditors and the Indonesian corporations to deal with corporate debt in contrast to the previous hands-off policy
- The willingness to deal with the social implications of the crisis.

A similar assessment was made in the evaluations conducted by the Fund on its programmes in Thailand, Indonesia and Korea, written one year after. It was stated that these changes were made by the Fund because it had not expected that the crisis would be so devastating (Lane 1999). And, as for the government of Indonesia, if there were circumstances that constrained the team earlier, these had changed by January 1998.

A new coordinating council, the Council for Enhancement of National Economics and Financial Resilience, was set up on 21 January 1998. The council was formed to coordinate and monitor the implementation of the new Fund-supported programme. The council had 12 members that included two Minister Coordinators, four Cabinet Ministers and the Governor of BI, three individuals representing the private sector with Professor Widjojo Nitisastro as the Secretary General and Dr. Fuad Bawasir, the Director General of Taxation as Deputy Secretary General. The council was led by President Soeharto as the chairman. In addition an expert team was also set up, which comprised of the Minister for Trade and Industry as the chairman and four members, high officials from variety of institutions. Basically, the new council comprised of members of the Monetary Board or the economic team that negotiated the stand-by agreement with the Fund and some people representing the private sector.

The President also asked the Fund to appoint a senior official, whose task was *liaising* directly between President Soeharto and the Managing Director or the Deputy Managing Director of the Fund. The Fund immediately appointed Mr. Prabhan Naverkar, who had only recently retired from his last post as Deputy Managing Director, after a very long career at the Fund.

Clearly, there were signs of new seriousness on the part of both the government and the Fund to make the programme work. In less than two weeks after the signing of the LOI, the blanket guarantee was adopted. IBRA was established with Dr. Bambang Subianto, the Director General of Financial Institution of the Ministry of Finance, appointed as its director. By early February 1998 most national banks had signed agreements with Bank Indonesia to join the guarantee scheme. Bank Indonesia transferred the supervision and restructuring process of 54 problem banks to the newly formed institution as stipulated in the programme.

The urgently needed programme for corporate debt restructuring was initiated with technical assistance from the Fund. A team entrusted to design a framework for corporate debt restructuring on a volunteer basis was formed and headed by Mr. Radius Prawiro (a former Minister and Governor of Bank Indonesia who served many years in the Cabinet).

Two committees were set up, a Steering Committee that represented creditors, and a Contact Committee that represented debtors. The Contact Committee was formed from members of a team on private foreign debts, which had been set up in December 1997. Among the members of the Steering Committee were a former official of the Bank of England, a banker from Standard Chartered and the CEO of UBS East Asia.[12]

The Fund also changed its team leader for Indonesia. From the preparation for the first LOI until the last week of January 1998, the team leader for the Fund was Dr. Bijan B. Aghevli, the Deputy Director for Asia Pacific (APD). However, by the end of January 1998, the team was headed directly by Hubert Neiss, Director for APD. With his longer experience, including several years as Chief Representative for Indonesia in the 1970s, and his ability to communicate well with Indonesian officials, working relations between Indonesia and the Fund had better prospects. The change in personnel contributed to a better environment for programme implementation.

The Market Knows Better

Why did a stronger programme with better preparation and follow-up steps still fail to produce a turning point for financial and economic recovery? Did the market know better? Let us try to shed some light to get better understanding on this seeming contradiction here.

The picture that appeared in many newspapers, of President Soeharto signing documents and Michel Camdessus watching with his arms crossed, became very well known throughout Indonesia. The picture seemed to many Indonesians a show of arrogance or condescension on the part of the managing director. For some time afterward Mr. Camdessus had to explain to journalists that he had not meant to show his disrespect, let alone to insult the President.

The signing was indeed unique for other reasons. As I said before it is uncommon for the president of a country to sign an LOI it is usually signed by a minister of finance. In the case of Indonesia in 1997, the Minister of Finance and Governor of the Central Bank signed the document. However, since April 1998 the signatories of the document have been the Minister coordinator for the Economy and Finance together with the Minister of Finance and the Governor of Bank Indonesia.

Certainly there is no specific rule on this matter. However, it has been the practice for Indonesia that the Governor of Bank Indonesia represents the government of Indonesia and holds the post as governor for Indonesia in the Fund, while the Minister of Finance holds the post of Indonesia's governor in the World Bank. In other words, these two officials are the Indonesia's formal representatives on the boards of governors of the two institutions.

President Soeharto had also negotiated with Fund officials on the substance of the programme. This was also very rare. But I am sure that there was another important point that he wanted to underline here. It is my contention that he did this to show the public his displeasure and loss of trust in the monetary authorities. As if to underline this, the two officials were not even invited to the signing ceremony.

He made this message even clearer through the decision to set up a new council to replace the former team, and to ask for a senior official of the Fund to act as a direct liaison between him and Mr. Camdessus. My working relationship with the President, that had been deteriorating since the bank closures, became even more strained. My communication with him was mostly done through Professor Widjojo Nitisastro, who was appointed secretary general of the new council and Minister Moerdiono. As it turned out, in less than three weeks, he would sack me from my post.

The new LOI was also unusual in that its contents seemed to demonstrate the President's willingness to make sweeping structural improvements, as the Fund demanded. Notably, the programme would abolish some special treatments or monopoly practices that had been enjoyed by interest groups close to the President.

The programmes to abolish Bulog's import monopoly except for rice; the clove and plywood monopolies in trade, the termination of special tax treatments for the national car project and off-budget and budget financing for the airplane industry, were all antithetical to President Soeharto's interests. Even the plan to grant autonomy to the central bank was in contrast to past practice. Frankly, I could not believe my eyes reading the draft, because I knew so well that these were his pet projects.

It seems that in reality, President Soeharto took all the proposals for discarding monopoly practices and special treatments for some projects as personal criticisms. In other words, the President must have considered the steps for structural reform as efforts to spoil his fun. So, the proposals must have caused some resentment on his part.

It was my conjecture that despite the fact that he signed it, he did not accept the programme wholeheartedly. In a meeting of the newly formed council on 21 January 1998 the President explained that what he decided in the LOI was what the market demanded. However, he reiterated that "for us, our Indonesian brand had to stay". He further said that "the national development that was based on the development trilogy as stated in the state guidelines had been securely ingrained in our society. However, it was as if wiped out by the last six months of financial turmoil".

The tone of his statements seemed to argue that, even though we had our agreement with the Fund as formulated in the LOI, the path of Indonesian development should be unchanged. During this meeting there were two occasions when he signalled his reluctance to implement the programme exactly as stipulated. One was on the proposal for foreign investors to fully own companies. He said that although this had been our decision he was actually uncomfortable with it. The other one was on Indonesia's concept of a balanced budget. He stated with a little bit of disgust that "it's up to the Fund to call our balanced budget a deficit budget, but it's balanced to us".

However, Mr. Camdessus and the Fund saw the President's involvement as a welcome change of heart and sign of commitment to implement the programme. Some who knew the President and understood the environment at this time, felt that it was naïve to think that there was serious commitment on the part of the President to actually implement the programme. In any case, objectively speaking, the programme was an improvement of the first one and it was certainly not wrong for the Fund to have higher expectations.

However, the Fund was wrong, at least in terms of a more stable rupiah. The market made its own assessment, and no longer believed in the ability of the government to cope or deliver. In the foreign exchange market, dollar buying continued. Foreign banks and investors no longer trusted the viability of Indonesian banks. They joined others in buying dollars and in withdrawing their outstanding loans and refusing to give roll-overs on their past loans or accepting letters of credit issued by Indonesian banks.

The loss of credibility was not confined to just the banking sector and the government's ability to manage the economy. By this time, the loss of credibility was already seeping through the political system and national leadership in general. Whatever the government or the Fund did in terms of enhancing the adjustment programme to address the financial and economic problems, the market and the public had already decided to distrust the capacity and commitment of the government in the fight against the crisis.

A more serious study should be conducted to answer questions related to the failure of the second adjustment programme. In the first programme the market and the public had lost their trust in the government efforts to cope with the problems due to the bank closures and inconsistent implementation of reform. The second better organized programme still did not convince the market and the public.

6

Bank Indonesia and the Crisis

Controversial Issues

Several steps that were taken by the government and the central bank during the crisis have become the subject of public debate in Indonesia and unfortunately have not been resolved to the present. Some policies have even become controversial, due partly to the lack of clarity on the part of many concerning what had been the real issues or the reasoning behind steps taken.

I will discuss three of them, namely the policy of granting liquidity support to banks; the debates on fixing the currency to the dollar in a currency board arrangement; and the issues associated with granting autonomy to the central bank.

My discussions here will not guarantee the disappearance of the controversies if the differences resulted from ideology or vested interests, in particular if "tribalism" is involved (Budiman 1999).

Liquidity Support to Banks

In tandem with the bank closures of November 1997, the most controversial policy launched during the crisis was the liquidity support to banks in distress that Bank Indonesia provided.

Was this a government or a central bank policy? What was the reasoning in either case? How should the losses arising from the liquidity support be apportioned between institutions? Who should be held responsible for the policy and its implications? How did the government deal with the alleged corruption?

The liquidity support to banks that Bank Indonesia provided during the crisis became controversial when the Supreme Audit Board issued two reports on the audits conducted in fulfillment of a request by the Parliament. The first one was a general audit report with a disclaimer, which the Agency issued in November 1999. The issuing of an audit report with a disclaimer is automatically read as a sign of problems in the audited institution, i.e. Bank Indonesia in this case. The second report was on an investigative audit on the central bank due to alleged possible criminal acts of corruption. The second report, which was issued in July 2000, specifically mentioned suspicion of possible criminal acts, either in the usage of the funds by the receiving banks or the provision of the funds by the central bank, or both. This time the report was publicly announced in a press conference held by the Supreme Audit Board.[1]

At the time of writing how the controversy around the alleged possible corruption will ultimately be resolved is not clear. However, since the end of 2000 the Attorney General's Office (AGO) has investigated and prosecuted a number of bank owners and CEOs of banks suspected of corruption. The AGO also interrogated Bank Indonesia's officials from the banking supervision, accounting, foreign exchange, and legal departments and others, including a number of directors and managing directors working during my governorship, and myself. A number of cases that involved some bankers associated with the receiving banks and three former managing directors of Bank Indonesia have been brought to trial.

At issue were the huge amount of funds involved, the possible huge losses that could occur, and the sense of unfairness due to public perception that banks owners and bankers, including central bankers, were the parties that had benefited, and because of their mistakes, ultimately it was the taxpayers who had to bear the burden.

I think public perceptions were also tinged with misunderstandings, misgivings, or preconceptions. The public perception about bank owners and bankers in Indonesia has been, not without grounds, that they symbolize the social ills of Indonesia, in particular the rampant practices of corruption, collusion and nepotism of the New Order government. Some argue that they were the benefactors of all the funds provided by the central bank that brought the economy to the verge of bankruptcy. It is unfair, so the argument continues, that the taxpayers have to bail them out. This is very appealing publicly, but it contains some flaws nonetheless.

In this argument, the role of Bank Indonesia, which has not been well understood by many either, has been confused with the real problem of structural weaknesses in the banking sector and banking supervision. The criticisms against Bank Indonesia's policies also indicate a lack of appreciation or refusal to accept the fact that the actions were taken in the midst of an extraordinary financial crisis.

It is not surprising that in a non-transparent environment with weak governance in both the public and private sectors, a central bank step — to provide liquidity support to banks suffering from distress due to bank runs in accordance with its function as lender of last resort and in effect implementing a government policy (that of not closing banks temporarily) — ultimately turned into a controversy. It became messier when, in the process of addressing other considerations, including political and group interests that came into play from the auditor's report through to the investigation as well as the court prosecution.

In fact, the issues associated with the liquidity support were already raised in reports circulated via the Internet in November 1997, which were published as a booklet entitled *Conspiracy to Rock Soeharto*.[2]

What is liquidity support?

What is Bank Indonesia liquidity support? What are the justifications for the central bank providing liquidity support? And why did the central bank provide liquidity support to particular banks only?

Bank Indonesia liquidity support is a facility that the central bank provides to banks suffering from a systemic liquidity mismatch to prevent the banking sector from collapsing. The liquidity support that the central bank provides actually comprises of a number of liquidity facilities to address different liquidity problems and to suit the conditions of the recipient banks.

The banking sector, which for most developing or emerging countries like Indonesia dominated the national payment system through its role in financial intermediation and as a source of financing, by the nature of its operations could at any time face problems of a liquidity mismatch. The central bank, as lender of last resort for the banking system and the guardian of the payment system, equipped itself with different liquidity support schemes. The terms that are generally known are "discount window" or "re-discount facility".

The term in Bahasa Indonesia, Bantuan Likuiditas Bank Indonesia (BLBI) was only publicly known in early 1998 when it was mentioned in the second LOI. Public comments showed a lack of understanding about what BLBI entailed. One comment was, "As it turned out Bank Indonesia had been giving this liquidity support to banks, even prior to the crisis".

Different schemes of liquidity support had been with Bank Indonesia since its transformation into the central bank of the Republic in 1953. As with any other central bank, Bank Indonesia is the lender of last resort for the Indonesian banking industry.

Bank Indonesia liquidity supports are all liquidity facilities provided by Bank Indonesia outside credits. The Bank Indonesia Liquidity Credits (Kredit Likuiditas Bank Indonesia or KLBI) are loans provided by the central bank to commercial banks at subsidized interest rates to support government programmes, such as loans to finance small and medium-scale industry, cooperatives or loans to support self-sufficiency in rice. So, the broad definition of Bank Indonesia liquidity support includes all facilities provided by the central bank for the banking sector outside these KLBI schemes.

If we describe the liquidity support as all various forms of Bank Indonesia liquidity to banks, there were altogether 15 facilities. The 15 facilities could be grouped into five as follows:

1. Liquidity support to banks for resolving liquidity mismatches. In the central bank operation there were two types of liquidity support in this category, one for a very short term of between 15–30 days (Discount Facility I) and another for a short term, between 90–150 days (Discount Facility II) with promissory notes as collateral.

2. Liquidity support to banks in the context of the central bank

open market operation. In this operation Bank Indonesia rediscounted promissory notes or other debt instruments of commercial banks, both through auctions and direct deals.

3. Liquidity support in the context of bank rescuing or nursing programmes conducted by the central bank. Bank Indonesia gave support to bank restructuring of problem banks through mergers and acquisitions in the forms of emergency or subordinated loans.

4. Liquidity support to banks facing runs in the context of stabilizing the banking industry and the payment system. The facilities were in the form of drawings by banks from their funds with the central bank used for fulfillment of the reserve requirements, and the exemption for banks to participate in daily clearing in spite of their negative balance with the central bank.

5. Liquidity support to banks in the context of defending market confidence in the banking sector. These facilities were in the form of advances by the central bank to the government for payment to small deposit holders of liquidated banks, advances for the implementation of blanket guarantees and advances for payments of banks' arrears to their foreign counterparts for trade financing and inter-bank debt exchange offers.

Bank Indonesia's liquidity support in the first two categories are instruments that most central banks provide in their operation as monetary authorities and lender of last resort. Prior to the crisis Bank Indonesia had been using these instruments in its operation. The third one had also been resorted to in its operation to give incentives to investors that had workable plans to invest in problem banks that could be rescued through merger and acquisition. In other words, the liquidity support that Bank Indonesia had used under normal conditions, prior to the crisis.

Liquidity support during the crisis

When the crisis struck the national economy Bank Indonesia resorted to liquidity supports that would be suitable to confronting the challenge, namely the last two categories. These forms of support were resorted to when Bank Indonesia detected that the national economy was facing a contagion that endangered the banking sector and the payment system could collapse altogether.

But how did the Bank Indonesia liquidity support actually develop? The financial turmoil that struck Indonesia in July 1997 started to cause problems for the banking sector when, in defense of the currency slide, the central bank took steps to limit liquidity. After the currency float in mid-August the government and the central bank tightened liquidity further. The policy was executed through a combination of interest rate increase, expenditure reduction by the government as well as administrative intervention. The last one was in the form of an instruction by the Minister of Finance for state enterprises to transfer their bank deposits into Bank Indonesia certificates (SBIs).

In the meantime, out of concern about the safety of their deposits people started to withdraw their bank deposits from a number of banks. This process caused a number of banks to feel the brunt from scarcity of liquidity in the inter-bank money market, which fuelled the crisis.

Bank Indonesia responded by providing banks that suffered from liquidity problems with liquidity support through different schemes. Since the problem was systemic, faced by an increasing number of banks over time, the most dominant form of support was one through the mechanism of the daily clearing of banks' transactions.

All banks participate in daily clearing to check their liquidity position after their daily operations. A bank that experienced a negative balance with the central bank as shown in the clearing process is given a day to settle the obligation. This bank would get the funds by borrowing in the inter-bank money market.

During the crisis, more banks suffered liquidity problems due to massive deposits and savings withdrawals. In the meantime the inter-bank money market did not function well, even banks with excess liquidity did not want to lend to other banks. Increasing numbers of banks were forced to rely on alternatives. They started using their own funds that were put aside with the central bank for the reserve requirements. But massive deposit withdrawals continued. Bank Indonesia liquidity support was the last resort for these banks to enable them to continue operating. What Bank Indonesia actually decided was to allow banks having negative balances to continue participating in the clearing process.

Bank Indonesia's decision to help banks having liquidity problems during the crisis was based on President Soeharto's policy of not liquidating banks to avoid social tension or unrest prior to and during the general election in October 1997. Bank Indonesia provided liquidity support to banks in need indiscriminately. The number of banks that received liquidity support in different forms during the crisis up to 1999 was 164.[3]

In normal conditions the liquidity support was mostly the discount facilities and the rediscount of banks' promissory notes. These instruments carried predetermined tenors and better safeguard measures for Bank Indonesia. The receiving banks had to produce collaterals for using the facilities.

However, in the middle of distress and crisis, conditions were very fluid and demanded faster mechanisms to address the pressing problems. A bank confronted with a run could go from a liquidity problem into insolvency within days. Here, time was of the essence and quick procedure was very important. In the face of the pressing risk of a collapsing banking sector and expectation that the crisis would be short term, Bank Indonesia was forced to act swiftly to provide liquidity support to banks through the clearing process. Banks having liquidity problems were allowed to continue participating in clearing irrespective of whether they had positive or negative balances with Bank Indonesia.

The downside was that this did not have the safeguard measures as the other facilities. But, the expectation was for the crisis to be over shortly, and the banks would be able to recover the lost deposits in the longer run, and to operate normally. The banking industry would be saved from collapse and banks would be able to pay back their obligation to the central bank.

However, when the crisis did not recede and problems continued to get worse, Bank Indonesia on several occasions changed the facility that was given to banks into more secured ones, the discount facilities I and II. By end-1997 all these provisions were even transformed into a more secure rediscount facility.

As it turned out, the crisis lingered on in spite of further measures like the adoption of blanket guarantees and the formation of a special institution to deal with problem banks (IBRA). In April 1998 the government and Bank Indonesia resorted to a longer-term facility to support bank restructuring through a programme of bank re-capitalization for both state-owned and private banks.

The provision in the programme of bank re-capitalization was for banks' owners to provide 20 per cent of the capital needed for the banks to have a capital adequacy ratio (CAR) of 4, while the government bore 80 per cent of the needed capital. As an obvious implication of the huge amount of liquidity support that banks received from Bank Indonesia (which was also followed by even much larger amounts of funds for bank re-capitalization after the crisis) government ownership of banks increased to more than 80 per cent of total banking assets.

Other forms of liquidity support were advances made by Bank Indonesia for financing different items owed by problem banks. These included payment for small deposits of the liquidated banks in November 1997, the adoption of blanket guarantees and payment of banks' arrears to their foreign counterparts in accordance with the agreement between national banks and foreign banks, known as Frankfurt agreement of June 1998. These obligations were later transferred to the government or IBRA for more transparent resolution in addition to freeing Bank Indonesia from making the payments.

The controversy over liquidity support

The saying that "failure is an orphan" seems to be fitting to ask the question of who should be held accountable for the policy for providing liquidity support to banks? This issue became a public debate after the Parliamentary Commission on Bank Indonesia Liquidity Support summoned officials and former officials of Bank Indonesia and the Ministry of Finance to testify in front of the Commission in February 2000.

These officials and former officials, including the governor and the former governor of Bank Indonesia and former Ministers of Finance, were asked to give their testimony on the issue of whether the decision on providing liquidity support was made by the central bank alone or together with the government. In other words, whether the policy to provide liquidity support was a Bank Indonesia policy or Government of Indonesia policy. It became a public controversy after a statement made by three former ministers of finance claiming that the policy for providing the liquidity support was not a government policy, and that the central bank made the decision out of its misunderstanding of government policy.[4]

However, the Commission in its November 2000 report on the investigation of the liquidity support issue concluded that the decision for Bank Indonesia to provide liquidity supports to banks during the crisis was a government policy to resolve the financial and banking crisis. The Commission recognized that the decision to provide liquidity support to banks was based on crisis conditions.[5]

To make a balanced assessment, it is important to get an overview of the whole issue, including the roles of the President and the Indonesian government as well as Bank Indonesia.

As mentioned before, based on the 1992 Banking Act, the central bank adopted a case-by-case approach in the implementation of the policy to restructure problem banks. In this approach, a variety of steps were taken to make the ailing banks healthy. These steps ranged from requiring a bank to increase capital or to write-off bad debts to assisting the bank to be acquired or merged. Only if these efforts failed, and if allowing the bank to continue its operations would endanger the stability of the banking system, would liquidation proceedings be pursued. In short, Bank Indonesia would make a recommendation to the Ministry of Finance for liquidating a problem bank only after all other avenues were exhausted.

The case-by-case method of bank restructuring was discarded when the number of problem banks increased. Bank Indonesia still continuing its efforts to mediate and provide incentives for investors who had workable plans for rescuing problem banks. However, the methods for resolving problem banks became more systemic, taking into consideration all relevant aspects of bank restructuring, including the costs and benefits of each alternative.

In December 1996, I, as the Governor of Bank Indonesia, accompanied by two managing directors in charge of bank supervision, proposed to President Soeharto to start liquidation proceedings on seven problem banks that did not have good prospects for rescue. The President did not approve our proposal. Instead, he instructed Bank Indonesia to finalize a draft of the government decree on bank closures. The reason was because at this time there was no specific regulation on bank liquidation. At this time should a bank be liquidated, corporate bankruptcy regulations would be applied. One of the problems was that banks could not treat deposit holders as priority creditors to receive repayment prior to other creditors. In other words, even if there was deposit insurance, the payment to deposit holders of liquidated banks could only be done together with payment to other creditors. There was no provision to prioritize payments for depositors. Deposit holders and other creditors are competitors. A government decree on bank liquidation was ultimately issued toward the end of 1996, i.e. the Government Regulation of the R.I. No. 68, 1996.

On April 1997 Bank Indonesia came back with a similar report on bank closures. It was quite ironic that in fact the President then approved the proposal for closure of the seven problem banks. However, he asked that the execution be postponed until after the general election and the general session of the People's Consultative Assembly. This in effect meant that the closures could only be implemented after March 1998.

Unfortunately, by July 1997 the financial crisis struck Indonesia. The number of problem banks increased. Ultimately, in November 1997, under a Fund-supported programme, 16 insolvent banks were closed including the original seven.

Bank Indonesia decided to provide liquidity support in the form of allowing banks suffering from negative balances with the central bank to participate in clearing when all the signals of distress were clearly detected in the banking sector in mid-August 1997.

It turned out that the government decision to float the currency in 14 August 1997 shocked Indonesian business, including the banking sector. The uncertainties of the foreign exchange rate created panic among the business community, with its high degree of foreign exchange exposure, mostly unhedged, and used for financing loans in speculative projects. They started to buy dollars heavily, the financing of which caused a liquidity crunch in the banking sector. The liquidity crunch was signalled by the liquidation (selling) of SBIs holdings by banks, including large banks. The inter-bank rate started to increase as well. At this time Bank Indonesia also learned from similar developments in Thailand when the baht started to crumble.

Confronted with a liquidity shortage in the banking sector and the President's instruction not to liquidate banks, Bank Indonesia decided to let banks stay in the red with the central bank to continue participating in the daily clearing. During these fragile times even rumours about a bank suffering losses in bank clearing could cause a run on that bank. And a bank run could easily trigger runs on other banks. Thus, the decision to let banks with negative balances participate in clearing was based on the government policy for temporarily not liquidating banks.

Both the case-by-case as well as systemic method of bank restructuring involved costs. The cost of bank restructuring has always been substantial. Someone ultimately has to bear the cost. The cost of bank restructuring through a variety of facilities to Bank Indonesia as the provider of these facilities ultimately constituted what was known as BLBI.

The biggest part of the liquidity support was the negative balances of banks with Bank Indonesia that was used to finance mass withdrawals of funds from most banks in the banking industry. The flight to safety occurred when market confidence in the banking sector was lost partly in reaction to the bank closures in November 1997. As a result the banking sector suffered runs and there was a risk that the payment system would collapse. The negative balance of commercial banks with Bank Indonesia kept worsening.

The table below shows the negative balance of commercial banks increasing from 1.4 trillion rupiah in July 1997 to 5.3 trillion rupiah by end-1997, and 48.4 trillion rupiah by February 1998. The size of banks' negative balances kept increasing despite efforts by Bank Indonesia, with the support of the government, to substitute the facility with a better liquidity support instrument and to stop allowing banks to run negative balances.

In a broad definition of liquidity support, we should also include other types of facilities. First, the advances made by Bank Indonesia for financing the repayment of deposits up to 20 million rupiah. Later on, based on a presidential instruction, the Minister of Finance decided that repayments would be conducted for all deposit holders of the liquidated banks. The advances amounted to 5.7 trillion rupiah (Table 8). Second, advances for financing related to the adoption of blanket guarantees, and for payment of banks' arrears on trade finance to foreign banks. Bank Indonesia also issued a new discount facility in March 1998. In total, Bank Indonesia liquidity support skyrocketed from 10.9 trillion rupiah in July 1997 to 62.9 trillion rupiah at the end of 1997, 96 trillion rupiah at the end of February 1998, 173.4 trillion rupiah in 1998 and 178.6 trillion rupiah in 1999.

TABLE 8
Bank Indonesia Liquidity Support, 1997–99
(rupiah billion)

	1997 (Jul)	1997	1998 (Feb)	1998	1999
Extended Lending					
Subordinated	7,954	9,422	9,383	8,915	7,237
Emergency	351	475	475	449	421
Bridging[1]	—	1,706	5,335	—	—
Discount Facility					
Disfa I	—	678	—	—	—
Disfa II	—	747	747	—	—
New Disfa[2]	—	—	—	30,610	—
Debit Balance					
Overdraft	1,394	15,343	48,385	16,859	1,000
Facility covering Ov[3]	—	—	—	54,573	—
Rediscount Facility					
SBPU	1,167	5,079	5,856	1,018	—
Special SBPU[4]		29,479	29,479	23,903	7,242
Others					
Trade arrears[s]	—	—	—	11,781	—
Gov. bonds				20,000	162,712
Total	**10,866**	**62,929**	**96,029**	**173,443**	**178,612**

Notes: [1] Advances by Bank Indonesia to pay for small depositor holders, ultimately all depositors of liquidated banks

[2] New discount facility, introduced in March 1998.

[3] To cover negative balances of banks with Bank Indonesia in the forms of discount facilities I and II.

[4] Rediscount facility to replace liquidity supports previously received by banks, introduced in December 1997.

Source: Rearrangement of Table 30, IMF, *Indonesia: Statistical Appendix* (Washington: IMF, October 2000), p. 33.

Liquidity support and the Government

What then was the government's role in the policy to provide liquidity support to banks during the crisis? Bank Indonesia had been put into a position of having to help these banks with liquidity support because it did not have the authority to close them at the time.

In a way, the liquidity shortage that initially was caused by government actions to defend the rupiah had forced Bank Indonesia to resort to its lender of last resort function.

In the early part of the crisis, prior to the involvement of the IMF, the government issued an explicit directive on the provision of liquidity support to banks on 3 September 1997 to the Cabinet.

On liquidity support the directives stated as follows:

(1) Healthy national banks that suffered from liquidity problems should temporarily be helped with liquidity

(2) Banks that are really unhealthy should be put under a programme of merger and acquisition with healthy banks. If the efforts failed these banks would be liquidated with a view to protect the interest of deposit holders, especially small depositors.[6]

In the first LOI, which itemized the government adjustment programme for addressing the crisis, several references were made that showed the government's involvement in the liquidity support policy:

(1) The government did not guarantee repayment of the liabilities of liquidated banks, except for small depositors up to the maximum of 20 million rupiah (around US$5,000). The repayment would be done through Bank Indonesia advance, but the government would finance it. This would be done until a deposit insurance scheme is adopted (First LOI, point 21)

(2) The government would phase out in stages quasi-fiscal operations of Bank Indonesia, as in the case of Bank Indonesia liquidity credits for government programmes. The government would show all subsidies transparently in the budget (First LOI, point 35)

(3) Bank Indonesia would streamline its lender of last resort function (First LOI, point 36)

In the second LOI it was stated that:

Since the crisis began, Bank Indonesia's monetary strategy has been to support the rupiah exchange rate, and limit any increase in inflation, by maintaining a firm monetary stance. The execution of this policy, however, has been hampered by problems in the banking system. Following the closure of 16 banks in November last year, customers concerned about the safety of private banks have been shifting sizeable amounts of deposits

to state and foreign banks, while some have been withdrawing funds
from the banking system entirely (Second LOI, point 14).

Furthermore, this document that itemized the Fund-supported
programme through a stand-by arrangement also stated explicitly about
the central bank liquidity support to the banking sector as an effort
to defend the banking system from collapsing. The document stated
that

> The movements in deposit have greatly complicated the task of monetary
> policy, because they have led to bifurcation of the banking system. By
> mid-November, a large number of banks were facing growing liquidity
> shortages, and were unable to obtain sufficient funds in the inter-bank
> market to cover this gap, even after paying interest rates ranging up to
> 75 per cent. At the same time, another smaller groups of banks were
> becoming increasingly liquid, and were trading among themselves at a
> relatively low Jibor of about 15 per cent. As this segmentation continued
> to increase, while the stress on the banking system intensified, Bank
> Indonesia was compelled to act. It provided banks in distress with
> liquidity support, while withdrawing funds from banks with excess
> liquidity, thereby raising JIBOR to over 30 per cent in early December,
> where it has since remained (Second LOI, point 15).

These passages of the government documents showed that the liquidity
support that Bank Indonesia provided for banks during the crisis was a
step that the central bank was compelled to take in an effort to prevent
the banking sector and payment system from collapsing. The decision
was based on the Bank Indonesia Act of 1968 that provided Bank
Indonesia with authority as the lender of last resort to provide banks
with liquidity they desperately needed in the face of runs. The decision
was based on government policy not to close banks temporarily as well
as an explicit presidential instruction for the monetary authorities to
help banks with liquidity problems.

The policy to liquidate 16 banks in November 1997, which ultimately
caused bank runs, was surely a government policy as a part of a
comprehensive financial restructuring programme. The financial
restructuring itself was one of the pillars of the Fund-supported
adjustment programme agreed to by the government to address the
crisis. In the policy to liquidate banks, the government decided to pay
back the owners of bank deposits of up to 20 million rupiah. The
payment was made using Bank Indonesia advances. However, it was
explicitly stipulated in the programme that the financing of the payment

would be borne by the government. In late February 1998 the government decided to make payments also to the rest of the depositors in the liquidated banks in the same manner as the payment to small depositors.

In late January 1998 the government decided to adopt a blanket guarantee that covered both the assets and the liabilities of national banks which subscribed to the programme. The payment for the blanket guarantee was also borne by the government budget.

As a part of the corporate debt restructuring programme in June 1998, an agreement was reached between international banks as creditors to Indonesian corporations and the steering committee representing Indonesian corporations for setting up a scheme for corporate debt restructuring on a voluntary basis. The agreement was later known as the Frankfurt Agreement. The agreement stipulated government guarantees for Indonesian banks' exposure to international banks. The government had to make payments for past arrears of Indonesian banks as a requirement for the resumption of international banks' facility on trade finance and inter-bank debt exchange offers. Bank Indonesia made an advance to pay the arrears with the understanding that it would be borne by the government.

In August 1998 and thereafter, when the government started its programme of bank re-capitalization with a formula of 20 per cent of the value of capital to be paid by bank owners and the rest by the GOI, the institution in charge was IBRA. If Bank Indonesia was in charge, Bank Indonesia would have paid the 80 per cent of capital first, but the burden would later be borne by the government.

In conclusion, contrary to some claims made during the parliamentary hearings in February 2000, the decision by Bank Indonesia to provide liquidity support to the banking sector was neither a wrong interpretation of government policy nor was it in violation of the Central Bank Act. It was definitely not an abuse of power or authority bestowed to Bank Indonesia and by the Board of Directors, including the Governor as member and chairman of the Board.

Resolving problems of liquidity support

The issue lingers on with slim prospects for a quick solution. I will only discuss briefly the government's efforts to deal with the problems of liquidity support based on available documents and information, in particular from publications by Bank Indonesia, IMF staff and Sukowaluyo (Bank Indonesia 2002, Enoch et al. 2001 and Sukowaluyo 2001).

The policy for providing the liquidity support continued at least until early 1999, almost a full year after my departure from Bank Indonesia.

There are two ongoing types of resolutions, political and legal.[7]

In terms of a political solution, the Parliament had set up a Working Committee on Bank Indonesia Liquidity Supports, which conducted hearings with officials from the Ministry of Finance and Bank Indonesia, bankers and other parties to come up with resolution for addressing the problems. The committee produced a report in March 2000 with the following conclusions:

- On the issue of determining which institution should be responsible on the policy to provide liquidity supports, the committee concluded that based on the Central Bank Act 1968 Bank Indonesia is a central bank that also functions as the government treasurer. The Governor, aside from heading the board was also a member of the Cabinet as well as member of the Monetary Board. This put the governor as both a decision-maker as well as the executioner of financial policy. Bank Indonesia implements the government financial policies. Bank Indonesia liquidity support is a government policy and the government should be responsible for it.
- On the possibility of any irregularities on the channelling and using of the funds the committee instructed the Supreme Audit Agency to conduct investigative audits on Bank Indonesia and receiving banks. From the audit the roles of each officials could be identified. The Governor of Bank Indonesia and the Minister of Finance should also take responsibility for the mistakes that Bank Indonesia committed.
- Should the audit find suspicion of any criminal act that caused losses to the government the Attorney General Office should investigate promptly.

Based on the investigative audit the Agency found that the liquidity support to the banking sector from 1996 to January 1999 amounted to 144.5 trillion rupiah. It was claimed that due to deviations in the channelling of the funds by the central bank and the uses by receiving banks, the government could suffer losses of 138.4 trillion rupiah or 95.7 per cent of the total liquidity support.

Bank Indonesia criticized the nature, procedure and findings of the audit:

- The audit was not an investigative audit, but it was a compliance audit instead. What was done was basically a general check on whether what had been done by the central bank has been in compliance with the rules and regulations. However, the rules and regulations were set up for normal conditions, while the liquidity support were provided in a crisis. The prevailing economic and financial conditions as well as the contagion that in fact compelled Bank Indonesia to take the decision to providing the facility were completely ignored in the audit. The deviations of policy from existing rules should not be interpreted as violations to the rule as what the audit was not a compliance audit.

- The audit did not take into consideration the function and authority of the central bank in conducting monetary and banking policy. Consideration was not taken in terms of whether the policy to provide liquidity support was outside the jurisdiction of Bank Indonesia, or whether the decision was a misuse of central bank authority.

- Bank Indonesia also criticized the conduct of the audit, whereby the auditors did not attempt to interview the former and present board members or hold any discussions with Bank Indonesia officials on the findings. Bank Indonesia also criticized the Agency for publicly releasing the report in a press conference.

There were other points of disagreements that Bank Indonesia noted in the book. For example, it was argued by the Agency that Bank Indonesia's advance for payment of deposits with the liquidated banks was a deviation from the rule of bank liquidation. The Agency refers to the government regulation on bank closure, which states that payments for deposit holders should be financed through the selling of assets of the liquidated banks.[8] Thus, according to the Agency, Bank Indonesia does not have any right to ask the government to bear the burden of financing. Here, the Agency completely ignored the fact that the decision to liquidate banks was a government policy, and that there was a prior agreement for the government to bear the burden of the financing as mentioned in the first LOI and a letter by the Minister of Finance to the Governor.[9]

The political resolution on the problem of the liquidity support had been strengthened by a legal solution. The legal solution was conducted through MSAA (Master Settlement and Acquisition Agreement), MRNIA (Master Refinancing and Note Issuance Agreement) and agreements between IBRA and bank owners on the repayments of what they owed to the government from the liquidity support they had previously received.

The legal resolution of the liquidity support has been more complex than the political solution. There are two issues here, the transfer of the right for repayment from the provision of the liquidity, and the steps taken by IBRA on the liquidity settlement.

On the first issue, the right for repayments of liquidity support was originally with Bank Indonesia as the provider of the facility to banks. With the establishment of IBRA in late January 1998 and the transfer of authority for bank restructuring of 54 problem banks to IBRA shortly thereafter, a transfer of authority for repayments of all facilities that were received previously by these banks to IBRA was a logical consequence. After all, the major justification for putting banks into the IBRA to be restructured was the amount of liquidity support that these banks received from Bank Indonesia.

On 6 February 1999 the Minister of Finance and the Governor of Bank Indonesia signed an agreement to subrogate the right for repayment of liquidity support from the central bank to the government, i.e. IBRA as the implementing institution. With this agreement, IBRA acquired a cession on the rights to repayment of the liquidity support owed by receiving banks to Bank Indonesia. The first batch of cessions involved the value of liquidity support outstanding as of 29 January 1999 as reported in the Supreme Audit Agency audit report on Bank Indonesia.

The transfer of cessions from Bank Indonesia to IBRA was effective on 22 February 1999. It involved 10 frozen banks, 5 banks that were taken over and 18 banks under a nursing programme; included in this transfer were the 16 previously liquidated banks. The total number of banks was 49, but since one of the liquidated banks — Bank Andromeda — did not receive liquidity support, the total number of banks involved in the transfer of cession was 48.

With the transfer of cession the collateral against the liquidity support submitted by receiving banks was also transferred from Bank Indonesia to IBRA. The collateral comprised of banks' assets, bank owners' assets and assets associated with group lending from 33 banks that was valued at 132.3 trillion rupiah or 99.8 per cent of the total liquidity support to these banks (132.8 trillion rupiah).

Bank Indonesia contends that the cession also included liquidity support to the 16 liquidated banks to the amount of 11.9 trillion rupiah. However, due to the opinion of the Supreme Audit Agency that considered this support a deviation, IBRA had not been willing to accept the cession from Bank Indonesia. This is another dispute on the status and legality of some liquidity support that has not been resolved.

In spite of the unresolved issues on the status of some forms of liquidity support, IBRA took steps to deal with the assets legally under its control in accordance with the agreement between the Minister of Finance and the Governor of Bank Indonesia of February 1999, including and in particular, the selling of assets.

The government had already channelled liquidity or funds to banks under a restructuring programme that included liquidity support, advances by IBRA, and payments against claims under the blanket guarantee. The responsibility to make payments on claims that arose from these facilities lies with IBRA.

IBRA took four legal steps in its efforts to get repayments from banks that had been receiving liquidity supports: transfer of assets through MSAA, MRNIA, conversion of liquidity support into capital participation in banks, and settlement of liabilities of principal bank owners.

MSAA is an agreement to solve obligation to pay by surrendering assets. This technique is offered to principal bank owners who owned adequate assets for the settlement of their obligation arising from the liquidity support they acquired before. IBRA would perform acquisition to the assets being surrendered.

There are two types of MSAA. First, those offered to principal owners of frozen banks or in the process of liquidation. The arrangement includes settlement of liquidity support the banks owed to IBRA, and group lending that violates legal lending limits. Second, those offered to principal owners of banks taken over by IBRA. The arrangement includes only group lending that violates legal lending limits. The liquidity support that the banks owed to IBRA in these cases were settled via conversion of the liquidity into capital participation.

The settlement of liquidity support through MRNIA is applied to principal bank owners who have surrendered assets to IBRA for the settlement of what they owe but are not enough to cover their total obligation. In the agreement, the bank owners acknowledge the unfulfilled obligation. For that they surrender additional assets that would be treated as personal and offer corporate guarantees for settling the rest of the debts at a stipulated time.

In Bank Indonesia's assessment, the resolutions through legal and political steps taken by the government have been encouraging. However, it turns out that Bank Indonesia has been too optimistic. The problems of the liquidity support linger on, both politically as well as legally, and the process of questioning Bank Indonesia officials continues.

Three former Managing Directors of Bank Indonesia have been prosecuted in court. Out of the three former Bank Indonesia's managing directors the state court in April 2003 sentenced one to 2.5 years imprisonment, and the remaining two to 3 years. It was curious that they were prosecuted under the Anti-Corruption Act, yet they were sentenced for their guilt for Bank Indonesia's policy of providing liquidity support to weak banks. It was explicitly stated in the verdict that they were not proven to have enriched themselves in the process. However, the High Court, after hearing their appeals in December 2003, overturned the verdict and freed them. It was mentioned in the High Court verdict that even though the three were proven to perform what they were accused of, i.e. providing liquidity support to banks, they could not be accused of conducting criminal acts. On the basis of this argument, the three former managing directors were freed. However, the state prosecutors appealed to the Supreme Court to reopen the case.

On 31 May 2002 it was announced by the Attorney General's office that I became a suspect in the BI liquidity support case on the basis of misusing my authority to provide liquidity support to banks that caused trillions of rupiah of losses to the government.[10] I had been undergoing interrogation by a group of state attorneys for close to two weeks in June 2003. Many witnesses had also been summoned by the Attorney General's Office to testify in my case. A number of lawyers from academia and a former minister had already made testimonies either as expert witnesses or defence witnesses. In March 2004, the Attorney General's Office issued a letter to stop the investigation of my case on the grounds of absence of evidence of wrongdoing on my part.

In the meantime in terms of political aspects of the solution the Economic and Finance Commission of the Parliament issued a new resolution on 3 July 2003, which reiterated that the liquidity support policy is a government policy designed by the Government and Bank Indonesia in the crisis, and that Bank Indonesia implemented the policy in an effort to save the monetary and banking system as well as the national economy.[11]

Public debate: some notes

The controversy over the liquidity support to ailing banks has been fuelled by a general lack of clear information and also the complexity of the monetary policies during the early stages of the crisis.

- Bank Indonesia liquidity support to the banking sector in the face of shortages due to runs during the crisis raised public debate and controversy after the Supreme Audit Agency announced its findings from general and investigative audits on Bank Indonesia on November 1999 and August 2000 respectively.

- At issue was the magnitude of the possible loss to the budget, which ultimately would have to be borne by the taxpayers. Allegations of corruption relating to both the bankers and the receiving parties as well as officials of Bank Indonesia as the party that was said to have made the decision also added to the debate. With weak legal and judicial institutions and intense politicking, the whole issue has become messy without clear prospects for a quick resolution.

- On the possible losses to the government budget, several points should be noted. First, the total amount of the possible losses that the Supreme Audit Agency claimed in the audit report was based on the total amount granted by the central bank to the banking sector. One aspect that was totally ignored in the calculations had been the possibility of fund and other assets recovery. Even if the recovery rate was low, the magnitude of the losses has to include the estimate of assets recovery. The fact that there was no reference to the possible recovery is incredible. Second, the first check should be whether the receiving banks acknowledged the amount of funds that they received. The liquidity support that was acknowledged by banks would become *assets of the government*, to be managed by IBRA. Only after this process was complete could an estimate of the possible losses be made, that is the *total funds received minus the expected recovery of the assets*.

- It is curious that the public has not been comparing the liquidity support policy and bank re-capitalization policy. Liquidity support supplemented the banks' short-term assets so as to meet short-term payment obligations, while recapitalization injected new long-term assets to make good accumulated losses, and thus to enable banks to meet the minimum CAR. It is my contention that Bank Indonesia's liquidity support can be seen as a down payment on guarding the banking system from collapsing (Djiwandono 2004). In terms of the magnitude, the bank recapitalization programme cost the government close to *three times as much* as the liquidity support.

- Liquidity support, either to one or two banks in a normal period or indiscriminately during distress and crisis, is not based on any motivation to save bank owners or any individual bank from possible losses. Instead, it is provided on the basis of Bank Indonesia's function as lender of last resort to avoid the banking sector from collapsing. In effect, the decision was based on saving the national economy from collapsing, which was part of the function of Bank Indonesia prior to the granting of independent status, as a government institution with an obligation to implement government policy. The fact that altogether 164 out of 238 banks received liquidity support from the central bank should confirm that the facilities were not exclusively provided to selected banks.

- The lack of a consistent banking policy — not closing banks prior to the coming of the Fund, followed by bank closures in November 1997, and back to not closing banks, and back again to liquidating banks in August 1998 — definitely raised confusion in the market to say the least. This was, however, due to the dynamic of the crisis. And for better or worse this was a policy of the government that Bank Indonesia was part of. In the period prior to its independent status Bank Indonesia could not act other than implement government policy as stated in the Central Bank Act of 1968.

- Public perception has been biased against Bank Indonesia's decision to provide the support as well as the weakness of its supervision on banks that were accused of misusing the funds they received. With respect to weak banking supervision, even if sometime public perception has not always been completely correct, no one would argue against it. However, faulting Bank Indonesia's decision on the granting of liquidity support on this basis does not seem to be fair either.

- The arguments against Bank Indonesia have been based on the investigative audit findings conducted by the Supreme Audit Agency, which strongly argues this case. As Bank Indonesia has strongly argued, the problem with the audit is the implied refusal to recognize the presence of an emergency situation. The other problem was to criminalize a decision made by the Board of Bank Indonesia, which was based on solid legal grounds and a policy of a legitimate government.

In short, misunderstandings and misinformation on the complexity of banks and central bank operations easily led to presumptions that constrained a proper perspective on a problem as complex as liquidity support. Since the credibility of the government institutions and officials, including the central bank at this time, was very weak it seemed inconceivable to the public that facilities involving trillions of rupiah were provided without kickbacks to the officials involved in the process. Liquidity support issues are complicated and problems linger on without clear-cut resolutions. In the meantime, officials who are straight and clean have been punished in various ways for having to bear the scarlett letter.

Puzzle over the Currency Board

The proposal for the adoption of a pegged rate exchange system with a currency board arrangement in late January 1998 not long after the government renewed its commitment to implement a Fund-supported programme to address the crisis has been full of unanswered questions to the present. Since the technique of a currency board arrangement has generally been known as a currency board system or CBS, I will use this term hereafter.

What actually the system of exchange that was proposed or what was the difference between the proposed system and the standard concept of CBS? Who invited Prof. Steve H. Hanke, an economist known to be proponent of CBS, to come to Indonesia? How, in the midst of a crisis, could someone who was a total stranger to the economic team, let alone the general public in Indonesia, be appointed as an adviser to the newly established Council for Enhancing the Resiliency of Economics and Finance (henceforth the Economic Resilience Council, known in Indonesia as DPK-EKU)? Why did the President drop the proposal and why did it pop up again from time to time? These are questions on the sudden surge and equally sudden disappearance of a proposal to adopt CBS that have not been satisfactorily answered.

Despite its brevity it is important to understand the debate on the proposal to adopt a CBS at a very volatile period. It is very important for macroeconomic policy to appreciate the subtle struggle of the episode, in order to learn from it.

Possible motivation

What happened at the beginning of 1998 has to be put properly in the history of the management of the national economy. It is still unclear who actually invited Prof. Steve H. Hanke to the President's circle. After the President's decision not to adopt the scheme, public discussion of the issue ceased. One can only conjecture that the group most likely to be responsible for inviting the professor to Indonesia must be some people close to the President's children. Indeed some of them, like businessmen close to the President's family, Peter Gonta and Tanri Abeng (who was appointed to the newly formed Economic Resilience Council) argued on television or made public statements about how powerfully a CBS could solve the financial crisis and fight speculators. The formal invitation to Prof. Hanke to be an adviser to the new council was made by the Deputy Secretary General of the council, Dr. Fuad Bawazir.

Steve H. Hanke is a professor of Applied Economics at the Department of Geography and Environmental Engineering, Johns Hopkins University, Baltimore. He was known as a proponent of the adoption of CBS for countries suffering from hyperinflation. He was also known to be the vice chairman of the Friedberg Mercantile Group, a hedge fund involved in currency trading. It was rumoured that at end-1997 the company had profited a lot from trading in Southeast Asian currencies, including the rupiah.[12]

Hanke had produced books and papers on currency boards (for example, Hanke and Schuler 1994). The system had proven to work in many cases, the most prominent having been Hong Kong, and until its recent collapse, Argentina. Prior to the collapse of Argentina's economy and President Eduardo Duhalde's decision to abandon the system in April 2002, it was even acknowledged as one of the pillars within the new bipolar foreign exchange system (Fischer 2001).

Most studies or writings on the Asian crisis argue that one of the common problems that the crisis economies confronted was that they adopted a fixed exchange system, or in the new conventional wisdom on an exchange rate system, a soft fixed or soft pegged system (Fischer 2001). The soft pegged or soft fixed system is an exchange system that fixed the exchange rate of a currency or pegged it to a strong currency. However, the fix or peg was not supported with its necessary institutions or arrangement, like a sound banking system, legal system and commensurate international reserves. This is to be distinguished from a hard fixed or hard pegged system as in the case of a currency board, or a fixed system with foreign exchange control, as the experience of Malaysia.

The question here is whether the proponents of a fixed rate for the rupiah and the CBS used this reasoning when they made the proposal in January 1998 to President Soeharto? Again, one can only conjecture or even speculate about it. I am convinced that this was not the proponents' major consideration. I am afraid their reasons were more pragmatic than that.

It was alleged that the actual aim for fixing the rupiah to be 50 per cent stronger than the current rate was to bail out those corporations suffering from maturing external debts due to the rupiah's nose-dive. It was reported in the media that Hanke's proposal was to fix the rupiah to the dollar at the rate of 5,000 rupiah to one dollar, when the rate was 10,000 rupiah to one dollar. This seems to be a very crude and simple argument. However, it does not seem to be too far-fetched, as the corporate sector was indeed facing problems since the floating of the rupiah, and the President's conies were prominent members of this group.

Why was President Soeharto interested in the proposal and was he serious about it? Was he merely trying to show his displeasure with the Fund? The last question is relevant because that there was public disappointment with the Fund.

Some have argued saying that it was indeed a ploy for President Soeharto to bide for time and to create displeasure against the Fund.

I do not agree with the above argument. It is my contention that the President was serious about adopting Hanke's fixed exchange system. There are several factors that support my view:

- First, from the time the crisis struck until my dismissal I observed that President Soeharto saw the crisis as a purely monetary or financial problem. More specifically, that the problem was the drastic depreciation of rupiah due to speculative activities by hedge funds. On several occasions, upon listening to or reading reports on the currency depreciation by the economic team, he made written or oral comments which expressed his disgust: "This (the weakening of the rupiah) must be due to the works of currency speculation", "There must be people playing around with it" or "There is an intention to discredit the government".

- Second, the President saw the crisis as a short-term problem of rupiah depreciation that would last for several weeks only. This was shown in his note on the economic team's first daily reports on the development of the rupiah by just after the rupiah's float: "Follow the rupiah development closely everyday for two to three weeks".

- Third, I believe that his contention was that, since the crisis was a short-run monetary and financial problem, he expected that the Monetary Council, in particular the Minister of Finance and the Governor of Bank Indonesia should be able to find a solution rapidly. The fact that the crisis became long-drawn and that he had to be "humiliated" by begging for the Fund's help, something that he actually despised, had made him anxious. All of these made him easily lured to alternative solutions beyond the steps that had been taken so far.

- Fourth, since the inception of the Fund-supported programme, in particular after the bank closures, his trust and patience with the monetary authorities was deteriorating. His trips abroad and his worsening health had also physically constrained communication between him and the monetary authorities during this period. It is my contention that his decision to form a new economic resilience board, and the appointment of a special liaison officer to the Fund, were his ways of showing his distrust of the Minister of Finance and the Governor as the principal officials dealing with the crisis.

- Fifth, the President was very concerned by further worsening rupiah depreciation by end-January 1998. This had pushed him towards finding a drastic resolution to address the financial crisis. He wanted to get the monetary problem behind him so that he could concentrate on his political agenda for his re-election in the General Assembly of the People Consultative Assembly, which was due to start 1 March 1998.

- Sixth, in January 1998, President Soeharto instructed several high officials from Bank Indonesia and the Ministry of Finance, including managing directors and the director general to draft a bill on the adoption of CBS and the supporting documents without my knowledge. The President also summoned the leadership of the Parliament to assist him in getting the bill enacted without delay.[13] This team was in constant contact with Hanke in doing the assignment.

Professor Hanke seemed to successfully convince the President that if he took his advice Indonesia could get rid of the rupiah problem and at the same time silence the speculators. This was an attractive proposition that must have been hard for the President to reject. Out of expediency and his lack of faith in his central bank Governor and Minister of Finance, the President was determined to adopt a fixed exchange system and CBS.

Aborting CBS

It is curious that in spite of the President's actions, including instructing a group of officials to prepare a study and asking for the support of the Parliament, he aborted the plan and abandoned Hanke's proposal?

I can only conjecture about the President's change of mind. There were both external as well as internal factors that seemed to contribute to his decision not to adopt the CBS.

The IMF wanted a floating exchange system. During a short period in mid-February 1998 the G-7 mounted pressure on President Soeharto to reject the idea of adopting a fixed exchange system with CBS. Through different ways, from telephone calls to high-level visits, the G-7 governments sent a strong message to the President to stick with the Fund-supported programme and forget about a CBS. Several leading officials, including former U.S. vice president Walter Mondale, Japanese Prime Minister Hashimoto, and German Minister of Finance Theo Waigel met with President Soeharto in Jakarta. In the meantime MD Michel Camdessus, Deputy Stanley Fischer, Secretary Rubin and Chairman Greenspan all made statements that in effect asked the government of Indonesia to abandon the plan for adopting CBS. The G-7 in their ministerial meeting also issued a similar statement.[14]

Meanwhile, the Monetary Board also submitted a memorandum to the President stating that various requirements had to be met first before a fixed exchange system with a CBS could be adopted. It should be noted that the memorandum was not phrased in a straightforward way. It was a professional memo in an environment during the New Order administration that always avoided directness. However, the reader of the memo would know that it was aimed at saying "don't do this". The memo was prepared by my deputies and sent to the President through the secretary general of the Economic Resiliency Council.

The memo basically explained what could and could not be done in a system with a CBS. It explained that all the present practices of subsidized credit facilities by the central bank could no longer be continued under the proposed new system. An important factor was the size of international reserves held by Bank Indonesia. If only a very narrow money supply was used, the international reserves needed would have been adequate. On this issue Bank Indonesia held a conservative position by using a broader money supply definition, which implied insufficient international reserves for supporting the proposed plan of adopting a CBS.

In the end the combination of external and domestic pressures worked to persuade President Soeharto to abandon the plan to adopt a fixed exchange system with CBS.

Side-effect of CBS

In early news coverage about my dismissal from my post as the governor of the central bank, the most popular explanation was that I was dismissed summarily by President Soeharto due to my disagreement with him on the CBS issue.

As with the other issues, we will never know the real reason for my dismissal. I can only say that this was possibly *one* of the reasons. But in my opinion there must had been more than just one reason for President Soeharto to decide on something that was unprecedented.

What follows is my assessment of the issues around the CBS.

I met with Professor Hanke only once during the period. At a meeting with him in the Minister of Finance's office in early February 1998, I presented my assessment of the problems that Indonesia faced and his proposal to adopt a CBS. I told him that what Indonesia was confronting then was severe loss of market and public confidence in three areas: the rupiah, the banking sector and the ability of Indonesian corporations to repay their debts. I told him that the adoption of a CBS, if implemented correctly, would at the most help to restore confidence in the currency. I told him that I could not see how his proposal would help our efforts to regain confidence in the banking sector nor the ability of the private corporations to repay their debts in foreign exchange. I even cautioned that the adoption of the system would push us into another problem of a heavy drain on reserves due to a surge of dollar buying.

I was also concerned about the lack of commitment on the part of the government (President) to let the system work, without intervention. I was concerned that immediately after its adoption, with a cheaper dollar, there would be strong pressure from the President's cronies for Bank Indonesia to release its reserves. My concern was that the Indonesian proponents for the adoption of CBS did not realize that one of the requirements for the technique was the *absence* of government intervention. An increase or decrease of reserves would only come from trade and capital account transactions, and that a change in reserves would change the money supply, and therefore interest rates. This should happen automatically without intervention by the government. I observed that the propensity for the government then, and even later, to intervene was very strong, which implied that letting the economy run on auto pilot would be an anomaly.

These were two things that could be taken for granted in the conduct of the government then. The central bank was part of the government. It did not have any autonomy. Thus, it would have been very difficult for Bank Indonesia to refuse the President's instructions to intervene. At the same time it had been clear on many occasions that the President had intervened on the pretext that he had a mandate from the People's Consultative Assembly. In short, with weak public and corporate governance, resorting to a system that required discipline by all parties not to intervene and to uphold the rule of law was tantamount to an invitation to failure.

With a private sector under pressure from unsustainable foreign exchange exposure, and their strong lobby through the President's family members, Bank Indonesia would have been in terrible position to have to fight against the intervention to compromise the management of foreign reserves. This argument may seem to be far-fetched, but, I am afraid, this was closer to the reason behind the proposal for adopting a CBS. In other words, the argument that the technique worked well in other countries was in fact irrelevant to Indonesia in early 1998.

Publicly, I indicated neither a preference for nor a rejection of a CBS. Every time I was queried, my answer was always the same: that we have to carefully study the costs and benefits of adopting a CBS before we could determine whether to go ahead. I made the same statement even after the Minister of Finance was compelled to say in front of a Parliamentary hearing that Indonesia was going to adopt a CBS. I am sure it was clear enough to the President that I was not in favour of the government adopting the system.

The public debate in Indonesia on the possibility for adopting a fixed exchange system with a CBS had been around for sometime. In February 2000, two years after he first proposed it, Hanke wrote a piece in the *Asian Wall Street Journal* arguing that my dismissal before the term ended was not due to my disagreement with President Soeharto, but it was due to the policy of providing liquidity support to the banking sector during the crisis.[15]

However, I am afraid he did this just to climb on the bandwagon during a public debate on the role of the central bank in providing liquidity support to banks during the crisis. It is doubtful that the President discussed my dismissal with Professor Hanke. Even if he did, the President knew that the liquidity support was part of his policy for helping banks. Just because the Supreme Audit Board held a view that most of the support provided to the banks could not be accounted to the government budget, in spite of the government's approval, Professor Hanke seemed eager to join the crowd placing the blame on Bank Indonesia under my leadership. In any case, there was no discussion on the loss to the central bank then.

I found his proposal for CBS and his claims to know so much about the Indonesian economy and finance typical of "experts" who visit Indonesia briefly. Here, the problem is not only that he claimed expertise on the Indonesian economy, but also in interpreting President Soeharto's thought. During the New Order era there was a good description about this kind of attitude: "Foreign professionals who stay in Indonesia for several weeks are 'experts'. After staying longer, they realize how much they don't know about Indonesia. And after staying much longer they become Indonesian, some are real experts, but most of them are not".

The public debate on a CBS came up again in May 2000 following the resumption of market pressure on the currency due to an open conflict between President Abdulrrachman Wahid and Governor Syahril Sabirin in a new era of the central bank's independent status. This time the *Asian Wall Street Journal* suggested in an editorial that the Indonesian government peg the rupiah to the dollar with a CBS.[16] I wrote a letter to the *ASWJ* editor showing my concern at the suggestion. I reiterated my argument that without strong discipline on the part of the government and other parties to let the system run on auto-pilot, and strong commitment for upholding the rule of law, the CBS would not work. I argued against its adoption.[17] With the collapse of the CBS in Argentina recently it is less likely that a new proposal for its adoption in Indonesia will emerge for sometime.

However, public discussion on what should be the proper exchange system for Indonesia seems to always be attractive, in particular whenever the rupiah is under pressure. In September 2000, when the currency was under pressure again, the 1999 Economics Nobel Laureate Professor Robert Mundell, was asked to join the debate when asked by a journalist about the issue. He made a statement supporting the idea for Indonesia to adopt a fixed exchange system. It became more interesting when Dow Jones Singapore reported that Mundell supported Hanke's proposal.[18]

I am afraid these kinds of statements and reports, with all due respect for his expertise, do not help Indonesia find solutions. As reported in the media, the statement was not careful enough with the claim that if

Malaysia was successful in fixing the ringgit, there was no excuse for Indonesia not to follow suit. This generalization is difficult to accept for those who understand the issues better. However, if one reads his statement carefully, Professor Mundell did qualify his opinion by saying "under the right circumstances". So the problem may actually lie in inaccurate reporting.

The major problem for Indonesia is to be consistent in implementing whatever system, technique or programme the government wants to adopt. Changing the system without putting in place the supporting institutions would not promise any sustainable solution. Professor Wing Thye Woo of the University of California at Davis stated correctly that "The main issue of the Washington Consensus was how to get the prices right, while after the Asian crisis it is how to get the institutions right."[19]

The Bumpy Road to an Independent Central Bank

As mentioned before one of the crucial contributing factors of the Indonesian crisis was a weak banking or financial system. Closely related was the absence of a robust financial infrastructure, including an independent central bank.

Of course one cannot argue that the absence of an independent central bank was the sole problem that led to the financial and banking crisis in Indonesia. The transformation of Bank Indonesia into an independent central bank would certainly not be a panacea. Indeed, despite its independence since May 1999 the economy has not completely recovered. However, an independent central bank is an important issue in its own right, and not only in the context of the crisis.

A call for an Independent Central Bank

Indonesia started to adopt a system of independent central banking at the end of May 1998 when President Habibie decided to remove the Governor of Bank Indonesia from the Cabinet, thereby restoring the status of Bank Indonesia to its pre-1983 position. The Governor of Bank Indonesia no longer has ministerial rank and no longer carries a duty as an assistant to the President in his capacity as the head of the government. The legal basis for an independent Bank Indonesia was made official with the enactment of the new bill on Bank Indonesia a year after. It is explicitly mentioned in the new law (Law No. 23, of 1999) that Bank Indonesia is an independent state institution, free from government or other parties' intervention, except on matters specifically mentioned in the law.[20]

Discussions on the need to have an independent central bank in the country had actually been going on for some time before the decision by the Habibie government. But they were limited to seminars or parliamentary hearings with the Governor and the Board of Directors of Bank Indonesia. However, the issue became more pressing during economic crisis. In fact, it was raised during the negotiation for an IMF stand-by loan in October 1997. Ultimately, it became part of the conditionality of the Fund-supported programme and was specifically mentioned in the second LOI to the Fund.[21]

Why does an economy need an independent central bank in the first place? Independent central banking has been an accepted practice in most countries since the end of the 1980s, when more countries adopting a market economy after discarding economic planning. It was also mentioned as one of the requirements for joining the European Union in the Maastricht Treaty, for example.

However, as Blinder wrote "the term (independence) itself is somewhat vague and has occasionally been misused".[22] I agree with his assertion that the term independence should be interpreted to mean that the central bank has freedom to decide on how to pursue its goals, and that its decisions are hard for any other branch of the government to reverse. Basically what it meant here is that once the goals for the central bank to pursue have been decided, the government cannot intervene on how the institution is run. Stanley Fischer described this as the condition that the central bank should have instrument independence, but not goal independence.[23] This is to say that the goal itself does not have to be decided by the central bank. Indeed, I think the goal should not be determined, by the central bank, or the central bank alone. But, once it is determined no other institutions are allowed to intervene in the central bank's policy to achieve it.[24]

At the outset it should be noted that even though there are variety of modes of macroeconomic management in national economies, in general central banks' responsibilities include monetary management, a payment system and occasionally banking supervision. The actual system adopted by each economy varies with respect to what are the overall responsibilities, and the classification of major and secondary responsibilities.[25]

In general, the central bank has the authority over supplying base money and the responsibility over managing money supply and credits and thus, interest rate determination. There are cases whereby the government determines the rate of interest, but it is the responsibility of the central bank to maintain its stability.

The central bank may be solely or together with other institutions, responsible for managing exchange rates for certain objectives. In addition it may have the responsibility of managing international reserves. With respect to exchange rate determination the central bank may have the responsibility to determine the system of foreign exchange to adopt or to execute a foreign exchange system, which is predetermined by the government.

The central bank determines, and sometime holds the reserves of, commercial banks. With the banking system in place the central bank is also usually oversees the national payment system.

The central bank is usually responsible for maintaining the stability of a financial system through conducting banking supervision and acting as lender of last resort. However, recent developments in different economies has been for entrusting banking supervision together with other financial institutions to a separate agency outside the central bank. The Bank of Japan and Bank of England after gaining their independent status, were released from conducting banking supervision. In fact, presently the U.S. Federal Reserve Bank is one of the few major central banks still responsible for bank supervision.[26]

The central bank may also function as the government's banker. In fact, the central bank's original task was not to conduct monetary policy or support the banking system, but to finance government spending. This was what happened with the Bank of Sweden, the world's oldest central bank, in its early days. In economies that rely on exchange control, the central bank is usually responsible for its execution. Central banks may also manage government debt, while in different countries central banks also provide economic and financial advice to their respective governments.

In the early development of most emerging market economies, the central bank functioned more as the government's banker than a central bank. The central bank was often used as the major source of financing government budget deficits. However, together with financial sector development there has been distinct transformation of central banking towards a more clearly defined function to include the three core responsibilities — monetary management, the national payment system and banking supervision.

This development was influenced by a new approach to the financial sector's role in development originating in seminal works by Edward Shaw and Ronald McKinnon in the early seventies (Shaw 1973, McKinnon 1973). Their work showed that most developing countries suffered from a condition of *repressed finance* whereby the financial sector, including the central bank, was placed under control of the government in the name of economic development. As a result, the banking sector was underdeveloped to serve the economy as a financial intermediary. The economy was usually dominated by the government, which kept running budget deficits that had to be financed by the central bank.

The two seminal works had inspired the view that economic development would be served better by a liberalized financial sector or *financial deepening*. By arguing that financial deepening would support development better, these works gave theoretical basis for financial liberalization in the later periods.[27] Some economies started a process of financial liberalization or financial deepening, as it was known then, in the early seventies and eighties while others did so in the nineties.

Indonesia started financial deepening as early as in the late sixties with deposit rate liberalization and in the early seventies through freeing foreign exchange controls. But financial liberalization took its steady course only in the eighties.[28]

In this context macroeconomic management of a national economy is basically conducted through fiscal and monetary policy. In the early part of the emerging market economies when the state sector was still dominant, macroeconomic management usually focused on achieving growth and stability. With a tendency for the fiscal side to be more expansionary, monetary policy was aimed at supporting economic growth while checking inflationary pressures such that growth and stability could be achieved. Thus, with the expansionary tendency of development activities dominated by government, inflationary tendencies coould be checked by prudent monetary policy.

Monetary policy in a market economy is the major responsibility of the central bank. Conceptually, the more independent the central bank, the more effectively it can achieve monetary stability. Studies show that countries with independent central banks indeed tend to have lower inflation rates. And low inflation did not appear to come at the cost of slower growth. But, correlation, of course, does not prove causation — Germany's Reichsbank was statutorily independent when the country suffered hyperinflation in 1923.[29] Despite this, it is generally agreed that the more independent the central bank, the more effective its monetary policy. Thus more central bank independence or less government intervention is warranted for effective macroeconomic management.

However, recent developments showed that monetary stability is not just about price stability. In particular, monetary stability is not just having a low rate of inflation measured by an index of prices of consumer goods and services. With record low rates of inflation in the industrial economies lately, the world is still experiencing a financial crisis. Even with central bank independence in advanced countries the financial system may still be facing new challenges, namely assets inflation or economic bubbles on the one hand, and economic deflation on the other. Both seem to be developing at present, in the United States and Japan respectively, at a time when inflation is very much under control. This raises some challenges to the conventional wisdom that the monetary objective of a central bank is stable inflation measured by the consumer price index.

Macroeconomic management has become much more complicated. As the *Economist*'s World Economy Survey mentioned above,

> the role of central banks has traditionally been defined in terms of banks, money and inflation. Thus at the pinnacle of their power it is disconcerting that they still have to ask three questions. What is a bank? What is money? And what is inflation?

With new innovations in financial instruments and new techniques of financial intermediation in global finance, the concept of independent central banking may need to be redefined as well. As if in answer to this issue, at least partly, the IMF in a recent Interim Committee meeting produced a document that specifically listed definitions of a central bank, financial agencies, financial policies and government.[30]

Independent central banking in practice

The central bank in a market economy is responsible for the development of a national payment system to facilitate the national economy such that consumption, production, investment and trade activities can run effectively and efficiently. In money supply creation through a fractional banking system, the central bank is commonly in charge of determining reserve requirement policy, the development of payment system techniques, and the regulation and infrastructure development of a clearing system.

With respect to banking supervision, despite recent moves to put this responsibility outside central banking, it had been common in the past to put this under central bank responsibilities. Some studies show that banking supervision in most countries was executed by central banks. However, as Stanley Fischer argued, this has nothing to do with a basic principle of central banking.[31] As it was cited before, the new tendency has been to put banking supervision together with supervision of other financial institution under a separate autonomous body.

The Indonesian experience taught us that the crucial issue is to put supervision of banks and other financial intermediaries, like finance companies and multi-finance institutions together in the same institution. In addition, the supervisory authority should be an autonomous or independent body. In the modern world of new innovations and global finance, and in Indonesia, the tendency to have cross-ownership in different financial institutions, supervision of various but closely connected financial institutions is becoming ineffective and inefficient. Separate bodies of supervision would create more chances for overlapping of supervision over these institutions or the reverse. Both are unwarranted. This is irrespective of whether the supervisory authority is a part of an independent central bank or outside. But it is crucial that the supervisory authority should cover these closely related financial institutions and that it has an independent status.

The crisis in Indonesia also taught us that with the central bank holding the responsibilities for banking supervision and being lender of last resort, monetary management was sometime compromised. Monetary tightening, which was required for stabilizing the currency, could be compromised because of the complicating effects the step may impose on the rescued banks.

In less independent central banking such as in Indonesia before May 1999, its effectiveness in either function was reduced even further.[32] This bolstered the argument for a separate independent authority to supervise banks and other financial institutions.

Conceptually, the argument for independent central banking must be in reference to monetary management. And the independent status refers to the choice of instruments and policy execution. Of course, conceptually there are constraints that would limit the authorities in making the choice in policy objectives as well as instruments as Mundell's "holy trinity" or Krugman's "eternal triangle" reminds us.[33]

In reality, the power to manage money supply and bank credit gives the central bank huge leverage, particularly in developing economies where banking dominates the financial sector. In this context, for economies in which the central bank has the authority to control the rate of interest, the policy objective of the interest rate policy is usually predetermined. The following are policy goals in different systems mentioned by Fischer:

- Germany's Bundesbank is responsible for maintaining the value of the currency. It is also required to support the general economic policy of the government in so far as this is consistent with the objective of maintaining the value of the currency.
- Banque de France is responsible for maintaining price stability within the framework of the general economic policy of the government.
- The Central Bank of New Zealand is responsible for price stability.
- The Federal Reserve Bank of the United States has a more general objective, i.e. to safeguard long-term growth of money supply and credits which are in line with long-term growth of production, maximum employment, price stability and normal interest rates in the long run.

From all of these examples, generally the independence of a central bank is related to its function of conducting monetary policy for price stability and (or) the stability of the national currency. The status has to be legally determined. The Federal Reserve is probably the only exception, because it has responsibilities that are formulated in wide-ranging areas and yet it is considered one of the most independent central banks.[34]

If independence is not considered to be important, it is also unimportant to formulate the central bank's functions very specifically. In other words, very detailed formulation would not make any difference. This was the case with the Bank of England before the adoption of the new *Bank of England Act 1998*, which became the legal basis of its current operations.

By observing practices of central banks in 72 developing countries, Cukierman et al. (1992) in their study showed the following:

- There are 2 countries whose central banks are responsible only for maintaining price stability with rights to deviate from the policy of their respective governments;
- 17 countries whose central banks are responsible for maintaining price stability and other responsibilities in line with it;
- 22 countries whose central banks are responsible for price stability and other responsibilities not necessarily in line with price stability;
- 10 countries whose central banks are not given specified responsibilities, and
- 15 countries whose central banks are responsible for specific areas outside price stability.

Whether there are other areas of responsibilities or not, monetary management for price stability is well accepted as the main responsibility of the central bank in a national economy. And if more independence or less intervention is accepted as a condition for a market economy to function more efficiently, it should follow that for the central bank to function more effectively in achieving monetary stability it has to be given a more independent status.

The central bank of a national economy should be an instrument independent in executing monetary management for monetary stability. But, in order to exercise independence the central bank's function has to be legally specified, such that it has an autonomous authority in determining monetary instruments in pursuing its objective. In turn, the central bank has to exercise its independence in a transparent and accountable manner.

The lack of central bank independence and the crisis

Independent central banking as discussed above follows a normative concept of a central bank's role in a market economy. Now let me briefly discuss what has been practised in Indonesia in the recent past prior to the enactment of the new law on Bank Indonesia.

I would like to reiterate that, out of the three major functions of Bank Indonesia as Indonesia's central bank, the most important issue of independence centred on monetary management. But, with the benefit of hindsight I would argue that the intervention in Bank Indonesia's banking supervision authority was the trigger point of the drastic loss of confidence in the Indonesian banking sector in the wake of the crisis.

In Indonesia the monetary policy objective as specified in the law on Bank Indonesia of 1968 was to safeguard the value of the rupiah. This implied that the central bank is responsible for safeguarding the rupiah value in terms of prices of goods and services (price stability) and foreign currencies (exchange rate stability).

With respect to the central bank's role as the government bank, Indonesia developed a balanced budget policy concept, which was controversial, but was to a certain extent effective to contain fiscal impact on inflation.[35]

But even in the monetary management Bank Indonesia prior to the new law was legally not independent. Two points should be mentioned here to explain this position. First, the responsibility for monetary policy was placed in a monetary board chaired by the Minister of Finance. The Governor of Bank Indonesia was only a member together with other economic ministers, even though he/she had the right to deviate from the board's views. Second, since 1983 the governor of the central bank was given a status of a cabinet minister or member of cabinet. So, the central bank became part of the government and as a consequence the governor was legally as well as structurally not independent from the government.

Bank licencing was the responsibility of the Minister of Finance. But the Ministry of Finance could only issue a bank licence upon receiving a recommendation from the central bank. In other words, the central bank had responsibility for reviewing new proposals for bank licences whether or not requirements had been fulfilled, but not to issue bank licences. Banking supervision was the responsibility of the central bank, while supervision for other financial institutions was the Ministry of Finance.

With respect to the payment system, Indonesia had no substantive problems to face, except for the implications of the tremendous growth of fund flows due to rapid growth of economic activities that created an additional burden on the payment system. Together with new developments in global finance, monetary authorities faced new challenges. The volume of daily transactions of the dollar in the money market increased from a little over US$2 billion at the beginning of the nineties to more than US$8 billion just before the crisis. At the same time the daily volume of transactions in the capital market also increased tremendously. All of these resulted in tremendous increases in the volume of daily payments for financing transactions. The volume of payments that the central bank clearing system had to clear increased from 5 trillion rupiah per day at the beginning of the nineties to more than 20 trillion rupiah in 1996. These required the necessary institutional development of a payment system that could finance such a volume of transactions efficiently and safely.

The lack of Bank Indonesia's independence both in its goals as well as in its choice of instruments in monetary management had definitely constrained its effectiveness in the conduct of monetary management during the crisis. The following are instructive:

- Prior to the crisis Bank Indonesia had great difficulty in convincing the monetary board to raise compulsory reserve requirement for banks. Bank Indonesia only managed to raise the reserve requirement for commercial banks after several discussions with the board in 1995. The reserve requirement was raised in February 1996 from 2 to 3 per cent of the total third party's funds in the banks, and another one in April 1997 from 3 to 5 per cent.

- Bank Indonesia did not enjoy the freedom of determining exchange rate depreciation or appreciation since there was always some controversy between increasing the rate of depreciation for export purpose and the reverse for inflation control. In the context of a crawling peg and managed floating before the crisis the rupiah was undergoing a creeping depreciation. Bank Indonesia did not have the freedom to determine the size of the depreciation. The monetary board determined the size of the annual depreciation, and Bank Indonesia implemented the decision.[36]

- During the crisis, Bank Indonesia under the instruction of the monetary board was reluctantly resorting to an administrative intervention by instructing some state enterprises and semi-government foundations to transform their deposits with commercial banks into central bank certificates. This was done in August 1997 as a part of liquidity tightening.

- The reverse problem arose when the President in October and November 1997 gave instructions to reduce the tightness of liquidity by allocating bank credits to small and medium-scale enterprises. These actions for both tightening and loosening liquidity through administrative instructions were contrary to my belief that monetary policy should not be conducted by way of financial shocks, which could generate additional uncertainty (Djiwandono 1994, p. 44). With the benefit of hindsight it had been clear that in both cases the policy overshot its targets, and adding to the instability instead.

- Bank Indonesia's lack of autonomy constrained its policy to defend the stability of the rupiah. This was very much felt by Bank Indonesia when its proposal to raise SBI rates did not receive the green light from the President. To overcome the tricky situation Bank Indonesia started to intervene in the rupiah inter-bank market to push the JIBOR rates up even though the SBI rates remained constant.

- The President's intervention was apparent when he instructed commercial banks to provide loans to SMEs using funds from bank deposits belonging to state-owned enterprises, without the involvement of both the Minister of Finance and the Governor of Bank Indonesia.

- Bank Indonesia's position as bank supervision authority, which was not strong to start with, was further undermined with the closures of the 16 banks. The owner of a closed bank (Andromeda) purchased another (Alfa), destroying the weak credibility of the bank supervision authority. The legal suit by owners of two liquidated banks against the Minister of Finance and the Governor of Bank Indonesia in court added drama to the discrediting of the monetary authorities.

- The dismissal of four Bank Indonesia managing directors before their terms ended in December 1997 was a direct intervention by the President on the management of the central bank that pushed further the deterioration of the central bank's public credibility.

- The plan by the President to change the exchange rate system into a fixed exchange with CBS was another blatant example of interfering with the central bank's operations. The whole preparation for the aborted plan was orchestrated through direct instructions from the President to high officials from the Ministry of Finance and the central bank without my knowledge. All of these finally culminated in the President's decision to summarily dismiss me as the Governor of Bank Indonesia.

The bank closures were widely criticized as causing bank runs, which led to a banking crisis afterwards. It was indeed ironic that the closing of these insolvent banks, which was aimed at boosting market confidence, in effect eroding it completely.

Can one argue with confidence that the bank closures were indeed the cause of the banking crisis in Indonesia? I have written elsewhere on this issue.[37] Suffice to say that I do believe in closing insolvent banks as part of banking restructuring. But the crucial issue is that of the execution of the closures. In other words, the problem is related to the methods and timing of the closures.

The Indonesian experience of bank closure has some bearing on the issue of central bank independence due to the fact that Bank Indonesia also has the responsibility for banking supervision. Bank Indonesia's lack of independence in its conduct as bank supervision authority was clearly demonstrated in the problems related to the closing of the 16 banks. Judging from what happened with the rupiah, it was positive for a very short period, but soon the pressure became even stronger. And even the short-lived strengthening of the currency was of course helped by a joint intervention in the foreign exchange market by Bank Indonesia, the Monetary Authority of Singapore and the Bank of Japan.

Bank Indonesia's lack of independence turned out to be too costly. Government intervention in the process of bank closures and bank acquisition ultimately negated the positive impact of a policy that basically was sound. The erosion of public confidence in the banking system was further fuelled by the reactions of some of the President's family members who sued both the Minister of Finance and the Governor of Bank Indonesia in court to show their contempt for the Bank's decision.

In addition, as discussed earlier there seemed to be a natural conflict of interest for the central bank as both manager of monetary policy and lender of last resort. In a non-transparent environment with weak governance the problems were more complex. Lack of independence of bank supervisory authority allowed a variety of government interventions that ultimately constrained the central bank. During the crisis, both banking supervision and monetary management were rendered ineffective.

On the other hand the Asian crisis serves as a wake-up call for monetary authorities about the close relations between effective monetary policy and a sound banking system. The latter should include stringent and effective banking supervision. The need for policy coordination between monetary policy and banking soundness received more serious attention from monetary authorities as well pundits and international institutions only since the mid-nineties.[38]

With the benefit of hindsight, it has certainly become commonplace to say that effective monetary policy requires a robust banking system or that a sound banking system is a sine qua non for effective monetary policy. Also that financial liberalization should be accompanied or even preceded by strengthening banking supervision. All these are part of a newly found religion, which was not apparent prior to the Asian crisis.

The Indonesian experience taught us that indeed monetary policy is basically a macroeconomic issue that deals with short-term variables. Tight or loose monetary policy and low or high rates of interest policy are in general short-term issues. On the other hand policies to produce a sound banking system deals with microeconomic issues such as banking efficiency, bank soundness as minimally measured with respect to its capital, quality of assets, management performance, earnings and liquidity. The same things hold for prudential regulation and banking supervision and other financial infrastructure. These are all micro economic issues. In addition they are in general medium-term or even long-term issues.

While it seems correct to say that a sound banking system is required for effective monetary policy or macroeconomic management, it is less clear whether we can argue that an economy could both strengthen the financial sector and make effective monetary policy at the same time. This implies that a government run a programme that could produce a solution for both micro and long-term problems in combination with macro and short-term problems. This is the daunting task facing monetary authorities of crisis-ridden economies like Indonesia. This I think is a new challenge for both theory as well as policy formulation.[39]

The Indonesian experience definitely strengthens the argument for an independent central bank for effective monetary management. But the experience also showed that there are new challenges facing the monetary as well as the supervisory authorities. This is due to the well-established argument for the close functional relation between monetary management as the sole responsibility of an independent central bank, and the soundness of the banking system, which requires an independent and robust supervision.

For Bank Indonesia to exercise its authority as an independent institution it is imperative that its function as the central bank is clearly specified and its independent status stipulated in the Central Bank Act. In turn, Bank Indonesia should exercise its independence in a transparent and accountable manner. And to have credibility, Bank Indonesia should be run fully by professionals of high integrity, from the governor down to the lowest level of officials. Adherence to good governance and transparency is the key word for Bank Indonesia to be an effective independent central bank.

An independent Bank Indonesia — the Central Bank Act

Actually the government had started a process of granting independence to Bank Indonesia when the intention was put as one of the stipulations in the second LOI of 15 January 1998. Point 22 of the document states that Bank Indonesia would be granted autonomy in the formulation and implementation of monetary policy. It also stipulates that to ensure the central bank remains accountable, the inflation objective will continue to be decided by the government as a whole, but the policies for achieving this objective, such as changes in official interest rates, would be determined solely by the central bank. To institutionalize the autonomy of the central bank, a draft law would be submitted to Parliament by end of 1998, which would also include changes in the composition and mandate of the monetary board.

In fact the government programme to grant autonomy to Bank Indonesia had been implemented through a Presidential Decree on the granting of authority to Bank Indonesia in Monetary Management on 27 January 1998. Bank Indonesia used its newly acquired authority to raise interest rates of different tenors of SBIs. The rate of SBI interest for one to two days was raised from 14 per cent to 30 per cent in the day the decree was issued.

With the enactment of Act No. 23, 1999 Concerning the Central Bank, Bank Indonesia became a legitimate independent central bank. It stands as an autonomous institution, and according to the law, government or other institutions cannot intervene in its activities.

However, the impact of its independence on monetary management has not been demonstrated because of lingering problems.

Post "independence" problems seemed to start during President Abdulrachman Wahid's government, when there was an apparent move by the President to remove Governor Sabirin. As a result, relations between the government and Bank Indonesia were not harmonious during his presidency from October 1999 to July 2001.

The dispute became long drawn out with different twists that ultimately damaged monetary conditions and economic recovery. The dispute also resulted in public debate over whether the new law gave Bank Indonesia *too much* independence. Against this backdrop both the government and the Parliament proposed draft amendments to the new law. But a resolution that could be accepted by all parties never resulted, and the uncertainty continued.

With a view to providing a better solution, the government and the Fund jointly formed a panel to evaluate the different proposals for amending the central bank law. The panel comprised of two Indonesian experts (Dr Boediono, former Minister of Planning and former Managing Director of Bank Indonesia, and Dr. Remy Sjahdeni, former Managing Director of PT Bank Negara Indonensia) and two foreign experts (Dr. Roberto Zahler, former Governor of the Central Bank of Chile, Dr. Donald Brash, the current Governor of the Central Bank of New Zealand).

After holding discussions with the officials in the government, members of Parliament, the central bank management, representatives of banking sector and experts in April 2002, the panel submitted a report.[40]

The report based its recommendations on the criteria that viewed the independence of the central bank as including the following:

- Freedom for the central bank to set the stance for monetary policy in pursuit of its target (whether determined by the central bank alone, or in agreement with the government);
- Freedom to refuse to provide credit to the government;
- Sufficient financial resources so that the central bank does not have to go to the Parliament at frequent intervals for the resources with which to operate;

- A substantial measure of (but not absolute) security of tenure for the central bank's senior management; and
- Structures and procedures designed to ensure that the central bank is ultimately accountable to the people.

The panel noted that the law was modelled closely on that under which the Bundesbank operated, with a very high degree of independence from government and other parties. The suggestions were mostly to avoid efforts to weaken its independence, at the same time also insisting on the necessity to make the central bank accountable to the people.

Part of the problem that seemed to unfold during the arguments between the two parties came from different interpretations about the new law. There was an accusation to the President who, according to a media report, wanted to replace the governor by someone of his choice. Was he not committing an intervention into the operations of the central bank that was in violation to the law? However, there was also a legitimate question about whether the granting of autonomy to Bank Indonesia could go without accountability?

The episode was unfortunate in that both parties in the dispute seemed to use their own interpretation of the law to serve their narrow objectives at the cost of a bigger objective, the financial stability and economic recovery of Indonesia.

I am afraid the parties in the dispute between President Wahid and Governor Sabirin were not prepared to accept the actual meaning of the granting of an independent status to the central bank. The law is formulated clearly with the purpose of properly defining authorities of institutions that are entrusted with specific functions and responsibility. This is done to make accountability clear as to which institution is responsible for what. The fact that Mr. Pradjoto, a prominent Jakarta lawyer specializing in banking, commented on the dispute by saying that Bank Indonesia's attitude in exercising its independence was like "a state within state" indicates this kind of issue.[41]

The main objective for a complex organization that has many divisions is to make a clear-cut job description for each position and to assign accountability to each division such that every time a problem arises it can be identified quickly. But, all these many and complex divisions are interrelated functionally for they belong to one organization. This should be equally valid for different institutions within a nation–state. The granting of independence to the central bank and the prohibition for intervention by the government and other parties should not be interpreted to mean that when there is a problem in the national economy there is a freedom for each party to blame the others. Simple logic seemed to be thrown out by parties involved in the unfortunate dispute.

Macroeconomics also tells us that the real sector and the monetary sector are functionally interrelated even though each has its distinct characteristics. Economic policy and activities are aimed at enhancing welfare that has both the real as well as monetary variables. Economic welfare is measured in real variables, like gross domestic product. But the gross domestic products are measured in monetary units, like the rupiah, dollar or other currencies.

The monetary sector within an economy provides support for the functioning of the real sector so that it functions optimally. Even a monetary approach, which analyses the working of the national economy through its observations of monetary variables, the demand for and the supply of money, recognizes the working of the real sectors. But, resorting to a general equilibrium concept, the approach accepts that the development of monetary variables is a mirror image of the development of the real sector variables. This is like a person looking in the mirror and sees him or herself, except in reverse.

In inflation one usually views the process from the real sector side and describes the process as the presence of an excess demand for goods. A monetary approach views the same process as the presence of an excess supply of money. Both descriptions of an inflationary process are correct. It is an increase of the prices of goods and services as a result of the presence of excess demand for goods and services over their supply or a reduction in the value of currency as a result of excess supply of money over its demand.

In daily expression the description of inflation is even more realistic, i.e. a process of money chasing goods. People perceive that money is worth less, so people want to get rid of their money. Economists say there is excess money supply. But, this is equivalent to saying that there is scarcity of goods, such that people fight for acquiring them. Economists say there is excess demand for goods. It seems that the public views the process of inflation in a more comprehensive way compared to economists that used to be grouped as either Keynesian and monetarists.

Actually if one cares to read the new Bank Indonesia Law carefully, it is clear that the aim of granting autonomy to the central bank is not to make the institution stand outside the whole system of government, nor outside the real sectors. There are explicit stipulations that underlie the necessary cooperation between the government and Bank Indonesia. Article 43 of the law states that one or two Cabinet Ministers could attend the Board of Governor meetings without voting rights. Likewise, article 54 states that the government is required to solicit Bank Indonesia or to invite the governor to the cabinet meetings whenever they discuss monetary and banking issues, which have relevance for the central bank function. These underlie the objective for the government and the central bank to cooperate in their operation for the achievement of national interests, which must be prioritized over group or even private interests.

From the philosophy or spirit of the law that has to guide its operations, the established theory that supports its function and operations as well as explicit articles in the law of the central bank, there is no support for the fights between the government and the central bank that would ultimately benefit no one.

But aside from the dispute between the government and Bank Indonesia, it has also been the case that the new Central Bank Act has several weaknesses that could constrain its operations. Several stipulations may need to be changed or improved. They include two issues that I would like to discuss here, namely the formulation of the objectives of the central bank and the procedure for selecting governors and deputy governors.

The lack of clarity in the formulation of the above items could potentially cause disputes between the government and the central bank that could be damaging to the effectiveness of monetary policy to the detriment of the national economy. Likewise, the procedures and requirements for the selection of governor and deputy governors could constrain the aim of getting the best candidates for the jobs.

A brief look at details of the law confirms that all the necessary requirements for an independent central bank are clearly stipulated in the law, including a clear specification of its objective and function, the meaning of independence, transparency and accountability. This is definitely most welcome for the development of Indonesia's banking system.

In contrast to the former law which used a very broad definition of Bank Indonesia's objectives, the new law very specifically stated that the central bank has a single objective in its operation, i.e. to achieve and maintain the stability of the rupiah's value. The stability is referring to its relation to the prices of goods and services or the rate of inflation and its value in terms of other currencies, or the rates of exchange.

Bank Indonesia's main function encompasses three areas; formulating and implementing monetary policies, managing the payment system and supervising banks. In the explanatory notes of the law it is mentioned that in order for the central bank to achieve effectively and efficiently the stability objective, the three areas of its function should be integrated. It is not very clear as to what integrating these activities means. In a way this is somehow not in tune with the single objective of the central bank.

Article 7 of the new Central Bank Act states that the objective of Bank Indonesia is to achieve and defend the rupiah's stability. It is further stated in Article 11 of the Act that Bank Indonesia determines the rate of inflation as a target. The target has to be publicly announced. It becomes the guidance for Bank Indonesia to conduct monetary policy.

In the explanatory notes of the Act it was mentioned that the central bank determined the inflation target annually. In other words, Bank Indonesia has autonomy in determining the annual inflation rate as its target as part of the function to manage the stability of the currency. It is a goal and instrument-independent central bank. This is a major change from the former regulation that completely put the central bank under the wing of the government to support development.

However, since the central bank determines on its own the inflation target to achieve annually, it also has its downside. At least theoretically the central bank could determine an inflation target which turns out to be completely different from what the government assumed in the budget. If this arises it would be confusing for the market. For the private sector, it does not matter whether the inflation target is coming from the Ministry of Finance or the central bank. The private sector is only concerned about whether the target is achievable.

So, even though it seems to be a good idea for Bank Indonesia to have autonomy to determine the inflation target, there is a risk of creating unnecessary uncertainty in the market, which could undermine the effectiveness of monetary policy. In the explanatory notes it is only mentioned that should there be any difference — in the inflation target that the central bank determined and the assumptions the government used in the budget — the Parliament could ask the central bank to explain it. There is no stipulation as to whether reconciliation should be pursued.

It is curious to note that, with respect to the achievement of exchange rate stability, a different formulation is provided. On the exchange rate policy, the new law states that Indonesia adopts the exchange system that has been in place since 1970, i.e. a free exchange system. In addition, there is also a stipulation in the Law of Foreign Exchange System and Foreign Exchange Flows No. 24, 1999. Article 5 of the law stipulates that the government determines the exchange system from the system proposed by Bank Indonesia.

In global finance with its free flows of capital since the 1990s, it would be difficult to reconcile the stability of a currency in terms of its domestic inflation rate and the rate of exchange to other currencies. No reconciliation seems to be needed between the government and Bank Indonesia in terms of maintaining exchange rate stability, thanks to the formulation that has no risk of dispute here. The problem is not about the possible dispute between institutions.

However, conceptually there is a problem. The panel referred to above reminded us that central banks could not achieve both objectives simultaneously other than by sheer luck. It was specifically noted that

> Monetary Policy can be devoted to the achievement of an internal inflation rate, in which case the exchange rate will inevitably fluctuate; or to the maintenance of a stable exchange rate, in which case the inflation rate would tend towards the inflation rate of the country against whose currency the rupiah is linked.[42]

I think an amendment for the formulation of inflation targets is indeed in order. I am in support of instrument-independent central banking. Instead of Bank Indonesia determining its own annual inflation target it would be better for the market that the government in cooperation with the central bank determine it. And after the inflation target is determined, Bank Indonesia has autonomy to determine whatever means are necessary to achieve the target.

Another point I would like to make about the new law is the procedure for selecting the governor and deputy governors of Bank Indonesia. Article 41 of the new law stipulates that the President appoints the governor and the senior deputy governor with the confirmation of the Parliament. In the explanatory notes it was mentioned that the President submitted three to five candidates and the Parliament should confirm one from them. Similar stipulation is also provided for the selection of other deputy governors, except that the governor submits the candidates.

I see no merit for both the President and the governor to submit more than one candidate for each post. For every party concerned it is more efficient for the President and the governor to submit a single candidate for each post. The proposed candidate(s) should have passed their fit and proper tests, which should be done prior to the submission. The present stipulation that candidates for the post of deputy governor have to come from within the central bank also carries the risk of not finding the right person in the right place.

Conceptually there are some points that need clarification. It is stipulated that Bank Indonesia is granted an autonomous authority of supervising banks. By December 2002 Bank Indonesia is to hand over this authority to an independent financial supervisory body, which will be created at a later date. However, due to the very slow progress in integrating financial supervision, the date for the handover has been postponed to 2010. As a matter of expediency it is well understood that Bank Indonesia is still performing this task. However, keeping it with the central bank while other financial institutions were under a separate supervisory body would invite problems that I mentioned before. At the same time putting both monetary management and the task of supervising banks cum lender of last resort also faces the risk for compromising the two functions, which Indonesia experienced during the crisis.

It may not be as crucial, however a note on the task for managing the national payment system is in order here. I trust that among the three tasks, the one dealing with clearing of payments does not have the characteristics of a public good. In the future, the more advanced the private sector, the more reason for the central bank to let this task be provided by the private sector instead of the central bank.

The process and the kind of amendments that will ultimately be passed by the Parliament have not been resolved to the present.

Let me close the discussion on this issue by reiterating the obvious. No matter how important is the legal basis for central bank independence, it does not guarantee to make the central bank an effective institution in achieving its objective of monetary stability and serving as a solid financial infrastructure for a robust banking system; Bank Indonesia still has to earn its reputation as an independent central bank.

7

LESSONS FROM THE CRISIS

Some Facts

The Indonesian crisis has lingered on, becoming the worst in Asia. It may even be simply just the worst amongst crises countries that the world has experienced in the recent past. Even though this has been generally accepted as fact, it is still pertinent to ask why is this so. In particular the question is relevant if confronted with another well accepted claim that, at the outset, the relevant fundamentals of the Indonesian economy were either at par with or even better than other crisis countries in Asia, and that the initial policy responses by the government were considered prudent and timely.

Together with two other crisis countries in Asia, namely Thailand and the Republic of Korea, Indonesia asked the IMF to assist the government in designing and implementing policy adjustment programmes through the framework of stand-by arrangements.

It is instructive to compare some macroeconomic indicators on vulnerability to external shocks, as shown in Table 9. With respect to external trade performance, both export growth as well as current account deficits in the first five years of the 1990s, and 1996 for Indonesia were better than for Thailand and Korea. The growth of credits from commercial banks prior to the crisis was relatively better for Indonesia.

TABLE 9
Vulnerability Indicators

	Indonesia	Korea	Thailand	Malaysia
Domestic Debt/GDP ratio (average 1992–96)	50	50	87	82
Corporate Debt/Equity ratio				
1991	190	480	170	90
1996	200	640	340	200
Families' control of publicly traded companies (%)	67.3	24.9	51.9	42.6
State-owned companies (%)	15.2	19.9	24.1	34.8
Annual domestic credit growth (1992–96)	12	15	37	38
Exposure to Property loans[1]	25–30	15–25	30–40	30–40
Non-performing loans 1996[2]	8.8	0.8	7.7	3.9
Peak of Non-performing loans, 1998/99[3]	30–35	25–30	25–30	45.3
Short-term debt/reserves	188.9	217	121.5	45.3
Export growth (dollar value)[4]	9.1	–2.8	–4.5	0.9
Current Account 1991–95 (% of GDP)	–2.4	–1.8	–7.7	–7.6
Current Account 1996 (% of GDP)	–3.2	–4.4	–8.9	–4.4

Note: [1] Share of property lending to the private sector, end 1997 (% of total)
    [2] Official estimates (%)
    [3] estimates by J.P. Morgan
    [4] second half 1995/second half 1996
Source: Rearrangement of Table 2, Asian Crisis Countries: Vulnerability Indicators, Andrew Berg, *The Asia Crisis: Causes, Policy Responses, and Outcomes*, IMF Working Paper no. WP/99/138, p. 8 and Table 5, Assets of Corporate Relations with Banks and States, Qaizar Hussain and Clas Wihlborg, *Corporate Insolvency Procedures and Bank Behavior: A Study of Selected Asian Economies*, IMF Working Paper, WP/99/135, October 1999.

Other indicators, such as the ratio of domestic debt to GDP, the corporate debt to equity ratio, and the growth of bank loans to the property sector, are similar for all these countries.

However, it is also true that the percentage of non-performing loans in commercial banks in Indonesia was worse than in other countries, and so was the concentration of ownership of publicly traded companies. The ratio of short-term debt to international reserves in Indonesia was also worse than that of in Thailand, but better than Korea's. It is generally true that Indonesia's macro fundamentals prior to the crisis were better for some and similar for other indicators to those of Korea and Thailand.

The initial policy response to the rupiah's depreciation in early July 1997 was the widening of intervention bands by Bank Indonesia as dictated by a managed floating policy with a crawling depreciation. This action was accompanied by judicious interventions in the foreign exchange market, supported by monetary and fiscal measures to prevent further depreciation. However, when the policy was no longer tenable, the rupiah was floated in mid-August 1997. By this time all the neighbouring countries had already floated their currencies.

From this time on, the government was working hard, albeit in vain, towards a more coordinated prudent monetary and fiscal policy together with measures of liberalization in the real sectors.

Early in October 1997, when the problems had clearly changed into widespread financial distress that endangered market confidence, the government decided to invite the Fund to help the government recover market and public confidence. Inside Bank Indonesia, I used to refer to the adjustment measures that the Indonesian government implemented prior to the arrival of the Fund, as a "self imposed Fund programme" due to the similarities.

The IMF commended these Indonesian government policy responses. In fact, during the meeting of the Consultative Group on Indonesia (CGI) in Tokyo in mid July-1997, all representatives of the creditor countries and multilateral institutions who were present at the conference congratulated the Indonesian delegation on the preemptive, timely and prudent measures taken.[1]

The above observations cannot explain well, and in fact contradict, the fact that among the crisis countries Indonesia fared the worst. Some indicators that show the impacts of the crisis on different variables in the crisis countries are shown in the following table. The two most telling impacts were currency depreciation and the negative GDP growth.

TABLE 10
Impacts of Crisis, June '97–March '98
(per cent changes)

	Indonesia	Korea	Thailand	Malaysia
Nominal exchange rate	−75	−41	−38	−33
Real effective exchange rate	−63	−33	−27	−23
Nominal Interest Rate	32	12	8	3.5
Growth of GDP	−13.7	−5.8	−9.4	−6.7
Stock Index (US$)	−50	−46	−58	−79
Stock Index (national currency)	−27	−38	−18	−38

Source: Adapted from Table 5, Andrew Berg, "The Asia Crisis: Causes, Policy Responses, and Outcomes", IMF Working Paper, No. WP/99/138.

Using both nominal as well as real measurement of depreciation, the rupiah's depreciation was more severe than the three other currencies, as was the negative GDP growth. The decline in the capital market index was slightly better than that of Thailand and Malaysia, but it is worse than Korea's.

Other indicators confirm that Indonesia fared the worst. These include the frequency and severity of social and political tensions, including riots and demonstrations, and the number of unemployed. Furthermore, the other crisis countries have experienced recovery with some macro indicators, like exchange rates, interest rates and inflation rates, back to the pre-crisis levels or better. Korea has started to repay its loans from the Fund. Thailand did not make use of the last drawings of its SBA. And both countries are basically out of their respective Fund-supported programmes. In contrast, Indonesia up until the time of writing still had to suffer from the Fund's decision to postpone disbursement of the current stand-by loan due to disputes on some items of the conditionality.

A Protracted Crisis

There are a plethora of studies, writings and conferences about the Asian crisis. Different factors have been identified as the cause or origin of the crisis. Basically, there are two groups that hold different arguments for explaining the Asian crisis. The financial panic theory, which maintains that the crisis originated from a shift of market perception from bullishness to meltdown. Through a herd mentality, the shift of market perception caused capital reversals, which led to severe depreciation of currencies and the collapse of the exchange rates of host countries. The other theory holds that the crisis originates from weak domestic fundamentals, crony capitalism, corruption and other structural problems. The structural weaknesses of the affected national economies led to vulnerability of the financial market to external shocks. A variant of the latter theory pinpoints the weakness of the banking system as the origin of the crisis.[2]

It has also been generally accepted that there were two prominent factors in the Asian crisis, i.e. the weakness of the banking sector and unsustainable corporate debts. These factors have been identified as causes or at least as factors that exacerbated the crisis. The then First Deputy MD of the Fund, Stanley Fischer implied that the Asian financial crisis could have been mitigated if only the crisis countries implemented flexible exchange rate systems, focused more on the health of their financial systems, more transparency of the monetary authority in their report of foreign exchange reserves, and that Fund surveillance had been more vigilant.[3]

None of these approaches explains the depth of the Indonesian crisis. It is indeed true that the devil is in the detail in this case. Indonesia experienced some external shock as part of the effects of the Mexican crisis in the beginning of 1995, when the rupiah was under attack for several days. By resorting to the existing policy of managed floating, the central bank restored market confidence after conducting market interventions.

Likewise, one cannot satisfactorily explain the Indonesian crisis merely by saying that the origin of the crisis was domestic structural problems. The rupiah was also under attack in July 1996, after a fire that burnt down the headquarters of PDI-P, the Indonesian National Party headed by Megawati Soekarnoputri, and the riots that followed. In a similar manner, Bank Indonesia successfully stabilized the rupiah, merely by relying on the existing practice of exchange rate management.

With respect to the weak fundamentals, it is without doubt that these problems had been known and talked about publicly long before July 1997. Thus, it is curious to say that structural weaknesses are the origin of the Indonesian crisis while at the same time accepting the argument that the crisis started in July 1997.

It is even not entirely correct to take up Stanley Fischer's explanation that Indonesia was practicing a pegged or fixed exchange system prior to the crisis. The managed floating with creeping depreciation combined with a periodic widening of the intervention bands is definitely not a pegged or fixed system.[4] I would argue that the managed floating with creeping depreciation of the rupiah combined with intervention band widening had been part of the uniqueness of Indonesia's exchange rate management. Various studies on the Asian crisis also report that the Indonesian case is different from other crisis countries.[5] One could also say that Bank Indonesia intervened and used its international reserves very judiciously.

Bank Indonesia used a more rigid definition of international reserves than the gross reserve definition used by the Fund. This is the reason why, the so-called "US$43 billion bail out for Indonesia" included USD 5 billion of Indonesia's own reserves that was ready for use. This fund was in effect a "saving" that Indonesia made resulting from the different method of calculating international reserves between Bank Indonesia and the Fund. Finally, the Fund itself acknowledged that Indonesia had been very prudent in spending the international reserves for intervention.[6]

Of course, the other two remaining arguments, the health of the financial sector and the need for better surveillance, are pertinent to Indonesia. The whole banking sector was weak structurally. There were too many commercial banks with high percentages of non-performing loans and weak governance, while banking supervision was not carried out properly. And I can only underline what Dr Fischer said at the time about the need for stronger IMF surveillance on this matter.

I have argued on different occasions that the Indonesian crisis was a multifaceted one. Although triggered by an external shock, experience shows that external shock does not necessarily develop into a crisis of the magnitude that Indonesia experienced.[7] Similarly, domestic shock alone could not lead to a crisis of the same magnitude.

Thus, the two factors that had been identified as fundamental to the Asian crisis were well founded in the case of Indonesia. The banking system, which was still in a state of consolidation, was too weak to face a contagious external shock. Corporate debt in foreign exchange was indeed unsustainable, viewed from their relative as well as absolute magnitudes, in addition to being mostly short-term and unhedged. To make matters worse, a big percentage of these loans were used to finance speculative activities, like property development and to a certain degree, equities trading.

Be that as it may, the question remains, why did Indonesia ultimately suffer the most? There are some plausible explanations. If concentration of corporate ownership can be seen as a good indicator of crony capitalism, which is associated with inefficiencies, corruption and other illness of a national economy, then Indonesia indeed was ripe for a crisis.

Corporate ownership by the top 15 families in Indonesia as shown by Claessens et al. (1999, Table 1) was very concentrated — 67.3 per cent — as compared to Malaysia and Thailand (between 30–40 per cent) and Korea (between 15–25 per cent). If state ownership is added to this, the figure for Indonesia becomes 82.5 per cent. The concentration of ownership explains well the large percentages of nonperforming loans, and violation of legal lending limits committed by these corporations, which are associated with distress and crisis in banking. This phenomenon is closely related to other problems that made Indonesia the most vulnerable economy, namely corruption. Ultimately, this is rooted in the other institutional weaknesses that Indonesia is notoriously lacking, good governance and a sound legal as well as judiciary system.

The ratio of short-term corporate debt to international reserves prior to the crisis for Indonesia was also very high, 189 per cent. Only Korea surpasses it with 217 per cent. The ratios for Thailand and Malaysia are 121.5 per cent and 45 per cent respectively.

Political factors also apply if one takes the commencement of the Fund-supported programme as the starting point of a systemic adjustment policy to address the crisis. It seems instructive to notice that both Thailand and Korea experienced a change of government that facilitated policy implementation to stop the bleeding and start the recovery. Thailand had a new government in November 1997 that immediately strengthened the Fund-supported programme, which began in August 1997. Korea had the same experience: when the Fund came on board in December 1997, the incoming government was already involved in the process of negotiations.

This was not how it happened in Indonesia. The Soeharto government negotiated the first letter of intent (LOI) to the Fund, likewise the second and the third ones.[8] After Soeharto left office, he was succeeded by Habibie, who was perceived as Soeharto's crony. The real change of government came only in October 1999 when Abdulrachman Wahid was elected President, which was two years after the first LOI. If a change in government seems to facilitate smooth implementation of Fund-supported programmes, the fact that the change only came after two years also put Indonesia at a disadvantage.

There is also a contrast between Indonesia's approach to dealing with corporate debt with that of the other two countries. Both Thailand and Korea addressed the problem of corporate debt early in the process of their respective Fund-supported programmes. In contrast, Indonesia had problems addressing corporate debt.

An initial policy to address corporate debts was assembled sloppily in January 1998 or almost three months after the commencement of the Fund-supported programme. In June 1998 a rudimentary framework was formed (the Frankfurt Agreement) and only in September of that year was some scheme was established, the so-called "Jakarta Initiative". Some features of corporate debt resolution, such as "roll over", which are crucial to stop the bleeding of banks, did not come early enough for Indonesia.[9]

Similarly, bank restructuring was not prompt enough. There are two issues I would like to mention here. First, the notorious bank closures. With the benefit of hindsight, in particular if one compares Indonesia's case with that of Thailand's, it should be noted that there is a difference between closing banks and freezing financial institutions. Banks serve as the major implementing agents in the payment system while finance companies do not make a difference. Thailand initially froze finance companies, while Korea acted similarly with a number of merchant banks. Their closure did not directly disturb the payment system but the monetary authorities in both cases did not immediately close the insolvent institutions. Only after installing blanket guarantees in the system did the respective monetary authorities liquidate them.[10]

In contrast, Indonesia liquidated 16 banks on 1 November 1997, several days before the Executive Board decided to grant Indonesia a stand-by facility. In fact, the bank closures were a part of the *prior action* or measures that had to be taken prior to the Board's decision to grant stand-by loans. The impact of the bank closures were devastating as has been discussed in this book.

With respect to bank runs after the closures in November 1997, I find that arguments that the policy failed due to the absence of a deposit insurance scheme unconvincing. Indonesia designed a partial guarantee scheme at the time of the bank closures. Indeed, the guarantee covered only the small deposits, but this is what most deposit insurance schemes did. It should also be noted that the bank runs did not occur immediately after the announcement of the closures. In fact, the execution of the closures, which actually encompassed more than 400 bank offices nationwide, ran smoothly. This is aspect of the Bank Indonesia operation that was least appreciated or recognized, but which my colleagues and I at Bank Indonesia were proud of.

The bank runs involved big depositors who generally were not covered by normal deposit insurance. And it started something like two weeks after some unfortunate developments as explained before. Thus, with respect to criticisms about the absence of a deposit insurance scheme I would tend to agree if one referred to a blanket guarantee, covering all depositors, and not just a regular deposit insurance scheme. Indonesia implemented a blanket guarantee scheme only in January 1998, when the banking system was close to total collapse.

Thus, in the midst of economic distress, Indonesia had liquidated banks, which constituted the dominant part of the national payment system, without a blanket guarantee.

This does not mean that I do not support the liquidation of insolvent banks. However, the Indonesian experience of closing banks raises some issues that have to be carefully considered, i.e. how and when insolvent banks should be liquidated. Closing insolvent banks, even though it is a right decision, should not be done when market confidence is fragile. At issue then is not whether to liquidate insolvent banks, but when you should do it. Of course this does not necessarily solve the problem also as for some people, bank owners in particular, there is never be a proper time to close banks.

Inconsistency is the Problem

I subscribe to the idea that a "turning point" is crucial in addressing a financial and economic crisis. Here a turning point means an occasion which produces an end to the deterioration process arising from the crisis, leading towards recovery and beyond. Unfortunately, reversing deterioration is not a guarantee for a sustained recovery, and even less so for sustainable development.

In order for a turning point to spin-off a process of recovery, other important factors need to be present namely:

- Speedy recognition of the problems — especially in the face of contagion, "the sooner the better";
- Good and consistent policies followed by consistency of implementation; and
- A robust world economy.

In this respect, a change of government seems to be instrumental to the success of economic readjustment programmes. Of course the crucial factor is whether the government is willing to commit itself to addressing the contagion. This does not have to imply a change of government. However, it does seem easier for a new administration to be consistent in implementation of adjustment programmes, which often involved correction of policy errors of the previous government.

Except for the first few months, Indonesia has been dealing with the crisis for over six years through the Fund-supported programmes. During this period Indonesia experienced three changes of government. The Soeharto administration negotiated and implemented the first batch of adjustment programmes. In May 1998, President B.J. Habibie took over. The market perceived his administration as a continuation of the Soeharto government. So, in a way Indonesia experienced a credible change of government only in October 1999, when President Abdulrachman Wahid was elected President. However, President Wahid, who was well received by the market initially, could not sustain the momentum. Recovery did not materialize because he did not implement the programme consistently. In fact, inconsistency seemed to be a characteristic of his administration.

In July 2001 President Megawati took over the presidency and her new cabinet took the right initial policy steps that soon had a positive impact on strengthening and stabilizing the rupiah. Despite the world problems in security and economy associated with 9/11 and its aftermath, including the Bali and J.W. Marriot Hotel's bombings, and SARS, Megawati's government had been able to produce a semblance of social and political stability, which has been positive for currency stabilization and modest economy growth. Thus, a turning point has been produced and economic recovery begun.

There is no established definition of what constitutes a turning point that marks the end of a process — of deterioration in this case — and the beginning of another one (recovery). In a business cycle, economic expansion or a boom is followed by bust, with a turning point in between. A recession or depression is followed by a recovery.

In a multi-faceted crisis such as experienced by Indonesia, the turning point that stops the process of deterioration and starts a recovery process seems to depend on the political stability that could only be provided by the presence of a stable government, which was not provided by the governments before Megawati's.

The democratic change of government in Indonesia only occurred in October 1999, two years after the first LOI. However, the presence of a new and legitimate government does not in itself guarantee an economic recovery either. It only serves as a starting point for a process toward recovery that must be followed by consistent implementation of a good programme previously designed. Despite its legitimacy, President Wahid wasted a golden opportunity to consolidate the good start to his administration, which was very well supported by the public and the market both internally and externally, in addition to a more robust world economy in 1999. A more consistent policy would have produced a sustainable recovery, as we observed in both Thailand and Korea.

From the first adjustment programme in 1997 to the most recent one, hurdles that have constrained the success of the programme generally arose from inconsistent implementation. The inconsistency can come from, using Haggard's analysis, sins of *omission* — from the lack of administrative capacity and know-how. Or it may arise as the result of *commission*, in the form of forbearance to favoured parties.[11]

It could be argued that Indonesia has suffered from both weak institutions in designing and implementing a comprehensive programme of adjustments to confront the contagious crisis. Rampant cronyism and corruption embedded in the ersatz capitalism of Indonesia have been part and parcel of the weak institutions that also include weak legal and judiciary systems in addition to the often mentioned weak banking system. Certainly the lack of administrative capacity has played an important role in failure to design and implement robust adjustment policies.

However, more damaging must have been weak governance. The system suffered from what in Indonesia is popularly known as KKN or corruption, collusion and nepotism, which was rampant in the Soeharto's New Order government, and has continued in all the successive governments.

In addition, there has been a tendency for government officials to be lacking initiative and decisiveness, and becoming more risk-averse. In the new era of pressing demand for transparency and accountability, governments have been hesistant to make decisions that risk failure and invite criticism.

There have been inconsistencies of programme implementation in every administration. Several blatant inconsistencies committed by the Soeharto government hindered programme implementation. However, inconsistencies either in the policy design or implementation have not been the monopoly of the Soeharto government.

These are examples of inconsistencies in the implementation of the first LOI, signed by the government of Indonesia 31 October 1997:

- When the government announced the reactivation of 15 big development projects that were previously included in the postponed ones due to interventions by President Soeharto's family and cronies.

- At the outset of the programme, Soeharto's intervention also damaged the execution of the decision to liquidate 16 banks. The monetary authorities had to succumb to the pressure to grant the purchase of a small bank by one of Soeharto's sons who partly owned a bank that was liquidated in the 1 November 1997 bank closures.

- In addition, members of Soeharto's members of family, who partly owned some of the closed banks, sued the Governor of the Central Bank and the Minister of Finance in court, in protest against the government decision. Market confidence in the monetary authorities' and the government's will to implement the Fund-supported programme deteriorated drastically with the legal actions and the government decisions associated with them.

- Bank Indonesia was confronted with constraints in implementing agreed policy for monetary tightening during the initial efforts to defend the rupiah from severe depreciation. The Fund kept asking for Bank Indonesia to raise interest rates while Soeharto did not allow the Central Bank to do so. In fact, Soeharto instructed the Central Bank to lower lending rates to help the business community to resume their activities.[12] Granted that the effectiveness of a high rate of interest policy for strengthening currency is still debatable, the inconsistency did a lot of damage to the credibility of policy implementation.
- In January 1998 Soeharto signed a second LOI to the Fund, which in effect strengthened and improved the previous measures, which were agreed upon in the first LOI. These included discarding monopoly in clove trading and Bulog (the state agency for food procurement) imports, abolishing subsidies to the aircraft industry (IPTN), and the special treatment for the national car project. All were Soeharto's pet projects. The implementation of all these measures was long and winding such that in effect the old practices continued.
- Soeharto was playing with a dubious proposal from Steve Hanke for implementing a fixed exchange system with a currency board arrangement (CBS), which created an uproar among the G-7 leaders and the Fund. Instead of following the steps agreed upon in the negotiation, Soeharto wanted to follow a different path.

However, all the succeeding governments have committed similar inconsistencies, albeit to a lesser degree. These are some examples:

- Banking restructuring has been very slow, to a large extent due to pressures from different parties to deviate from the agreed programmes. The fact that IBRA, the Indonesian Bank Restructuring Agency, in less than four years of its existence already experienced seven changes in its management, attests to the presence of different interest groups. Corporate restructuring has also been incredibly slow.

- A fight between the government and Bank Indonesia over the management of the central bank during President Abdulrachman Wahid's government also shows a similar problem.
- The programme of privatization and its implementation has been confronted with constraints, which arise from different reasons, from conceptual, social, political, as well as personal interests.
- The policy to eradicate corruption and develop good governance in both the public and private sectors has been generally disappointing. In general law enforcement under all the post-Soeharto administrations has been poor, and the judiciary system remains weak.

Ambivalence towards the role of the Fund in the government's efforts to fight the financial and economic crisis has always been present among some groups of Indonesians, including those in the administration. In general, government policy relying on high rates of interest to defend the currency, issues related to the choice of the exchange rate system, including the use of capital controls or a currency board technique, implications of bank closures, the policy to help banks with liquidity support, and the implementation of blanket guarantees, have encountered strong criticism in the Parliament as well as in public debates.

Some of the concerns originate from early criticisms of the Fund's adjustment policy prescriptions to developing countries that were sometimes ineffective due to its reliance on a "one size fits all" type of programme. To be fair, the Fund has been learning this lesson, albeit only slowly.

Certainly the Fund could learn more lessons from the Indonesian experience in the last several years of muddling through. The Fund is definitely not free from at least contributing to the contagion as well as to Indonesia ultimately becoming an intractable case. For sure, corrections and adjustments have been made during the implementation of the programmes as well as institutionally in the Fund's operation, such as redesigning the Fund's conditionality and setting up the Independent Evaluation Office. However, the extensive involvement of the Fund staff and the more subtle management and stakeholders' influence in programme implementation must have played some role in the making of Indonesia's crisis:

- There are two areas that most seem to accept as either part of the cause or as factors that exacerbated the crisis, i.e. the weak banking sector and unsustainable corporate debt. Indonesia's unfortunate experience of the November 1997 bank closures and the hands off policy of the corporate debt problem at the outset reflect poor design, inconsistency and weak implementation of policies to cope with the crisis, not just by the Indonesian government but also by the Fund.

- The adoption of a blanket guarantee for the banking sector in late January 1998 became a controversy. Critics argued that a blanket guarantee was not warranted, while supporters criticized it as coming too late. The adoption of the blanket guarantee was a government decision. But the Fund was very much involved in the decision to adopt the scheme. The Fund staff argued that a blanket guarantee had to be adopted to save the banking industry from collapsing entirely. It should be noted here that, even if the cause of the problems originated domestically, certainly they also implicate the Fund. Professor Kim Dae-Hwan aptly describes a similar issue on the Korean crisis, as "home grown, but not home alone".[13] It is also curious that Thailand adopted a blanket guarantee prior to the announcement on the policy to freeze a number of financial institutions. Even if the Fund was not the originator of that policy, it should be noted that the Thai government went into a Fund-supported programme prior to Indonesia, and the blanket guarantee scheme was already well in place by the time Indonesia negotiated the arrangement with the Fund. This could also be said about the policy to deal with corporate debt.

- In the early stages of the programme, the Fund's inflexible requirement for a budget surplus of 1 per cent of GDP in 1998 turned out to be a disaster. The Fund retracted the decision in January 1998 to allow the government to implement a budget with a deficit of over 2 per cent of GDP. But it was too late; the market punished the rupiah severely due to the perception that the government's balanced budget was clearly in violation of the Fund's requirement.

- The bickering between the Wahid government and the Central Bank over the amendment of the Central Bank Law lasted longer than expected, which contributed to economic uncertainty.

TABLE 11
Indonesia's Letters of Intent

Date of Issue	Title
Megawati Government	
1. 10/12/2003	Indonesia — Letter of Intent
2. 16/09/2003	Indonesia — Letter of Intent
3. 11/06/2003	Indonesia — Letter of Intent
4. 18/03/2003	Indonesia — Letter of Intent, Memorandum of Economic and Financial Policies, and Technical Memorandum of Understanding
5. 20/11/2002	Indonesia — Letter of Intent
6. 09/04/2002	Indonesia — Letter of Intent
7. 13/12/2001	Indonesia — Letter of Intent, Memorandum of Economic and Financial Policies, and Technical Memorandum of Understanding
8. 27/8/2001	Indonesia — Memorandum of Economic and Financial Policies
9. 07/9/2000	Indonesia — Memorandum of Economic and Financial Policies
10. 31/7/2000	Memorandum of Economic and Financial Policies, Government of Indonesia and Bank Indonesia
11. 17/5/2000	Indonesia — Memorandum of Economic and Financial Policies
12. 20/1/2000	Indonesia — Memorandum of Economic and Financial Policies
Habibie Government	
13. 22/7/1999	Indonesia — Supplementary Memorandum of Economic and Financial Policies
14. 14/5/1999	Indonesia — Supplementary Memorandum of Economic and Financial Policies
15. 16/3/1999	Indonesia — Supplementary Memorandum of Economic and Financial Policies (Fourth Review Under the EFA)
16. 13/11/1998	Indonesia — Supplementary Memorandum of Economic and Financial Policies
17. 19/10/1998	Indonesia — Supplementary Memorandum of Economic and Financial Policies
18. 11/9/1998	Indonesia — Supplementary Memorandum of Economic and Financial Policies
19. 29/7/1998	Third Review Under the Stand-by Arrangement
20. 24/6/1998	Indonesia — Second Supplementary Memorandum of Economic and Financial Policies

TABLE 11   (*continued*)
Indonesia's Letters of Intent

Date of Issue	Title
	Soeharto Government
21. 10/4/1998	First Review Under the Stand-by Arrangement
22. 15/1/1998	Memo on Economic and Financial Policies
23. 31/10/1997	Memorandum of Economic and Financial Policies

Similarly, for several years the status of the five deputy governors of Bank Indonesia who officially resigned, but were on active duty, also caused confusion. On the one hand, there was a valid argument from the government to stress on some rule of accountability that goes hand in hand with independence. On the other hand, there was also a valid argument for the Fund to insist on guarding the independent status of the central bank by not changing the board of governors in any way not stipulated in the central bank law. The standstill definitely jeopardized the effectiveness of Bank Indonesia.

In sum, Indonesia became a basket case due to political instability reflected in frequent changes of government before a new government under President Megawati produced a turning point for financial and economic recovery.

IMF and the Crisis

What was the Fund's overall role in the Asian crisis and its aftermath? Did the Fund help the crisis countries to get out of the crisis? Did the Fund treat Indonesia differently from other crisis countries? To answer these questions accurately a more careful analysis is required. However, as a general observation, it is fair to say that the Fund had a prominent role in the crisis, for better and for worse, not least because three of the crisis countries in Asia went to the Fund for help.

Indeed, three countries entered into stand-by arrangements with the Fund in their respective efforts to fight against the onslaught of the financial crisis in 1997, i.e. Thailand (20 August), Indonesia (5 November) and Korea (4 December).[14] The Philippines was still under a precautionary arrangement with the Fund from before. Malaysia elected a different path in coping with the crisis, especially after the departure of Anwar Ibrahim from his posts as Deputy Prime Minister and Minister of Finance.

Part of the criticism has something to do with the natural tendency for people to deny their failure.

The Indonesian media has often reported government officials claiming that some unpopular measures were taken because of the Fund's insistence, for example, the bank closures or abolishing domestic oil subsidies. These are clearly efforts by some officials to suggest that the Fund determines policy.

The reverse of the above could also be read from some media reports on the Fund's insistence that these are the host governments' own programmes. This is implicitly saying that the Fund has nothing to do with them. The truth must lie somewhere in between.

This is also the problem of ownership of adjustment programmes, which the Fund under Horst Kohler's leadership tried to address as part of the process of learning the lessons from the Asian and other crises. I will discuss this briefly. But first let us discuss the issues that have been raised in general criticism of governments and the Fund in addressing the crisis.

Adjustment programmes in the framework of stand-by loans that the IMF granted to Asian crisis countries encountered criticism almost immediately. Well-known economists — amongst others, Joseph Stiglitz (Stiglitz 1998a, 1998b), Jeffrey Sachs (Radelet and Sachs 1998), Paul Krugman (Krugman 1998), Jagdish Bhagwati (Bhagwati 1998) have criticised the Fund's approach towards the Asian crisis. The criticism was louder after it became clear that the impacts of the Asian crisis was much worse than expected.

In Indonesia the IMF's role in the government's adjustment policy received so much criticism due to its poor results. But the criticism also originates from a lack of understanding or misunderstanding about the nature of different policies or about the conditionality of the Fund facility. Criticisms of the Fund's role in the crisis and of the officials who were responsible for inviting them came from different groups, including prominent senior government officials like the Minister of the National Development Planning of the Megawati government, Chairman of the People's Consultative Assembly or even the Vice President.[15]

In general the critics showed that the Asian financial crisis was different from the crisis that had developed in Latin American. Crisis in the Latin American economies in the 1980s and Mexico in 1994 originated in deficits in their budget that created disturbances in the balance of payments. In contrast Asian countries in general did not experience any budget deficits. Asian countries also generally have high rates of national savings that differ from Latin American countries.

Many critics have shown that despite the different problems that these countries were facing, the Fund advocated the same policy package. The IMF approach to any crisis is sometimes described as "one policy fits all", in particular regarding tight monetary policy or high interest rates to stabilize exchange rates. Arguably during the early period of the Fund-supported programme in Indonesia, the monetary stance was not as tight as it appeared.[16] The stabilization policy has also been blamed for causing adverse economic effects: recession, social dislocation and a host of problems.

The generally perceived IMF function is that of helping member countries deal with their balance of payments' problems through providing stand-by loans and technical assistance. The funds are put together with the member country's international reserves.

The problem that the public sees is currency depreciation or devaluation and its implications on routine economic activities. However, the balance of payments' problem that leads to exchange rate depreciation usually originates from or is associated with imbalances in the real sectors. Thus, a comprehensive programme to address the real problem is indeed warranted. But, dealing with the whole problem comprehensively by resorting to comprehensive adjustment programmes runs the risk of encountering many negative side-effects, as correctly demonstrated by some IMF critics.

According to the articles of agreement, the purposes of the IMF are among others,

> To facilitate the expansion and balanced growth to international trade, and to contribute thereby to the promotion and maintenance of high level of employment and real income and to the development of the productive resources of all members as primary objectives of economic policy.[17]

From this passage it is clear that the mandate of the IMF is comprehensive, encompassing monetary as well as real sectors of the national economies.

So, to say that IMF does not have any mandate to deal with the real sectors is not valid.[18]

However, the general perception seems to be that the IMF task is only helping member countries to deal with monetary issues and exchange rates. This leads to criticism about IMF's role in dealing with structural reforms particularly related to the IMF lack of expertise in handling of financial, institutions or legal and judicial institutions, and other issues related to governance and transparency, which figured prominently in the Indonesian adjustment programmes. In my observation, this criticism against the Fund has some validity. Similarly, criticizing the Fund for poor preparation in dealing with the crisis seems to have more credibility than accusing the Fund for overstepping its jurisdiction.

The IMF has also been criticized for its policy on the two problems that have been generally recognized as the causes of or at least the factors that exacerbated the Asian crisis, i.e. the weaknesses of the banking sector and unsustainable corporate debt. The IMF is either seen as lacking the expertise in dealing with the micro aspects of banking operations, which is crucial for the establishment of a sound banking sector, or that it is simply outside IMF's sphere of activity. A similar criticism was also levelled at IMF handling of corporate debt. The bank closures in November 1997 and the problems that followed demonstrated the first problem. The fact that Indonesia's corporate debt problem was addressed only after the second LOI in late January 1998 in a less than professional manner, and in contrast to the programmes that both Thailand and South Korea, seemed to show the lack of preparation and of expertise or willingness or both in the matter.

In the case of Indonesia, there were additional problems. Indonesia suffered tremendously from the bank closures in November 1997, but it is debatable whether other alternatives would have provided a better result. With respect to corporate debt it seems the problem was the Fund's lack of commitment early in its involvement through the stand-by arrangement. Both issues need more careful study to better evaluate what should have been done.

Some critics even went so far as to propose the closure of the IMF. An example was the criticism from two former U.S. Treasury Secretaries, William Simon and George Shultz, together with the former Chairman of Citicorp Walter Wriston.[19] Others, like the Meltzer Commission, suggested streamlining the Fund's activities to some core functions and responsibilities, which to a certain extent was in line with what has been developing within the Fund under the new management.[20]

At this juncture, the debate turned a bit ugly in Joseph Stiglitz's, *Globalization and Its Discontents*, which concentrates more on criticizing the Fund's role in the Asian crisis than discussing globalization. The book has not been much appreciated, especially by the Fund's staff who abandoned their usual restraint in counterattacking Stiglitz.[21]

Indonesia's experience could illustrate some of the actual issues with the Fund-supported programme that covers issues perceived to be outside the proper task of the institution. During the crisis, the government invited Paul Volcker,[22] to give his assessment of the development of the crisis and the programme to address it.

Volcker visited Jakarta on 10 to 12 January 1998. During his brief stay, he met with President Soeharto and the Economic Team to discuss the problems faced by Indonesia and steps to resolve them. When the Minister of Finance and myself received him in Minister Mar'ie Muhammad's office, he could not hide his surprise on the nature and number of issues included in the IMF-supported programme that had been proceeding for two months then. During the discussion, Volcker raised a question that was surely rhetorical, "What do these cloves and garlic have to do with monetary problems?"

Of course his question did not imply that he supported the government's granting of the clove trading monopoly to Tommy Soeharto, the President's favourite son. Nor did he agree with the monopoly on garlic imports. He was merely showed his astonishment that "trivial" problems like these were made part of the adjustment programme. The argument here is, even if these are relevant problems confronting the government, was it proper for the Fund to be involved in addressing them?

But I think that since monopoly practices were seen as part of the problem by Fund staff, they put these as part of the structural conditionality for the loan.

In a new era of global finance, economic management has to meet the requirements of micro-macro economic consistency that go together with transparency, accountability and good governance. Comparative advantage in microeconomic factors has to develop into competitive advantage. Comparative advantage in microeconomic factors has to develop into competitive advantage (Porter 1998). Of course this is not entirely new. Theoretical links between macroeconomics from micro foundations on the labour market and other areas had been developed since the 1960s.

The close interconnection of micro and macro issues in the management of banking and monetary of policy had been recognized before the Asian crisis, at least among academics associated with the Fund. This was demonstrated in the studies and publications on monetary policy and bank restructuring, amongst others those written by IMF staff (Lindgren 1996, Alexander 1997, Sundararajan 1991 and Enoch 1997).

However, it was the Asian financial crisis of 1997 that demonstrated the need to have consistency between macroeconomics and micro-economics, as argued by Dr. Jesus P. Estanislao, a former Minister of Finance of the Philippines. In addition, there is a need to run parallel tracks of fairness, accountability and transparency, as understood and accepted under globally accepted codes, norms or conventions.[23]

In the meantime, the IMF role in governments' efforts to address the Asian crisis became prominent due to the adoption of adjustment programmes by the three worst-hit crisis countries receiving stand-by loans. In each of the three countries, some micro-macro policy framework figured prominently in both financial and real sectors. In the real sectors the adjustment policies formed the structural conditionality in these stand-by arrangements.

In normal times, a programme of this nature, very complex and involving so many institutions in the implementation, must be preceded by a careful study weighing all the alternatives. The study is a must to get all the necessary information and data as well as the costs and benefits of every alternative available, determine the priorities, etc.

During the crisis governments of affected countries did not have time to weigh all the pros and cons for inviting the IMF and to assess alternatives, etc.

In Indonesia the decision to invite the IMF came after months of concerted but futile efforts by the monetary authorities. For one thing, the rupiah continued to depreciate. In fact, the problems seemed to be spreading from currency depreciation to the banking and other sectors of the economy rapidly. The government decided to invite the IMF to regain market and public confidence. For this, a process for acquiring a stand-by loan had to be followed, starting with a negotiation to formulate the adjustment programme.

Initially, in the framework of a precautionary arrangement, the plan was for the IMF team to come to Indonesia in October for a programme that would be launched in December 1997. However, the dynamic of the problems hastened the process and shifted the exercise into a full-scale stand-by arrangement with an Emergency Financing Mechanism (EFM).

The emergency procedure, in effect, shortened preparation time including negotiations with and decision by the Executive Board, for loan withdrawals. The facility was a good provision in terms of speeding the availability of funds. But the rapidity at which the programme was launched precluded more careful and better preparation. The Fund has admitted in its evaluation on the programmes for Thailand, Indonesia and Korea that some decisions had to be made on the basis of incomplete data and information (Lane 1999, p. 1).

The emergency procedure had only been introduced by the Fund in September 1995, after the Mexican crisis that clearly indicated the need for faster loan disbursement. However, the Indonesian experience showed that the emergency procedure was also associated with higher risk as there was not enough time for all parties to provide the necessary expert input, and accurate data.

It has become fashionable to criticize the IMF for prescribing monetary policies that are too stringent (although similar criticisms have been around since the stand-by arrangement was introduced in the 1950s).

However, the criticism of the Fund's involvement in its response to the Asian crisis was related to the rising number of structural adjustments that were perceived as being imposed. A case in point was the Indonesian LOI of April 1998, which contained a matrix listing 117 steps of structural reforms in fiscal, monetary, banks, investment, privatization, trade, environment, social safety net, and others.[24]

A more careful observation would suggest that the criticism relates to what is popularly known as "IMF therapy". It should be noted that the theory behind the Fund's adjustment programme was the late 1960s monetary approach to the balance of payments, based on the well-known J.J. Polak model (IMF 1977).

The basic tenet of the approach was to treat the balance of payments as a monetary phenomenon, which fitted well with the Fund's position as the guardian of international monetary stability. Even though the monetary approach to the balance of payments worked mostly with monetary variables, it was based on a general equilibrium assumption, which implied that what happened in the monetary variables reflected the real sectors. And thus, the financial programming of the Fund also observed the development of the real sectors. This had been a simple way for justifying the Fund adding structural adjustment of the real sectors. In the Fund-supported programme for developing countries, structural conditionality in the forms of structural benchmarks took on more prominence.[25]

One obvious defect of the monetary approach, in the context of the new environment of global finance with free flows of capital, has been its disregard of the importance of balance sheet effects (of banks). Experts have shown how the balance sheet effects worked during the financial crisis. Basically, an unsound banking sector could constrain the effectiveness of the macroeconomic policy for exchange rate stability. During a financial crisis, the monetary steps taken by the government could push an unsound banking sector into distress and crisis as in Indonesia.

I understood the complexity of the issues that the government had to deal with only during and after actively participating in the negotiation process for the formulation of the programme outlined in the first LOI. What troubled me was related to the fact that, even though macroeconomic problems that had to be addressed were interrelated with microeconomic problems, they were basically different in nature.

It has been widely recognized that monetary policy cannot be effectively implemented in the absence of a robust and sound financial sector, the banking sector in the Asian case, due to its dominant role in their economies. However, a sound banking sector had a lot to do with micro issues, like efficient management and corporate governance. In addition these are by nature medium or even long-term issues. It has also generally been understood that raising interest rates or enforcing tight monetary stance or conducting intervention in the foreign exchange market is a short-term solution. In short, structural adjustments are in general medium-term problems, while monetary policies offer temporary solutions.

Building legal institutions, an incorruptible judiciary, or improving corporate and state governance, can only be long-term goals. So, the problems to be addressed by the programme had different characteristics and their solutions required different time-frames. Even to realize and accept the facts that these are the actual problems to address might be difficult. And, to put them together in a comprehensive package in a two-week negotiation under distressing conditions turned out to be quite challenging to say the least. But this was still the easier part: to implement the programme consistently was even more difficult — as the Indonesian experience shows.

Finally, even if no problems are encountered in the formulation of the adjustment programme due to good cooperation by the host government and the Fund staff such that a workable, realistic Fund-supported programme could be launched, I still find something disconcerting about the process. Fund support is limited to a financial facility that is basically short-run liquidity in the form of balance of payment support. So, the Fund-supported programme looks more like an economic development plan, but the financing is limited to providing general short-term liquidity to support the receiving country's international reserves. Of course, in the Indonesian case as well as the others, there was support from the World Bank and the Asian Development Bank, which to a certain degree takes care of the problem raised here. However, the underlying problem remains.

I conveyed my initial observations to Stanley Fischer through my communication with him towards the end of 1997. He responded by promising that I would be given a forum in a Fund seminar for airing my concerns. I was provided with a forum months after my dismissal from the office. I put these observations more formally in a dinner speech that I gave during a symposium, "Towards the Restoration of Sound Banking System in Japan — Its Global Implications", organized by the IMF office in Tokyo and Kobe University's Research Institute for Economic and Business Administration, Kobe, 4 July 1998.[26]

In the new spirit of more transparency and governance, it is important to assess how the adjustment policies were formulated or designed. This is not to seek blame but in the spirit of learning from experience. With a clear idea of the negotiations with the Fund and subsequent decision-making, one would be able to assess the issue of ownership of adjustment programmes.

Legally, an LOI for a stand-by arrangement is a document containing the adjustment programme of a Fund member country asking for the use of Fund facilities. The facilities are in the form of the right to receive a stipulated loan. As part of the requirements, the government of the member country has to submit a set of measures or adjustment policies to correct the current problems in the balance of payments or the national economy. The programmes belong to the government that makes the proposal; thus, the Fund's claim that the programme is the host country's programme is technically accurate.

However, in a way the host country's claim that some of these measures originate from the Fund is also true. Fund facilities come with *conditionality*. Even if the measures to be implemented are genuinely proposed by the government, they are designed with a view of the Fund's conditionality. In fact, the details of any LOI are usually discussed or negotiated between the government and the Fund's staff before submission to the Fund for the approval. The actual measures and policies that constitute a set of adjustment programmes are the result of negotiation between the government and the Fund.[27]

The term "Fund-supported programme" used in reference to the arrangement properly reflects the reality that the adjustment programmes to be implemented are programmes that are constructed jointly by the government of the receiving member country and the Fund. Of course the government of the member country is the one that has to be responsible for the policies.

In this regard, Fund accountability should be in the form of not disowning any negative implications or even failures of any Fund-supported programme. It is unfortunate that the media in general credits the Fund too much for the successes and vilifies it too much for the failures of Fund-supported programmes, making recipient governments seem powerless.

In response to criticisms, the Managing Director Horst Kohler started to review the Fund's operations not long after assuming his position, in particular looking at *structural conditionality* for possible streamlining. In general, the improvements address the issue of the extent of structural conditionality that ultimately reduces the sense of ownership of the host government. The improvement is directed towards focusing on the core function of the Fund, i.e. maintaining monetary and balance of payment stability.[28]

The Fund also created a new *Independent Evaluation Office* that comprised of experts from the Fund as well as academics recruited to make a study and evaluation of the IMF role in three crisis countries, Indonesia, Korea and Brazil. The main objectives of the study were (1) to draw lessons for the staff, management and Executive Board of the IMF in its future operational work and (2) to identify the processes by which important decisions were made, with a view to increasing transparency.[29]

These moves by the Fund are commendable and may signal a turning point for the institution in response to calls by some of its critics to be less rigid without reducing its effectiveness. The turning point in some countries receiving stand-by loans was preceded by a change in their respective governments. This may also be the case with the Fund that launched changes since the new management with Horst Kohler at the helm.

The Asian crisis indeed acted as a wake-up call for the Fund, and other affected parties for that matter, to take a hard look at the role that this institution should play as guardian of world monetary and financial stability. The Fund is expected to a certain degree to act as a lender of last resort for member countries, in a world economy that is characterized by global finance with free capital movements. This is a very tall order. The fact that the Asian crisis turned out to be worse than most expectations had a profound impact on international efforts to reform the Fund and the other related institutions.

From my experience of negotiating the first LOI that constituted the Indonesian Fund-Supported Programme as well as my observation afterwards, I can see that the Fund has been making efforts to be more flexible, even though I cannot help but state that the process has been very slow indeed. The reform of the Fund's operations, especially when it comes to deciding on conditionality, is something that should really be welcomed.

However, I still have some general concerns. I think the Asian crisis has reminded many governments and the Fund as well as other institutions about the complexity of the problems any country faces with free movements of capital across national economies. Everyone has been convinced on the need for a sound financial system to support sustainable macroeconomic policies, which include recognition of the close linkages between business operations at a micro level and macroeconomic management, the financial and the real sectors of the economy, as well as between economic management and a social and political systems.

Against this backdrop, the Fund is reforming itself to focus its operations and surveillance on its core function. All are welcome moves in the right direction, but one problem remains. To negotiate

TABLE 12

Indonesia's Financial Position in the Fund as of 31 March 2002

I. Membership Status: Joined: 21 February 1967; Article VIII

II. General Resources Account:	**Rupiah Million**	**% Quota**
Quota	2,079.30	100.00
Fund holdings of currency	9,002.12	432.94
Reserve position in Fund	145.48	7.00
Holdings Exchange Rate		

III. SDR Department:	**Rupiah Million**	**% Allocation**
Net cumulative allocation	238.96	100.00
Holdings	17.70	7.41

IV. Outstanding Purchases and Loans:	**Rupiah Million**	**% Quota**
Stand-by arrangements	1,834.56	88.23
Extended arrangements	5,233.74	251.71

V. Latest Financial Arrangements:

Type	**Approval** Date	**Expiry** Date	**Amount Approved** (Rupiah Million)	**Amount Drawn** (Rupiah Million)
Quota			2,079.30	100.00
EFF	04 Feb 2000	31 Dec 2003	3,638.00	1,436.04
EFF	25 Aug 1998	04 Feb 2000	5,383.10	3,797.70
Stand-by	05 Nov 1997	25 Aug 1998	8,338.24	3,669.12

Source: IMF

and construct a programme encompassing all these elements in a short time, under stressful conditions, resorting to the only available instrument in the form of liquidity support from the Fund, is basically too much to ask.

Lessons for All Parties

What are the lessons from the Indonesian crisis and the various policies that have attempted to cope with it? From Indonesia's experience, and possibly that of other countries, I believe there are three crucial requirements for policies addressing contagion to be effective in the sense of producing a turning point and sustainable recovery. They are: prompt acknowledgment and acceptance of the crisis, prompt action to design workable adjustment policies, and consistent implementation. Strong growth in the world economy, the locomotives in particular, would of course help. In addition, a sustainable recovery should encompass a new paradigm for managing a national economy in the framework of global economics and finance that includes micro-macro consistency, governance and transparency within a democratic framework.

The implementation of the Indonesian adjustment policy has been littered with inconsistencies. Indeed, inconsistencies have been the main features of Indonesian policy implementation. Indonesia muddled through attempts to resolve the crisis by the governments under Soeharto, Habibie and Abdulrahman Wahid. Even the Megawati government seems to follow this pattern. Despite better macroeconomic conditions and prompt policy responses at the onset, Indonesia has experienced a protracted crisis.

Changes of government seemed to serve well to produce a turning points to stop economic deterioration in Korea and Thailand. To a certain degree, this has also been the case with Indonesia, but at a much slower pace. This seems to also be the case of changes in Fund policy. Serious efforts to improve the Fund structural conditionality and to focus its operations have come only after changes of the Fund management, from Michel Camdessus and Stanley Fischer to Horst Kohler and Anne Krueger, and other key positions in the management.

Relations between the present Indonesian government and the Fund seem to be in better shape. The Fund has been learning some lessons from managing the crisis in Indonesia as shown in its views on budget deficits, corporate debt, and social implications of the crisis. The Fund has been streamlining its structural conditionality. Similarly, the Indonesian economic team has been showing willingness to make the required adjustments.

However, the problems and challenges facing Megawati's government have been much more daunting, due to the continuing past practices of policy inconsistency and worsening world economic prospects. For example, facing a slowing down of the national economy, the government cannot automatically resort to the conventional policy of fiscal stimuli or loose monetary policy. With a budget already suffering from deficit, any fiscal stimuli is constrained already. And, to add to the constraints, the size of a budget deficit tolerated is predetermined in the performance criteria. Likewise, lowering the interest rate or adding base money is constrained by the performance criteria.

The government hand's are tied. The degree of freedom in macroeconomic management is limited, due to the existing Fund-supported programme. The nature and magnitude of the problems in a new environment of a learning process of democracy and transparency have even made the government seem occasionally indecisive, which ultimately adds to the problems. In fact inertia seems rampant.

Flexibility by both the Fund as well as the monetary authority should be in order here. The issues of tight monetary stance and a high rate of interest have come and gone. In the meantime some empirical studies have been demonstrating the ineffectiveness of high rates of interest for stabilizing exchange rates.[30]

Of course, to the claim that a high rate of interest is not an effective instrument for defending the exchange rate, one could cite how Hong Kong successfully saved its currency against the onslaught of a speculative attack in October 1997. A high rate of interest indeed does not impact negatively on economic growth in the short run. However, high rates of interest for a long period are definitely detrimental to economic growth. Problems will arise when the high rate of interest is extended for a long period.

During the crisis we observed a rapid shift of problems confronting banks from a liquidity crunch to solvency. A high rate of interest, which may be effective in the short run to strengthen the currency, could easily have negative implications in the long term.

In this respect, the new Fund policy of focusing on its core functions is definitely a step in the right direction. Included is its concern over the issue of ownership of the Fund-supported programme. The more cumbersome the conditionality, the more pressure by the superpowers to impose their own agenda on the structural conditionality of the Fund-supported programme, the more difficult would be for the government to consistently implement the programme.

Until 11 September 2001, all the problems and challenges facing President Megawati originated from the previous administration. However, the terrorist attacks in the US and the US-led response that triggered a world economic recession have been causing additional challenges for the President and her Cabinet. This time there is no strong US economy to serve as a locomotive to make the necessary pull. The Megawati government, which made a sensible start, seems also stalling to follow up the good start with the right steps to accelerate. The past government missed the chance to start a recovery process. The present government made a good start, but seems to be giving up before entering a recovery process.

Recent improvements have given some breathing space. But they cannot provide the national economy with more needed certainty and safety for doing business, returning parked capital abroad as well as new foreign investments. The political elite has not been forthcoming in terms of their resolve to address the national issues; it is unlikely that a breakthrough will come soon.

8

Epilogue

Caveat

Since the beginning, I have been confronted with a dilemma in the writing of this book. One motive for writing this book has been the wish to share with the public my observations, assessments as well as analysis about a crisis that has had an impact on all aspects of life in Indonesia. The crisis has been an extraordinary period for the Indonesian economy. However, due to my former position as one of the key players in the government, that strong wish has been clouded with an uneasy feeling concerning possible criticism of self-defence or self-justification about whatever role I played in it.

My assessments may, of course, be affected by hindsight, or even normative values as part of my wish for something to have happened, instead of what actually did happen. I have been aware of these issues from the beginning of the endeavour. I even blame its long-delayed completion to this dilemma.

However, I write this book not as an apologia. To those who in fact perceive it this way, I would like to assure you that this is not the intention.

The crisis and its implications and the effort to resolve them are still unfolding. So, the story will continue, even though the players have changed. Much has been written about the crisis, and I am sure there will be more accounts. It is hoped that this book will complement them. Through this the public could ultimately receive a complete and accurate picture of what went on during this important period.

I have also been confronted with a classic problem of history writing, i.e. to determine when to start and when to end. The issues and problems continue, which complicates the determination of when to end the narration. For practical reasons, the focus of these discussions has been on the period of my term at the central bank. So in general the analysis starts with the beginning of the financial crisis in July 1997 and ends with my dismissal in February 1998.

Many of the assessments or analyses in this book may have originated from discussions with my colleagues in Bank Indonesia or other institutions in the government. However, I have tried my best to identify the original sources in such cases.

This account is not based on interviews with other colleagues who were in charge during the crisis, my colleagues within the central bank nor those with authority over me. This book is more of putting together records, analyses and assessments of the events as I observed them. However, I am responsible for the assessments and evaluations which my colleagues or others may find incorrect or incomplete.

It is my wish that other players and observers of this very important, if unfortunate and sad, episode of our national economy will also publish their views and analyses so we will get a complete and accurate assessment of the multifaceted crisis that struck Indonesia. These efforts will contribute positively to the future management of our national economy, and enhance welfare and prosperity in a new development paradigm that cares more about equality, fairness, democracy and — one that respects governance and transparency.

A Multi-dimensional and Protracted Crisis

Several points below show the link between the short period of events that have been the focus of the discussions in this book and the periods prior to as well as after the crisis. These points show the problems confronting the national economy as well as the steps taken by the government to address them, which underline the questions and the possible answers to the multi-dimensional and protracted crisis that Indonesian has been experiencing.

Debate on the origin of the crisis

I would argue that Indonesia's crisis was multi-dimensional. Empirical studies on the Asian crisis have shown that Indonesia, despite its similarities with other crisis countries, showed unique characteristics.

The Indonesian crisis originated from an external shock in the foreign exchange market as part of the regional contagion. The financial shock revealed weaknesses of the national economy, both in the financial sector — the unsound banking system and unsustainable corporate debt in foreign exchange — and the real sectors, low efficiency and practices of crony capitalism. Through the failure of government policies to address problems, which include the Fund cum U.S. Treasury's roles, a vicious downward spiral revealed weaknesses in Indonesia's social and political fabric. Ultimately, Indonesia experienced a multi-dimensional crisis.

The argument here is in line with saying that weaknesses in the banking sector, corporate debt, the real sector as well as the socio-economy caused Indonesia's sensitivity to external shocks.

In the Indonesian crisis, the external financial shock served as a trigger to the domestic contagion. I would argue that the trigger did not have to be the financial shock from Thailand. In my opinion, if there was no external shock from Thailand, the trigger could have originated from social disorder of the nature that Indonesia experienced during the crisis.[1]

The political economy argument provides us with additional explanations. Most economists who accept the effect of the external triggers, whether from the herd instincts of market players or the moral hazard associated with a soft fixed-exchange system or the presence of government guarantees in bank lending, do not try to explain why people change their attitudes and take actions that trigger a chain reaction (contagion).

The political economy approach explains why the government would not allow the currency to depreciate rapidly, or to let corporations go under, in spite of its inability to implement the policy. The government's moves ultimately caused a moral hazard. These efforts were based on political calculation, either through the use of voting or other means, including protests and demonstrations (Haggard 2000, Horowitz and Heo 2001).

Programmes to address crisis

Adjustment steps and programmes to address the crisis had been formulated in the first two letters of intent to the Fund in October 1997 and January 1998. The Fund-supported adjustment programmes of Indonesia may stand as the most comprehensive programmes for addressing the crisis with the assistance of the multilateral institution. The programme comprised of a macroeconomic framework to solve the current account imbalances, supported by prudent monetary and fiscal policies, a comprehensive restructuring of financial institutions, economic reforms of the real sectors, and enhancing governance and transparency.

In spite of the general consensus on the crucial role of the weaknesses of the banking sector and unsustainable corporate debt, the Fund-supported programme did not fully address the issue until some time later. With respect to the corporate debt problem, aside from mentioning the amount and its composition in the first letter of intent, no attempt was made to deal with it in the early stages.

Efforts to deal with the corporate debt problem were only initiated after the signing of the second letter of intent in mid-January 1998. The follow-up has also been slow partly due to conflicts of interest.

It is my contention that the government's delay in addressing the corporate debt problem was caused by the Fund's reluctance to deal with the issue initially. As explained earlier, the Fund position on the issue was nothing more than telling the Indonesian government not to bail out the corporate debtors. While the government should not bail out corporate debts, a clear-cut policy for assisting companies in difficulty at the outset could have avoided the situation getting out of hand. But the fact that the problem has lingered must be due to the lack of government resolve to deal with the real issues. All parties ultimately fail the test of the requirement of "the sooner the better" in dealing with a crisis.

With respect to the comprehensive restructuring of the financial sector, the first two letters of intent had actually shown all the necessary steps. Included in these two documents were steps to liquidate 16 banks that turned controversial due to its failure to achieve what was intended. Closing insolvent banks is a correct decision. However, how and when to do it seems to be a more complex decision. The Indonesian experience seems to show that closing banks in a systemic way in a fragile banking industry is not advisable.

Several other steps, including the adoption of a blanket guarantee, the setting up of IBRA, improvement of banking institutions that included better legislation, and granting the central bank its independence, had all been formulated in the first two letters of intent. What emerged in all the other 16 letters of intent under the three presidents in succession up to President Megawati were a continuous process of adjustments and improvements in the process of implementing stand-by arrangements with the Fund.

I have discussed three areas of policy that could be classified as controversial: the decision to provide the banking sector with liquidity support during the crisis, the debates over adopting a fixed exchange system with a currency board, and granting the central bank its autonomy. Of the three, provision of liquidity support to banks during the crisis has been the most controversial. The policy started to become a controversy since the Supreme Audit Board's report on Bank Indonesia in July 2000 claimed that most of the liquidity support to banks was not in accordance with the general rules of the central bank. It was argued further that there were irregularities in the channelling of the facility as well as the utilization of the liquidity. The huge amount of the support, the alleged irregularities, and the implication of the burden to the government budget, have all caused the policy to become controversial.

Bank Indonesia, after some public debates, issued a formal statement maintaining its position that the liquidity support decision was an implementation of the government's policy not liquidating banks and to providing assistance to banks facing problems. The facility was given to prevent the banking sector from collapsing during the crisis. It was an implementation of government policy, which Bank Indonesia was part of and dependent upon, in its function as lender of last resort.

Public perception that the central bank and the receiving banks were at fault has been based largely on the claims of the Supreme Audit Board. The Central Bank has been wronged for providing liquidity support to banks, instead of freezing or liquidating them. The recipient banks have been criticized because of their misuses of the facility. Losses were incurred. Since the government has to bear the potential losses, there are allegations of corrupt practices in the central bank as well as the receiving banks. In its calculation of potential losses, the Supreme Audit Board added up all the liquidity support that had been provided up to a certain date, i.e. position as January 1999, i.e. 134.5 trillion rupiah.

It is unfortunate that Bank Indonesia only came up with its position on the issue very late. In a recent publication (Bank Indonesia 2002), the Central Bank shows that there were irregularities in the audit itself. The Central Bank's position is that the audit was a compliance audit and that it was based on a rule that was valid for normal conditions. But the situation during the crisis was completely different. Certainly, resorting to normal instruments would not have helped, thus the need to resort to liquidity support.

There is a strong tendency for many to forget the link between the liquidity support and the formation of IBRA. The public debate seems not to reflect the fact that IBRA was established to take care of problem banks. But why did Bank Indonesia submit those banks to IBRA's supervision? Bank Indonesia made the submission due to these banks' inability to repay the liquidity support that they had received. With the submission of these banks to IBRA, the right to claim the liquidity support went with the transfer.

It is unfortunate that the Supreme Audit Board also disregarded the link between the formation of IBRA and the liquidity support. Defining the potential loss to the state as the sum of all the liquidity support channelled by the central bank to the receiving banks with total disregard of asset recoveries by IBRA is definitely misleading. Even if there were mark-ups on the assets of banks and debtors of banks, there are some assets that cannot simply be dismissed. The correct potential loss should be calculated from the total liquidity support minus estimated asset recovery. Of course, in accounting terms all the liquidity support acknowledged by receiving banks become assets of the government (IBRA), and there is no loss until they are realized.

IBRA itself has suffered from political interventions since its birth. From its establishment in February 1998 to 2002, it already experienced six changes of director. The position of the director is in high demand and the disregard of the link between the liquidity support and the claims on assets associated with them must be due to the fact that IBRA has enormous authority over huge assets. At the same time, no one wants to deal with the liquidity support, which after all was one of the reasons for its formation. These changes constrain its performance.

The last point seems to confirm its dismal performance as compared to similar institutions in neighbouring countries. Up to the beginning of 2001, IBRA asset sales were only 7 per cent of the total assets it accepted at the beginning of its operations. This is a very poor performance compared to Thailand with 70 per cent, Korea with 48 per cent and Malaysia with 61 per cent.[2]

Exchange rate management

In terms of exchange rate policy, the government's initial response to the external shock was to stick with the current managed floating with a band by widening the band from 8 per cent to 12 per cent. By the time Indonesia took the step on 11 July 1997 it was the only exchange management that still relied on managed floating in the region. All the others were either already practicing a floating system or had turned to it. Ultimately, Indonesia adopted a floating system on 14 August 1997. This system has been maintained ever since, in spite of public debate now and then for resorting to a fixed system with a currency board. This would also include a fixed system with exchange control, Malaysian-style.

The business community and the public have been concerned that since the floating of the currency, Indonesia has been experiencing drastic depreciation of the rupiah and continuing uncertainty about the exchange rate. On the other hand, despite its continuing uncertainty and a rupiah that has been far from pre-crisis levels, the government and Bank Indonesia seem to be firm in their position to stick with a floating system.

In the meantime, new conventional wisdom seems to suggest that a sustainable exchange system is either a free-floating system or a hard-pegged (hard fixed) system. The fixed system means one with a currency board (Fischer 2001; Williamson 2000).[3] I would add in the hard fixed system, an arrangement for a fixed exchange system with exchange control, Malaysia-style. However, after the collapse of Argentina's currency board in May 2002, I am afraid less people will trust this technique.

In practice, the most important requirement for an exchange system is how consistently it is implemented. In the case of a fixed system with a currency board the consistency includes government discipline not to intervene in the market. The government has to see that the supporting institutions, including the legal system and the judiciary, work well. In the case of exchange control, the institution in charge has to execute its task transparently without intervention.

In a hard-pegged system as practiced in Hong Kong, aside from consistent implementation, the stability of its exchange rate is supported by ample reserves. It seems that for practical reasons an important factor that convinces the market is the size of foreign reserves held by its monetary authority as proposed by Martin Feldstein in his "self help guide to emerging markets" (Feldstein 1999).

In the case of a freely floating system the monetary authority cannot intervene in the market. It has not been clear whether countries that recently adopted a freely floating systems have indeed been disciplined enough not to make any market interventions. For sure, Indonesia has intervened in the market from time to time. In other words, a true freely floating system is still an exception.

An important determining factor for the market to make a move whenever confronted with changing conditions is the perception of market players. If an economy implements a fixed system, and the government is perceived to be unable to defend the system, market players would make a move to save their investments — similar to a flight to safety in banking — that would naturally adversely impact on the exchange rate. In the midst of huge, free flowing funds, the monetary authority would not be able to defend the currently adopted exchange system.

As explained before, the above phenomenon has been what many countries in Asia which adopted fixed or managed exchange systems experienced during the crisis. The market players held that these countries pegged their currencies to the dollar, and that these countries could not defend the system in the face of global funds freely flowing from place to place.

The main argument is as follows. Market perception was that the fixed exchange system adopted by the crisis countries was not sustainable and that the monetary authorities of these countries could not defend their exchange system due to weak fundamentals. In this condition, the monetary authorities were in a similar position to banks facing systemic runs.[4] Many central banks did, in effect, adopt systems not fundamentally different from the previous ones.[5] The question is why are market perceptions any different now? What is the rationale for arguing that market perception determines the sustainability of the exchange system that a country adopts? In this respect, despite popular arguments otherwise, it is difficult for me to accept claims that the pre-crisis exchange system in Indonesia was a fixed one.

The above questions, plus the experience of Malaysia with its exchange controls, seem to underline an argument that the real issue is not about the choice of exchange system, but about how to deal with the free flows of global capital.[6]

Postscript

Writing this book has taken far too long. Aside from my limited writing proficiency, this has also been due to a variety of reasons including deciding which issues to include, how detailed the discussions should be, the relevance of each issue, and the mentioning of names. In addition, there have been personal problems that have been distracting.

I have spent many days and hours testifying in public hearings in the Parliament and answering questions, the Police Headquarters in the process of interrogations by the Attorney General's Office, or testimonies in courts on cases of alleged corruptions in the provision and utilization of Bank Indonesia liquidity support. From end 1999 to the present all these testimonies and interrogations have cost me months of concentration and writing time. In May 2002, I was myself named as a suspect in a case alleging that, together with other members of Bank Indonesia's board of directors, I violated my authority by providing liquidity support to banks that caused trillion rupiahs worth of losses to the state.

The Indonesian crisis lingers on and recovery seems elusive.

Indonesia has been faring badly in comparison to the performance of other crisis countries that also resorted to the Fund's stand-by arrangements. Thailand, which asked for stand-by arrangement in August 1997, did not need to use the whole facility due to its faster recovery. Korea used up the whole facility. However, Korea has already made repayments on most of the facility (Supplement Reserve Facility) that the country received since December 1997. In the Fund evaluation of its support to the Asian crisis countries in 2000 the concern was for these countries becoming complacent because the Korean recovery happened so fast.[1]

The development of the crisis and its resolution in Korea and Thailand has been in reverse to what happened in Indonesia. If the two other countries no longer need the Fund and the stand-by arrangements, Indonesia is badly in need of both the Fund as well as its support for gaining back market confidence

By the end of 2000 or two years after the beginning of the IMF's involvement in Indonesia's efforts to address the crisis, Indonesia had experienced four cancellations of its withdrawals of the loan due to non-compliance or delay in the fulfillment of the conditionality. In the same year, the World Bank, ADB and the Japanese government postponed disbursements of some of their loans. So, it was clear that the multilateral institutions as well as other governments had used the Fund's decision as their reference. Similarly, negotiations with the government's creditors, both in the Paris Club, as well as the London Club, depended on the Fund's review of the implementation of the stand-by arrangements.

I am sure the players in the capital as well as the currency and financial markets also used the Fund's evaluations on Indonesia when making decisions. Given the lack of reliable information from Indonesia's monetary authorities themselves, their dependence on the Fund's evaluations is high. In addition, the Asian crisis has caused most financial supervisary authorities to be more stringent. On top of this, the world economy post-11 September 2001 has been tainted with shocking events like the bearish capital markets due to plummeting "dotcom" companies, the fall of Enron and Andersen and their aftermath, the weakening of the mighty dollar, etc. These uncertainties looming over the world economy and global finance only create additional constraints for the sustainable recovery of the Indonesian economy.

These realities that are sometimes ignored or least misunderstood by Indonesian politicians or even some government officials at the cost of the country's recovery. On the other hand, there has also been a tendency for government officials and politicians to display helplessness in the face of the complexity and enormity of the problems. Since the problems have become more complex and increasingly larger over time and since any action the government takes bears a bigger risk of failure, there is a tendency for the government to take no action, to wait and see. The government's inertia and the market's wait-and-see attitude can only make things worse.

In the face of a less promising world economy and uncertain financial prospects, what could be said about the main discussions of this book on managing the central bank as part of the national efforts toward sustainable recovery? I think the most important message that I would like to share here is that a better understanding about the past problems is still very important. In a dynamic environment it may seem a waste of time to look back, after all the future is still uncertain, so what's the use of assessing the past which will not repeat itself? However, I think looking back is still important, even in a dynamic world. We could at least not repeat old mistakes in the new environment.

In the longer term, it is imperative for policymakers to understand the interconnections and the implications of one particular policy on another. Only in this manner will decision-makers see the possible consequences of choosing a particular path and be prepared to bear the risks of their decisions.

In the midst of a high degree of uncertainty and inertia, for fear of taking risks, decision-makers may optimize their policies by being eclectic. In monetary economics and finance some would argue for some "rule" instead of "discretion" due to their belief that the monetary sector should not add to the uncertainties of the real sector. Recently, the contagion effect has hit other sectors. I am referring to how Andersen collapsed due to the herd instinct of its clients abandoning the company in the manner of bank clients deserting their bank in a bank run. In this environment, eclecticism could build confidence in stages, both for the policymakers, as well as the market players who observe the process. In this manner, uncertainties that have constrained all parties could be avoided. Certainties could be constructed in stages together with confidence building. This could give a clear perspective for the market players and the general public in their respective activities for getting out of a downward spiral to move to a virtuous cycle of sustainable development.

Indonesia's efforts to pinpoint who was responsible for the crisis, with popular targets being former officials, outsiders (like the Fund or speculators), or the system, has not been able to shed light on how our nation can emerge from the doldrums. Even in valid cases, this has not been a productive way to find a resolution. The crisis sometimes seems to continue to linger on, with no sign of a full recovery.

It is hoped that a clearer picture of all the old problems and issues as well as policies implemented, will emerge. This is very important for formulating steps to be taken by the government, the private sector and the general public to form a synergy for economic recovery and development in a new paradigm of democracy, governance and transparency.

Notes

Prologue: The Crisis and Me

1   This stipulation is similar to Article 48 of the new Central Bank Law No. 23, 1999.

2   The SEACEN Governors are governors of central banks and heads of monetary authorities, comprising Korea, Malaysia, Mongolia, Myanmar, Nepal, the Philippines, Singapore, Ceylon, China-Taipei, Thailand and Indonesia. During this meeting there were only 10 members, since Mongolia had not joined yet. However, governors of the Central Banks of Samoa, Tonga and Fiji were also present as guests.

3   See *Republika*, 16 February 1998 and *Gatra*, 21 February 1998, which reported the plan to replace me with Syahril Sabirin.

4   Several dailies and weeklies in Jakarta, including *Business News*, *Merdeka*, *Republika*, *Jawa Post*, *Tiras*, and others, carried similar reports in their 20 February 1998 edition.

5   *Suara Pembaruan*, 18 February 1998, http://suarapembaruan.com/News/1998/02/180298/Headline/h102/h102htm. Several newspapers in Jakarta reported the government's announcement with titles such: "Soedradjad goes back to the Campus" and "Soedradjad will go back to his Teaching Job".

6   For examples, see "Soedradjad's Voice after his Freedom", *Merdeka Minggu*, February 1998, and "It's Embarrassing, Retreating before the War is Over", *Republika*, 10 February 1998.

7   All of these reports were published in *Suara Pembaruan*, 11 February 1998, http://www.suarapembaruan.com/News/1988/02/110298/Ekonomi/ekl/ekl.html.

8   Several sources told me that President Soeharto always did his reading, including several Indonesian papers, every day after his morning prayers. So he must have followed the debate about the CBS as reported in the press.

9   Taken from several editions of *Suara Pembaruan*, some statements were made after their meetings with President Soeharto between the second to last week of February 1998. One of the reports was entitled "G-7 asked Indonesia to

Cancel its Plan to Adopt CBS", http://suarapembaruan.com/News/1998/02/220298/Headline/hioi/hioi.html.

10 *Prospek*, 2 March 1998.

11 *Xpos*, no. 08/I, 21–27 February, 1998. The last attack had appeared in the publication *Konspirasi Menggoyang Soeharto*. [Conspiracy to Rock Soeharto]. (Kumpulan Selebaran Paling Aktual, November 1997).

12 See footnote 24, Chap. 4.

Chapter 1: Introduction

1 He seemed to think that the Indonesian crisis tarnished his image as Indonesia's "Father of Development".

2 See Peter Montagnon and Sander Thoenes, "Rupiah's Defensive Walls Turned out to be Built on Sand", *Financial Times*, Weekend, 14–15 March 1998, and Jose Manuel Tesoro, "Once a Castle in the Sand: The Central Banker is Focused on Rebuilding", *Asiaweek*, 6 February 1998.

Chapter 2: Origin of the Crisis and Early Responses

1 Bank Indonesia, *Report for the Financial Year 1994/95* (Jakarta: Bank Indonesia, May 1995), p. 23.

2 It should be mentioned here that during that period, the daily volume of foreign exchange trading in Jakarta was approximately US$4 billion. This daily trading had been increasing from US$1.5 billion in early 1980s, to US$8 billion in mid-1997.

3 Flights to safety by rich Indonesians transforming their rupiah assets into dollars have occurred every time social tensions rose, whether they originated from economic, social or political causes. Dollar purchase has been popular since the government made the rupiah convertible in the 1970s. Traditionally, the flight to safety was done through buying land or gold.

4 See also, Overview of the Proceeding of a Conference on Macroeconomic Issues for Asian Countries, organized by Bank Indonesia and the IMF, Jakarta 7–8 November 1996, *Macroeconomic Issues Facing Asean Countries*, edited by John Hicklin, David Robinson and Anoop Singh (Washington D.C.: IMF, 1997).

5 Articles and books on the Asian crisis flourished almost immediately upon its outbreak. Some authors used more dramatic expressions, like Leo Gough, *Asia Meltdown* (Oxford: Capstone, 1998), Callum Henderson, *Asia Falling* (New York: MacGraw-Hill 1998), Michael Backman, *Asian Elipse*, (Singapore: John Wiley & Sons 2001).

6 Institute of International Finance, *Capital Flows to Emerging Economies* (Washington D.C.: IIF, 29 January 1998). Also see a description by the World Bank that mentioned the downgrading of Indonesia's sovereign and corporate ratings by Standard & Poor's and Moody's during this short period in

"Indonesia in Crisis: A Macroeconomic Update", a document produced by the World Bank for the Paris meeting of the Consultative Group on Indonesia (CGI) in July 1998.

7   Stephan Haggard raised this issue. His study attempts to address the question of why market sentiment changed (Haggard 2000).

8   World Bank, "Addressing the Social Impacts of the Crisis in Indonesia: A Background Note for the 1998 CGI", mimeo.

9   This figure is the lowest estimate of private capital outflows in that year. Other estimates put the figures between US$25 billion and US$40 billion.

10 As quoted by Lim Say Boon in his column, "The Art of the Possible", *Far Eastern Economic Review (FEER)*, 4 February 1999.

11 See Kevin Muehring, "Grasping Greenspanomics", *Institutional Investor*, (June 1993), and David M. Jones, *The Politics of Money: The Fed under Alan Greenspan*, (New York: NYIF Corp. Simon Schuster, 1991).

12 The conceptual argument of the managed floating system was explained in the Bank Indonesia annual report in my first year as governor, *Bank Indonesia: Report for the Financial Year 1993/94* (Jakarta: Bank Indonesia, May 1994), and the following year. I explained the concept and its ramifications on different occasions to the banking community.

13 Callum Henderson, in his book, *Asia Falling*, wrote an accurate explanation of the concept based on an interview with me before its publication.

14 See, "Exchange Rate Policy", *Bank Indonesia, Annual Report, 1994/95* (Jakarta: Bank Indonesia, 1995).

15 The CGI is a forum between the government of Indonesia and its creditor countries or institutions, which was formed in 1990 to replace the previous similar forum, the Intergovernmental Group on Indonesia (IGGI) formed in the late 1960s. The IGGI comprised of 18 countries plus a number of multilateral agencies, like the World Bank, the IMF, the Asian Development Bank, the UNDP, and other institutions. The Minister of Development Aid from the Netherlands chaired the IGGI.

16 See Andrew Berg, "The Asia Crisis: Causes, Policy Responses, and Outcomes", IMF Working Paper, no. 138, 1999, Table 3, p. 15.

17 The annual interest rate for Bank Indonesia certificates (SBI) with two-month maturity was raised from 11 per cent to 22 per cent, while the three month SBI rate was raised from 11.5 per cent to 30 per cent.

18 The prominent issues in hearings of Bank Indonesia's Governor in the Finance and Banking Committee of the Parliament prior to the crisis were the high percentage of non-performing loans of commercial banks, the related issue of bank lending and violations of the legal lending, limits. All these problems reflected unsound banking practices. See also the study by Imam Sugema "Banking Sector and Economic Collapses".

19 Two books that record and analyse these matters comprehensively are Binhadi, *Financial Sector Deregulation, Banking Development and Monetary Policy: The Indonesian Experience 1983–1993* (Jakarta: IBI, 1995) and David C. Cole and Betty F. Slade, *Building a Modern Financial System* (New York: Cambridge University Press, 1996).

20 The announcement was widely reported in the media, amongst others, "Ten Steps to Stimulate Economic Recovery", *Republika*, 4 September 1997.

21 President's Directives and Decisions in Special Cabinet Meeting on Economics, Finance, Development Supervision, Production and Distribution (Jakarta: Bina Graha, 1997, mimeo).

22 Taken from *Gatra*, 18 October 1997.

23 "Camdessus Announces IMF Support for Indonesia's Economic Program", IMF News Brief, no. 97/19, 8 October 1997.

24 The initial correspondence between the GOI and the IMF as well as the Indonesian Executive Director clearly used the term "precautionary arrangement". After the arrival of the IMF mission, this became "stand-by arrangement".

25 There is sometimes confusion as to what constitutes an LOI and an MEFP. On the IMF website, http://www.imf.org/external/np/loi/mempuba.html, the definitions of LOI and MEFP are identical. Publicly, both the letter and the MEFP are usually called the letter of intent. Strictly speaking, the LOI is the covering letter that explains the aim of the member country for requesting to use the IMF facility by submitting an adjustment programme that explains all the steps to be taken to address the problems that the member country is currently facing.

26 Indonesia's quota then was 1.497 billion rupiah, or US$2.078 billion.

27 See *Indonesia: Summary of Disbursements and Repayments*, January 1970–31 August 2000 in the IMF website, /http://www.imf.org/external/np/tre…ey=440&stardate=1970&enddate=2000.

28 Indonesia reentered the IMF at the beginning of the New Order government under President Soeharto in February 1967, after leaving the institution during the heyday of the previous government under Soekarno.

29 As an example, *Suara Pembaruan* reporting government critics, like Dr. Rizal Ramli, "Don't Hurry to Ask for IMF Support", 9 October 1997.

30 On the different IMF facilities, see IMF, "Financial Organization and Operations of the IMF", Pamphlet Series No. 45, and Review of Fund Facilities — Preliminary Considerations, 2 March 2000, http://www.imf.org/external/np/pdr/fac/2000/index.html.

31 Paul Blustein in his book, *The Chastening: Inside the Crisis that Rocked the Global Financial System and Humbled the IMF* (New York: Public Affairs, 2001), showed that in all crisis countries which sought IMF help, Thailand, Indonesia, Korea,

Russia and Brazil, intervention by the G-7, and the United States in particular, in the formulation of IMF-supported programmes in these countries was apparent.

32   See Indonesia's LOI to the IMF, 31 October 1997, item number 21.

33   See "IMF's Prolonged Role in Indonesia Questioned", *Jakarta Post*, 15 December 2001.

34   See also Robert W. Hefner, *Civil Islam: Muslims and Democratization in Indonesia* (Princeton, NY: Princeton University Press, 2000), pp. 201–7.

35   As mentioned by Dr. Stanley Fischer to the Governor of Bank Indonesia, in the follow up to our meeting in Jakarta on 1 October 1997, the term being used was "precautionary". Likewise, a letter written by Indonesian ED in IMF, Dr. Subarjo Joyosumarto on 2 October 1997 to the GOI mentioned "An IMF Mission to Study the Possibility of Implementing a Precautionary Arrangement".

Chapter 3: Stabilization and Reform Programmes

1   Aside from the side letters and the letter on intervention, these documents can be downloaded from the IMF website, http://www.imf.org/external/np/loi/html/.

2   The Southeast Asian Group comprises of Brunei Darussalam, Cambodia, Fiji, Indonesia, Lao PDR, Malaysia, Myanmar, Nepal, Singapore, Thailand, Tonga, and Vietnam.

3   IMF News Briefs, No. 97/22, "Camdessus Comments on Indonesia's Actions", (31 October 1997).

4   In Indonesia, liquidating gold reserves, or even lending it, is always avoided by the government for the "psychological" reasons that doing so might create the wrong impression that the government is going bankrupt.

5   Bank Indonesia announcement, "Siaran Pers" (Press News), 15 May 2000.

6   IMF Staff Report, *Recovery from the Asian Crisis and the Role of the IMF*, http://www.imf. org/external/np/exr/ib/2000/062300.html/.

7   See also, William E. Alexander et al., *Systemic Bank Restructuring and Macroeconomic Policy* (Washington D.C.: IMF, 1997), and Stijn Claessens et al., "Financial Restructuring in East Asia: Half Way There?". World Bank Financial Sector Discussion Paper No. 3, 1999.

8   IMF, *Strengthening the Bank Rehabilitation Effort*, volume II and I (Washington D.C.: IMF, December 1997). The team that dealt with the bank restructuring programme under the stand-by arrangement continued the study. The team also included staff from the U.S. Treasury and ADB. The team made reports, in March, Jun, and August 1998 respectively, entitled, "Resolving the Banking Crisis: Bank Restructuring and Related Issues", prepared by Charles Enoch et al., mimeo.

9   Hassanali Mehran et al., "Indonesia: Bank Liquidation and Resolution", Washington D.C.: IMF, 31 August 1994, mimeo.

10   *Suara Pembaruan*, 10 November 1997.

11   In the Indonesian banking system then, based on the prudential measures that were calculated from their compliance to the requirements concerning adequacy of capital, assets quality, management, earnings and liquidity (CAMEL), bank soundness was classified using a four step rating system that included sound, fairly sound, poor and unsound (Binhadi 1995, p. 244).

12   In the past, bank restructuring was based on a conventional restructuring programme permitted under the Banking Law of 1992 on a case-by-case basis, with involvement of the central bank.

13   The policy for providing exporters with a pre-shipment facility was introduced as part of a policy to selectively assist the real sector that was experiencing pressure from the high interest rates in bank lending. The scheme was only available for a limited number of exporters in commodities selected by the Department of Trade and Industry. In total only 20 exporters resorted to the facility. A large company (Texmaco Group) close to President Soeharto which misused the facility marred the image of the programme itself.

14   In a recent conference in Hakone, Japan, I mentioned this episode in front of Professor Sakikabara, the former Japanese Vice-Minister of Finance, who was in charge then. He commented that the main reason for not continuing the operation was because it was no longer effective (Conference on "Market and Diplomacy", organized by the Japan Institute for International Affairs, Hakone, 9–10, March 2002)

15   From October to December 1997, cash withdrawals from the banking sector amounted to 4.5 trillion rupiah (approximately US$10 billion), while in the first three weeks of January 1998, withdrawals were totalled 7.4 trillion rupiah (equivalent to more than US$9 billion).

16   IMF, "Stand-by Arrangement — Review Under the Emergency Financing Procedures", Prepared by the IMF Asia Pacific Department, 7 January 1998, mimeo.

17   The data that was compiled from this short period at a later date was adopted by the Indonesian Debt Restructuring Agency (INDRA), formed in January 1998.

Chapter 4: Poor Programme Implementation

1   On the filing and subsequent withdrawal of the suits against the Minister of Finance and Bank Indonesia Governor, see for instance, Michael Richardson, "Suharto's Son Sue Government", *IHT*, 6 November 1997; "Bambang Drops his Lawsuit over Bail", *AWSJ*, 13 November 1997.

2   IMF, "Indonesia: Stand-by Arrangement — Review Under the Emergency Financing Procedures", Asia and Pacific Department, Approved by Bijan B. Aghevli and Joaquin Ferran, 7 January 1998, p. 14, mimeo.

3   Ibid., p. 23.

4   It was later revealed that President Soeharto had suffered his first stroke.

5   Point 2 of Presidential Instruction in the Cabinet Meeting of 3 September 1997.

6   The Minister of Finance and the Governor of Bank Indonesia made statements about not closing more banks after reporting to the President (*Suara Pembaruan*, 4 November 1997). The government policy not to close more banks was reiterated by President Soeharto after announcing the second LOI (*Suara Pembaruan*, 16 January 1998).

7   If the funds spent by MAS and BOJ in the joint intervention in November 1997 were counted as withdrawal of loans from Japan and Singapore in the programme, there was US$1.5 billion of disbursement from these sources.

8   See Paul Blustein's assessment of the role of the IMF and the U.S. Treasury in the Korean case in *The Chastening…*, ch. 5.

9   Joon-Ho Hahm, "Financial Restructuring in Korea: The Crisis and Its Resolution", in *East Asia's Financial System: Evolution and Crisis*, edited by Seiichi Mauyama et al., pp. 109–44 (Singapore: ISEAS, 1999).

10   The maximum payment was decided during the meeting between the President and the Monetary Board in preparation for the bank closures. Since in 1992 the government had guaranteed payments up to a maximum of 10 million rupiah, I was proposing that the government raise the amount to 30 million rupiah. The Minister of Finance opted for 20 million rupiah, acknowledging that the burden would ultimately be borne by the budget. And this was the amount that the President agreed to.

11   See Lindgren 1999, p. 22.

12   Read C. Brown's comment from the Fund on my paper, *The Banking Sector in an Emerging Market: The Case of Indonesia*, in Charles Enoch and John H. Green (Enoch and Green 1997).

13   Communiqué of the Interim Committee of the Board of Governors of the International Monetary Fund, Press Release No. 96/46 (Washington D.C.: IMF, 29 September 1996).

14   *Warta Ekonomi*, No. 26/Th IX/17, November 1997.

15   *Suara Pembaruan*, 8 December 1997, http://www.suarapembaruan.com/News..12/081297/Ekonomi/eko15.html.

16   *Suara Pembaruan*, 4 November 1997.

17   *Suara Pembaruan*, 16 January 1998.

18   The Parliamentary Committee to investigate Bank Indonesia's liquidity support summoned the Governor, the Deputy Governors and myself in February 2000 to testify.

19 "President's Instructions and Decisions at the Special Cabinet Meeting on Economics, Finance and Production and Distribution", Jakarta: Bina Graha, 3 September 1997, mimeo.

20 "RI Worst in Corporate Governance: Survey", *Jakarta Post*, 19 June 2000.

21 "*Konspirasi Menggoyang Soeharto*".

22 This was of course ignored when the government decided to do so in compliance with part of the conditionality (prior action) of the Fund's stand-by arrangement.

23 In accordance with Article 29 (1) and 32 (3), of Central Bank Act No. 13, 1968.

24 "Kalau nggak bisa diselamat ditutup saja" [If it is not possible for a bank to be saved it should be liquidated], *Bisnis Indonesia*, 5 October 1997.

25 The data was taken from Liliana Rojas-Suarez, "Proper Sequencing of Financial Market Liberalization: Learning from the Chilean Experience, Table II", paper presented at a workshop of the Asian Policy Forum, the ADB Institute, Shanghai, 27 February 2002.

Chapter 5: Stronger Programme with Weak Commitment

1 IMF, "Indonesia: Stand-By Arrangement—Review Under the Emergency Financing Procedure", a confidential document prepared by the Asia and Pacific Department, 7 January 1998, mimeo.

2 These observations were made during the discussion in the Board concerning the Review of the Indonesian SBA by the Fund as contained in a report by the Alternate Executive Director for Southeast Asia Group, 8 January 1998, mimeo.

3 *Suara Pembaruan*, 14 November 1997.

4 *Suara Pembaruan*, December 1997.

5 *Kompas*, 19 June 2000.

6 Syahril Sabirin was only sworn in a couple of days after since the President wanted the change immediately, although Sabirin had asked for several days to return from Washington, D.C.

7 IMF, "Stand-by Arrangement", op. cit.

8 Since 1968 the government had adhered to the construct of a balanced budget that was not actually balanced in the ordinary sense. The idea was that the government limited itself to foreign sources of financing. Thus, the budget could have a deficit, but, the deficit could not be financed through domestic borrowing or by printing money. The deficit had to be financed through foreign loans and aid. In this construct the total budget, which included foreign loans and foreign aid, should be balanced. In other words, the budget allowed a deficit to the amount of the foreign loans and aid utilized during the fiscal year.

9   A letter written by the IMF's Southeast Asia Executive Director, Mr. Zamani Abdul Ghani from Malaysia, who tabled a protest to Managing Director Camdessus on the matter. The report appeared in the *Washington Post*, 7 January 1998, while Mr. Zamani's letter was dated 14 January 1998.

10   *Annual Report of Bank Indonesia 1998/99* (Jakarta: Bank Indonesia, May 1999), chapter 5. See also LOI, 15 January 1998 and 29 July 1998.

11   Taken from confidential memos from Fund staff to the Indonesian team on necessary steps to be taken to implement the new programme, dated 18 January and 23 January 1998 (mimeo), and *Annual Report of Bank Indonensia 1998/99*, chap. 5.

12   *Suara Pembaruan*, 7 February 1998.

Chapter 6: Bank Indonesia and the Crisis

1   Supreme Audit Board, press release "Special Audit Report on The Provision and Usage of Bank Indonesia Liquidity Supports", 4 August 2000.

2   *Konspirasi Menggoyang Soeharto*.

3   See J. Soedradjad Djiwandono, "Liquidity Support to Banks during Indonesia's Financial Crisis", *BIES*, (April 2004).

4   "Former Ministers of Finance and Bank Indonesia's Governor Exchanged Accusations on Who is Responsible for Bank Indonesia Liquidity Supports", *Suara Pembaruan*, 2 October 2000, http://suarapembaruan.com/News/2000/02/10/Ekonomi/ek07.html.

5   Bank Indonesia, *Mengurai Benang Kusut BLBI* [To untangle the winding knot of Bank Indonesia liquidity supports] (Jakarta: Bank Indonesia, 2002), p. 94.

6   "President's Instructions and Decisions in the Cabinet Meeting on Economics and Finance, Development Supervision, Production and Distribution", Jakarta: Bina Graha, 3 September 1997, point 8.

7   Bank Indonesia, *Mengurai Benang Kusut BLBI*, op. cit.

8   Government Regulation No. 25, 1999.

9   See First LOI, point 2. This was also mentioned in a letter from the Minister of Finance to the Governor of Bank Indonesia, 20 February 1998.

10   *Jakarta Post*, 1 June 2002.

11   Taken from a press release by Bank Indonesia's Public Relations Unit, 3 July 2003.

12   In one of his visits to Jakarta it was reported that Professor Hanke stayed at the Shangri La Hotel under the alias of Simon Holland, and his stay was paid for by Astra International. However, it is difficult to establish a link between President Soeharto and Astra International, except that one of its then directors was in the inner circle of the Cendana family. *AWSJ*, 24 February 1998.

[13] The parliamentary leadership's support was reported in the media as "Mar'ie (the Minister of Finance): Indonesia will adopt CBS", http://www.suarapembaruan.com/News/1998/02/110298/headline/h101/h101.html.

[14] Several editions of *Suara Pembaruan* from the second and third weeks of February 1998, http://suarapembaruan.com/News/1998/02/220298/headline/hioi/hioi.html.

[15] Steve H. Hanke, "Indonesia's Central Bank Goes Bust", *AWSJ*, 17 February 2000.

[16] "Indonesia Déjà Vu", Editorial, *ASWJ*, 15 May 2000.

[17] "I am Amazed", *ASWJ*, 25 May 2000.

[18] "Nobel Laureate Mundell Supports Rupiah Peg for Indonesia", Dow Jones, Singapore, 4 September 2000, http://asis.biz.yahoo.com/.../Nobel_Laureate_Mundell_Supports_Rupiah_Peg_for_Indonesia.htm9/4/00.

[19] Intervention by Prof. Wing Thye Woo in a workshop on "Sequencing of Financial Liberalization and Regional Trade Implications of PRC", organized by ADBI, held in Shanghai, 8 May 2002.

[20] Article 4 of Law No. 23 of 1999 Concerning the Central Bank.

[21] Letter from President Soeharto to Mr. Camdessus and the "Memorandum of Economic and Financial Policies", 15 January 1998, mimeo.

[22] Alan S. Blinder, *Central Banking in Theory and Practice* (Cambridge, MA: MIT Press, 1998), p. 53.

[23] Stanley Fischer, "Modern Central Banking", in F. Capie et al., *The Future of Central Banking* (Cambridge University Press, 1994).

[24] For example, in New Zealand the government determines the goal for monetary policy, i.e. the inflation rate. But, beyond that it is up to the Central Bank of New Zealand to choose its instrument(s) for achieving the predetermined rate of inflation.

[25] See Stanley Fischer, "Modern Central Banking", in Capie, et al. (1994) and *Central Banking in Developing Countries*, edited by Maxwell J. Fry et al. (London: Routledge, 1996).

[26] See "Survey: The World Economy", supplement of the Economist, 25 September–1 October 1999.

[27] Edward S. Shaw, *Financial Deepening in Economic Development* (New York: Oxford University Press 1973), and Ronald I. McKinnon, *Money and Capital in Economic Development*, (Washington D.C.: Brookings Institution, 1973).

[20] The most important of which was the easing of bank licencing in October 1988. The Indonesian banking sector enjoyed a tremendous expansion in terms of both mobilization of funds and lending as well as the number of banks.

[29] "Survey: The World Economy" in *the Economist*, 25 September 1999, p. 4.

[30] IMF, "Communiqué of the Interim Committee of the Board of Governors of the International Monetary Fund", 26 September 1999, mimeo.

[31] Stanley Fischer, "Modern Central Banking", op cit., p. 4.

[32] Stijn Claessens et al., *Financial Restructuring in East Asia: Halfway There?* World Bank Financial Discussion Paper no. 3.

[33] Paul Krugman, *The Eternal Triangle: Explaining International Financial Perplexity*, http://web.mit.edu/krugman/www/triangle.html.

[34] Study by Cukierman (1992, Fig. 5) shows that only the Bundesbank surpasses the Fed in term of independence.

[35] Granted, Indonesia's balanced budget concept, which treated the rupiah value of foreign loans and aid as development revenue, defied proper definitions of government revenue. However, the concept had successfully forced the government not to borrow domestically nor the central bank to finance a budget deficit. This actually implied that the balanced budget concept, which had been practiced in Indonesia since 1968, had been contributing to prudent fiscal policy, which was the trademark of Indonesia's macroeconomic management until the crisis. However, there was also some leakage when the government registered "off-budget" expenditure.

[36] It was sometimes strange that the Indonesian government had to hear contrasting advice from the two sister institutions, the World Bank and the Fund, in this respect.

[37] "Bank Indonesia and the Recent Crisis", *BIES* 36, (April 2000): 47–72.

[38] IMF studies on these matters were reported in Lindgren et al, *Bank Soundness and Macroeconomic Policy* (D.C.: 1996) and Enoch and Green, *Banking Soundness and Monetary Policy* (1997).

[39] Richard Cooper in his comment on Steve Radelet's and Jeffrey Sachs' work specifically mentions that the soundness of banking systems should be an objective of monetary policy (Brookings Papers on Economic Activity, 1, 1998). See also Manuel Guitian, "Banking Soundness: The Other Dimension of Monetary Policy" in Enoch and Green (1997), pp. 41–62. In this paper Guitian showed that a sound banking system should stand on its own as an objective of monetary policy.

[40] "Panel Report on Proposed Amendments of Bank Indonesia Law", April 2001, mimeo.

[41] *Tempo Interaktif*, 3 June 2000.

[42] "Panel Report on Proposed Amendments of Bank Indonesia Law", April 2001, mimeo, p. 4.

Chapter 7: Lessons from the Crisis

[1] The Consultative Group on Indonesia (CGI) is a forum organized by the World Bank, which comprises of 18 countries and many multilateral

institutions, that provide the government of Indonesia with loans and grants for development.

2   See for instance, Haggard, *The Political Economy of the Asian Financial Crisis*.

3   Stanley Fischer, "Asia and the IMF", remarks at the Institute of Policy Studies, Singapore, 1 June 2001, http://www.imf.org/external/np/speeches/2001/060101.htm.

4   From 1994 to 1996 the intervention bands were widened six times, while the nominal rate of the rupiah was depreciated 4–5 per cent annually.

5   See, for example, Graciela L. Kaminsky, "Currency and Banking Crises: The Early Warning of Distress", IMF Working Paper no. WP/99/178, December 1999.

6   See IMF, *Structural Conditionality in Fund-Supported Programmes*, Box 8, p. 40 http://www.imf.org/external/np/pdr/cond/2001/eng/index.htm.

7   See, J. Soedradjad Djiwandono, "Bank Indonesia and the Recent Crisis", BIES 36, no. 1 (April 2000).

8   As detailed in Chapter 5, the second LOI was even unique because, no longer trusting the Minister of Finance and the Governor of Bank Indonesia, Soeharto personally negotiated the programmes and signed the document.

9   This is conjectured from the sequence of events in the Asian crisis as listed by Lindgren et al., *Financial Sector Crisis and Restructuring*, op. cit.

10   See David C. Cole and Betty F. Slade, "Comments on the IMF Report on IMF-Supported Programmes in Indonesia, Thailand and Korea: A Preliminary Assessment," 2 February 1999, mimeo.

11   Haggard, *The Political Economy of the Asian Financial Crisis*, op. cit., p. 8.

12   It should be noted that Bank Indonesia did not enjoy its independent status until the enactment of the new Central Bank Law in May 1999.

13   Dae-Hwan Kim, "Globalization and the IMF-Controlled Economy: The Case of Korea", a paper presented in a seminar at the Southeast Asian Studies Programme, the National University of Singapore, July 2001, mimeo.

14   See Lindgren et al., *Financial Sector Crisis and Restructuring* and Timothy Lane et al., "IMF — Supported Programs in Indonesia, Korea, and Thailand: A Preliminary Assessment", (1999), and Jack Boorman et al., "Managing Financial Crises: The Experience of East Asia" (2000).

15   As an example, see the policy brief by Minister Kwik Kian Gie entitled "Indonesian Economic Reform: What Went Wrong", in a recent seminar "Lessons from the Indonesian Transition: Setting a Future Reform Agenda", organized by UNSFIR-Bappenas, Jakarta, 24–25 February 2004, mimeo.

16   See Jack Boorman, "Life with the IMF: Indonesian Choices for the Future", paper presented at the 15th Congress of the Indonesian Economists Association, Malang, 15 July 2003, http://www.imf.org/external/country/idn/index.

[17] Article I, (ii), Article of Agreement of the International Monetary Fund. http://www.imf.org/external/pubs/ft/aa/index.htm.

[18] Note also arguments presented by Stanley Fischer on this matter, *Presentation to the International Financial Institution Advisory Commission*, Washington D.C., 2 February 2000, http://www.imf.org/external/np/speeches/2000/020200.htm.

[19] George Shultz, William Simon and Walter Wriston in "Who Needs the IMF?", *Wall Street Journal*, 3 January 1998.

[20] See the Meltzer Commission Report on the International Financial Institution Advisory Commission, http://www.house.gov/jec/imf/imfpage.htm.

[21] See, for example, Kenneth Rogoff, "Open Letter to Joseph Stiglitz", http://www.imf.org/external/np/vc/2002/070202.htm.

[22] Paul Volcker is Former Chairman of the Board of Governors, Federal Reserve System, United States, 1979–87.

[23] Jesus P. Estanislao, "Paradigm for Policy and Institutional Arrangements in a Global Market Era", a paper presented at a conference on Asia-Pacific Cooperation, organized by Japan Institute of International affairs, Hakone, Japan, 8–9 March, 2002.

[24] IMF, "Structural Conditionality in Fund-Supported Program", 16 February 2001, Box 8, p. 40 http://www.imf.org/external/np/pdr/cond/2001/eng/index.htm.

[25] Ibid.

[26] "Banking System Soundness and Macroeconomic Management: The Recent Indonesian Experience", http://www.pacific.net.id/pakar/sj and J. Soedradjad Djiwandono, "Monetary Policy and the Banking System in Indonesia: Some Lessons", the Fifth India-ASEAN Eminent Person Lecture, Research and Information System for the Non-Aligned and Other Developing Countries (RIS), New Delhi, 2 September 1998.

[27] This is an easy target for domestic politicking. The critics, either incoming government officials referring to their predecessors, or others, could easily dub the participants in the negotiation as lackeys or mouthpieces of the Fund.

[28] Letter by MD Horst Kohler to the Fund officials, Streamlining Structural Conditionality, 18 September 2000, a cable address by the Managing Director, to the Heads of Departments and Offices. See also "Conditionality in Fund-Supported Programmes — Overview", http://www.imf.org/external/np/pdr/cond/2001/eng/overview.

[29] See "The Role of the IMF in Recent Capital Account Crises — Draft Issues Papers/Terms of Reference for an Evaluation by Independent Evaluation Office", Independent Evaluation Office of the IMF, April 2002, mimeo.

30 See, for example, Iwan J. Azis, "Modeling Crisis Evolution and Counterfactual Policy Simulations: A Country Case Study", ADB Institute Working Paper 23, Tokyo: ADB Institute, August 2001.

Chapter 8: Epilogue

1 I would like to thank Professor Anne Booth for raising this issue during one of my presentations at ISEAS in May 2001.
2 Quoted from a World Bank study by Mark Landler, "For Indonesia Solvency is Political", *New York Times*, 20 April 2001.
3 See also Morris Goldstein, *Managed Floating Plus* (Washington, D.C.: Institute for International Economics, 2002). The plus is to denote the requirements in the monetary management for inflation targeting and aggressive measures to discourage currency mismatching.
4 See that arguments about including the ratio of short-term debts to international reserves in the macro fundamentals as proposed by Steve Radelet and Jeffrey Sachs (1998).
5 Of course a different meaning of intervention is used here. In the fixed system, the monetary authority is legally required to intervene to defend the system. In a floating system, the intervention is to slow down the depreciation to defend a certain rate.
6 See, Marias Vernengo, "Exchange Rate Regimes and Capital Control", *Challenge*, November 2000.

Postscript

1 IMF, "Recovery from the Asian Crisis and the Role of the IMF", June 2000, http://www.imf.org/external/np/exr/ib/2000/062300.htm.

References

a. Books and Articles

Adams, Charles et al. *International Capital Market: Development, Prospects and Key Policy Issues*. Washington D.C.: IMF, 1998.

Alexander, William E. et al., eds. *Systemic Bank Restructuring and Macroeconomic Policy*. Washington D.C.: IMF, 1997.

Arndt, H.W. and Hal Hill, eds. *Southeast Asia's Economic Crisis: Origins, Lessons and the Way Forward*. Singapore: ISEAS, 1999.

Azis, Iwan J. "Modeling Crisis Evolution and Counterfactual Policy Simulation: A Country Case Study". ADB Institute Working Paper 23. Tokyo: ADB Institute, 2001.

Backman, Michael. *Asian Eclipse: Exposing the Dark Side of Business in Asia*. Singapore: John Wiley & Sons (Asia), revised 2001.

Bank Indonesia. *Laporan Tahunan* (Annual Report), 1993/94, 1994/95, 1995/96, 1996/97 and 1997/98.

―――. *Mengurai Benang Kusut BLBI* (To Untangle the Confusing Bank Indonesia Liquidity Support). Jakarta: Bank Indonesia, 2002.

Berg, Andrew. "The Asia Crisis: Causes, Policy Responses, and Outcomes". IMF Working Paper, WP/99/138. Washington D.C.: IMF, 1999.

Berthelemy, Jean-Claude and Tommy Koh, eds. *The Asian Crisis: A New Agenda for Euro-Asian Cooperation*. Singapore: World Scientific, 1998.

Bhagwati, Jagdish. "The Capital Myth". *Foreign Affairs* (May–June 1998): 7–13.

Binhadi. *Financial Sector Deregulation, Banking Development and Monetary Policy: The Indonesian Experience, 1983–1993*. Jakarta: IBI, 1995.

Blinder, Alan S. *Central Banking in Theory and Practice*. Cambridge, MA: MIT Press, 1999.

Blustein, Paul. *The Chastening: Inside the Crisis that Rocked the Global Financial System and Humbled the IMF*. New York: Public Affairs, 2001.

Boorman, Jack, Timothy Lane, et al. "Managing Financial Crisis: The Experience in East Asia". IMF Working Paper, WP/00/107. Washington D.C.: IMF, 2000.

Boorman, Jack. "Life with the IMF: Indonesia's Choices for the Future", http://www.imf.org/external/country/idn/index, 2003.

Boughton, James M. *Different Strokes? Common and Uncommon Responses to Financial Crisis.* IMF Working Paper, WP/01/12. Washington D.C.: IMF, 2001.

Budiman, Arief. Capitalism, Tribalism and Religion. Mimeograph, 1999, unpublished.

Bussiere, Matthieu and Christian Mulder. "Political Instability and Economic Vulnerability". IMF Working Paper, No WP/99/46. Washington D.C.: IMF,, 1999.

Capie, Forest et al. *The Future of Central Banking: The Tercentenary Symposium of The Bank of England.* Cambridge: Cambridge University Press, 1994.

Cerra, Valerie and Sweta Chaman Saxena. "Contagion, Monsoon, and Domestic Turmoil in Indonesia: A Case Study in the Asian Currency Crisis". IMF Working Paper, No WP/00/60. Washington D.C.: IMF, 2000.

Claessens, Stijn, et al. "Financial Restructuring in East Asia: Halfway There?" Financial Sector Discussion Paper No 3. Washington D.C.: World Bank, 1999.

Claessens, Stijn. *Systemic Bank and Corporate Restructuring: Experiences and Lessons for East Asia.* Washington D.C.: World Bank, 1998.

Claessens, Stijn et al. "Financial Restructuring in Banking and Corporate Sector Crisis: What Policies to Pursue?". NBER Working Paper Bibliographic Entry, http://papers.nber.org/papers/W8386, 2001.

Cohen, Benjamin. *The Geography of Money.* Ithaca, NY: Cornell University Press, 1998.

Cole, David C. and Betty F. Slade. *Building a Modern Financial System: The Indonesian Experience.* Cambridge: Cambridge University Press, 1996.

————. "Comments on the IMF Report on IMF-Supported Programs in Indonesia, Thailand, and Korea: A Preliminary Assessment". Mimeograph.

Colt, C.C. and N.S. Keith. *28 Days: A History of the Banking Crisis.* New York: Greenberg Publisher, 1933.

Cukierman, A., Steven B. Webb and Bilai Heyapi. "Measuring the Independence of Central Banks and its Effects on Policy Outcomes". *World Bank Economic Review* 6, no. 3 (1992): 353–98.

Delhaise, Philippe F. *Asia in Crisis: The Implosion of the Banking and Finance System.* Singapore: John Wiley & Sons (Asia), 1998.

Djiwandono, J. Soedradjad. *Perdagangan dan Pembangunan.* Jakarta: LP3ES, 1992.

————. *Ekonomi Makro Dalam Dinamisme Perekonomian Dunia: Tantangan Bagi Pendekatan dan Kebijaksanaan Makro.* Jakarta: Fakultas Ekonomi, Universitas Indonesia, 1994.

————. "Bank Indonesia and The Recent Crisis", *Bulletin of Indonesian Economic Studies* 36 no. 1 (2000): 47–72.

————. "Central Banking Reform in Indonesia". *Asia Business Law Review* 28, pp. 53–62, 2000b.

———. "The Muddling Through of Crisis Management in Indonesia: A Case for Central Bank Independence". In *Capital Flows Without Crisis? Reconciling Capital Mobility and Economic Stability*, edited by Dipak Dasgupta, Marc Uzan and Dominic Wilson. London: Routledge Taylor and Francis, 2001.

———. "Liquidity Support to Banks During Indonesia's Financial Crisis". *Bulletin of Indonesian Economic Studies* 40, no. 1 (April 2004): 59–75.

Drucker, Peter F. "The Changed World Economy". *Foreign Affairs* 64, no. 4 (1986).

Dziobek, Claudia and Ceyla Plazarbasioglu. *Lessons from Systemic Bank Restructuring, Economic Issues*. Washington D.C.: IMF, 1998.

Eatwell, John and Lance Taylor. *Global Finance and Risk: The Case for International Regulation*. New York: New Press, 2000.

Effros, Robert C., eds. *Current Legal Issues Affecting Central Banking*. Washington D.C.: IMF, 1995.

Eichengreen, Barry. *Globalizing Capital*. Princeton, NJ: Princeton University Press, 1996.

———. *European Monetary Unification: Theory, Practice, and Analysis*. Cambridge, MA: MIT Press, 1997.

Enoch, Charles and John H. Green. *Banking Soundness and Monetary Policy: Issues and Experiences in the Global Economy*. Washington D.C.: IMF, 1997.

Enoch, Charles, Gillian Garcia, and V. Sundararajan. "Recapitalizing Banks with Public Funds: Selected Issues". IMF Working Paper, WP no/99/139. Washington D.C.: IMF, 1999.

Enoch, Charles. "Intervention in Banks During Banking Crises: The Experience of Indonesia". IMF Policy Discussion Paper, No PDP/00/2. Washington D.C.: IMF, 2000.

Evans, Owen, Alfredo M. Leone, Mahinder Gill and Paul Hilbers. "Macro Prudential Indicators of Financial System Soundness". IMF Occasional Paper no 192. Washington D.C.: IMF, 2000.

Feldstein, Martin. "A Self-Help Guide for Emerging Markets". *Foreign Affairs* 78, no. 2 (1999).

Fischer, Stanley. On the Need for an International Lender of Last Resort, http://www.imf.org/external/np/speeches/1999/010399.html., 1999.

———. "Exchange Rate Regimes: Is the Bipolar View Correct?" http://www.imf.org, 2001.

———. "Asia and the IMF", Remarks at the Institute of Policy Studies, Singapore, June 2001. http://www.imf.org/external/np/speeches/2001/060101.htm. 2001.

Forester, Geoff, ed. *Post Soeharto Indonesia: Renewal or Chaos?* Singapore: ISEAS, 1999.

Fry, Maxwell J., Charles A.E. Goodhart and Alvaro Almeida. *Central Banking in Developing Countries*. London: Routledge, 1996.

Frydl, Edward J. "The Length and Cost of Banking Crisis". IMF Working Paper, and No WP/99/30. Washington D.C.: IMF, 1999.

Goldstein, Morris. *The Asian Financial Crisis: Causes, Cures, and Systemic Implications*. Washington D.C.: Institute for International Economics, 1998.

———. *Managed Floating Plus*. Washington D.C.: Institute for International Economics, 2002.

Goldstein, Morris, Graciela L. Kaminsky and Carmen M. Reinhart. *Assessing Financial Vulnerability: An Early Warning System for Emerging Markets*. Washington D.C., IMF, 2000.

Gough, Leo. *Asia Meltdown: The End of The Miracle*. Oxford, UK: Capstone Publishing, 1998.

Haggard, Stephan. *The Political Economy of the Asian Crisis*. Washington D.C.: Institute for International Economics, 2000.

Hanke, Steve H. and Kurt Schuler. *Currency Board for Developing Countries: A Handbook*. San Francisco: Institute for Contemporary Studies, 1994.

Hausmann, Ricardo and Liliana Rojas-Suarez. *Banking Crisis in Latin America*. Washington D.C.: Inter-American Development Bank, 1997.

Henderson, Callum. *Asia Falling*. New York: McGraw-Hill, 1998.

Hicklin, John, David Robinson and Anoop Singh, eds. *Macroeconomic Issues Facing Asean Countries*. Washington D.C.: IMF, 1997.

Hill, Hal. *The Indonesian Economy in Crisis: Causes, Consequences and Lessons*, Singapore: ISEAS, 1999.

Hunter, William C., George G. Kaufman and Thomas H. Krueger, eds. *The Asian Financial Crisis: Origins, Implications, and Solutions*. Boston, MA: Kluwer Academic Publishers, 1999.

Hussain, Qaizar and Clas Wihlborg. "Corporate Insolvency Procedures and Bank Behavior: A Study of Selected Asian Countries". IMF Working Paper, WP/99/135. Washington D.C.: IMF, 1999.

International Monetary Fund. *Monetary Approach to the Balance of Payments*. Washington D.C.: IMF, 1977.

———. *Financial Organization and Operation of the IMF*. Pamphlet Series no. 45, Washington D.C.: IMF, 1998.

———. *Review of Fund Facilities — Preliminary Considerations*. Washington D.C.: IMF, 2000.

———. How We Lend. Washington D.C.: IMF http://www.imf.org./external/np/exr/facts/howlend.html, 1999.

———. *Recovery from the Asian Crisis and the Role of the IMF*, Washington D.C.: IMF. http://www.imf.org./external/np/exr/ib/2000/062300.html, 1999.

———. "Indonesia: Anatomy of a Banking Crisis, Two Years of Living Dangerously, 1997–99". IMF Working Paper, No WP/01/52, May 2001.

———. *Indonesia: Selected Issues*. Washington D.C.: IMF, October 2000.

————. *Exchange Rate Regimes in an Increasingly Integrated World Economy.* http://www.imf.org/external/np/exr/ib/2000/062600.htm, 2000.

————. *Conditionality in Fund-Supported Programs — Overview.* http://www.imf.org./external/np/pdr/cond/2001/ eng/overview/index.htm.

Johnston, R. Barry. *Sequencing Capital account Liberalizations and Financial Sector Reform*, Paper on Policy Analysis and Assessment of the IMF. PPAA/98/8 Washington D.C.: IMF, 1998.

Jones, David M. *The Politics of Money: The Fed under Alan Greenspan.* New York: NYIF Corp., Simon Schuster, 1991.

Kaminsky, Graciela L. *Currency and Banking Crises: The Early Warning Distress,* Working Paper IMF, WP/99/178. Washington D.C.: IMF, 1999.

Kenward, Lloyd. "What Has Been Happening at Bank Indonesia?" *BIES* 35, no. 1 (1999).

Kindleberger, Charles P. *Maniacs, Panics and Crashes: A History of Financial Crises.* New York: John Wiley & Sons, 1996.

Krugman, Paul. *What Happened to Asia?* http://www.mit.edu/people/krugman/index/html, 1998.

Lane, Timothy et al. *IMF-Supported Programs in Indonesia, Korea and Thailand, A Preliminary Assessment.* Washington D.C.: IMF, 1999.

Lindgren, Carl-Johan, et al. eds. *Bank Soundness and Macroeconomic Policy.* Washington D.C.: IMF, 1996.

————. *Financial Sector Crisis and Restructuring: Lessons from Asia.* Washington D.C.: IMF, 1999.

Masuyama, Seiichi, et al. *East Asia's Financial Systems: Evolution and Crisis.* Singapore: ISEAS, 1999.

McKinnon Ronald I. *Money and Capital in Economic Development.* Washington D.C.: The Brookings Institution, 1973.

Mehran, Hassanali et al. *Indonesia: Bank Liquidation and Resolution.* Washington D.C.: IMF, 1994.

McLeod, Ross H. and Ross Garnaut, eds. *East Asia in Crisis: From Being a Miracle to Needing One.* New York: Routledge, 1998.

Pangestu, Mari and Manggi Habir. "The Boom, Bust, and Restructuring of Indonesian Banks". IMF Working Paper, WP/02/66. Washington D.C.: IMF, 2002.

Pomelearno, M. *The East Asia Crisis and Corporate Finances: The Untold Story.* World Bank Working Paper, No. WPS 1900, Washington D.C.: The World Bank, 1998.

Porter, Michael E. *The Competitive Advantage of A Nation.* New York: Free Press, 1998.

Radelet, Steven and Jeffrey Sachs. "The East-Asian Financial Crisis: Diagnosis, Remedies, Prospects". Brookings Papers on Economic Activity. Washington D.C.: Brookings Institution, 1998.

Rahardjo, Dawam (Team Coordinator). *Bank Indonesia dalam Kisaran Sejarah Bangsa* ([Bank Indonesia in the History of the Nation]). Jakarta: PT Pustaka LP3ES, 1995.

Shaw, Edward S. *Financial Deepening in Economic Development*. New York: Oxford University Press, 1973.

Sheng, Andrew, ed. *Bank Restructuring*. Washington D.C.: World Bank, 1996.

―――. The Crisis of Money in the 21st Century, Guest Lecture, Hong Kong: City University of Hong Kong. Mimeograph, 1998.

Solomon, Robert. *Money on the Move: The Revolution in the International Finance since 1980*. Washington D.C.: Brookings Institution, 1999.

Stiglitz, Joseph. "Responding to Economic Crisis: Policy Alternatives for Equitable Recovery and Development". http://www.worldbank.org/html/extdr/extme/jssp092998.html, 1998a.

―――. "Sound Finance and Sustainable Development in Asia". http://www.worldbank. org/html/extdr/extme/jssp031298.html, 1998b.

―――. *Globalization and its Discontents*. New York: W.W. Norton Company, 2002.

Stone, Mark R. "Corporate Debt Restructuring in East Asia: Some Lessons from International Experience. Paper on Policy Analysis and Assessment". PPAA/98/13. Washington D.C.: IMF, 1998.

Sugema, Iman. Banking Sector and Economic Collapses: Lessons from Indonesia. Bogor University, unpublished.

Sukowaluyo Mintorahardjo. *BLBI Simalakama* (BLBI Dilemma). Jakarta: Riset Ekonomi Sosial Indonesia, 2001.

Sundararajan, V. and Tomas J.T. Balino, eds. *Banking Crises: Cases and Issues*. Washington D.C.: IMF, 1991.

World Bank. *The East Asian Miracle: Economic Growth and Public Policy*. Oxford: Oxford University Press, 1993.

―――. *East Asia: The Road to Recovery*. Washington D.C.: International Bank for Reconstruction and Development, 1998.

―――. *East Asia: Recovery and Beyond*. Washington D.C.: International Bank for Reconstruction and Development, 2000.

Williamson, John. *The Crawling Band as an Exchange Regime*. Washington D.C.: Institute for International Economics, 1996.

―――. *Exchange Rate Regimes for Emerging Markets: Reviving the Intermediate Option*. Washington D.C.: Institute for International Economics, 2000.

Yoshihara, Kunio. *The Rise of Ersatz Capitalism in Southeast Asia*. Singapore: Oxford University Press, 1998.

b. Laws and Regulations

Undang-Undang Republik Indonesia nomor 13 tahun 1968 tentang Bank Sentral [Law of the Republic of Indonesia Number 13 of 1968 concerning the Central Bank]

Undang-Undang Republik Indonesia nomor 7 tahun 1992 tentang Perbankan [Law of the Republic of Indonesia Number 7 of 1992 Concerning Banking]

Keputusan Presiden nomor 23 Tahun 1998 tentang Pemberian Kewenangan Kepada Bank Indonesia di Bidang Pengendalian Moneter

Peraturan Pemerintah Republik Indonesia nomor 68 tahun 1996 tentang Ketentuan dan Tata Cara Pencabutan Izin Usaha, Pembubaran dan Likuidasi Bank

[Government Regulation of the Republic of Indonesia number 68 of 1996 Concerning Provision and Procedure for Revocation of the Business Licence, Dissolution and Liquidation of a Bank]

[President of the Republic of Indonesia Decree Number 23 of 1998 Concerning the Granting of Monetary Management Authority to Bank Indonesia]

Undang-undang Republik Indonesia nomor 23 tahun 1999 tentang Bank Sentral

[Law of the Republic of Indonesia Number 23 of 1999 Concerning the Central Bank]

Index

Anti-Corruption Act, 184
Asian crisis
    difference with Latin American
        crisis, 236
    impact, 221
    two views, 22, 23
Asian currencies
    depreciation, 43
Asian Development Bank (ADB), 242
    loans, disbursements of, 88, 259
Assistant Minister Coordinator for
    Economy, Finance and Industry
    (EKUIN), 8
Attorney General's Office, 166, 184
Bank Alfa, 133
    purchase of, 109
Bank Andromeda, 138
    liquidation, 33
Bank Bumi Daya, 94
Bank Central Asia (BCA), 94, 126
bank commissioners
    role, enhanced, 136
Bank Dagang Nasional Indonesia
    (BDNI), 94
Bank Danamon, 94, 126
bank deposits
    transferring to SBIs, 170
Bank Indonesia
    certificates (SBIs), 51, 53, 174, see
        also SBI rates

crisis management, 15
fire, incident of, 149, 150
Governor, dismissal of, 1–3
independence issue, 196–200,
    203–9
intervention band, 38
liquidity support, 176
managing directors, dismissal of,
    3, 150
non-independence, cost of, 207
post-independence problems, 210
President's intervention, 206
reserves, table of, 87
supervision of banks, handing
    over, 216
Bank Indonesia Law, 213
Bank Indonesia Liquidity Credits,
    168
banking sector, see banking system
banking system
    collapse, 151–53
    distress, in, 51–63
    lack of transparency, 125
    legal and regulatory framework,
        81
    loss of confidence, 119
    problems, 27
    restructuring, 15, 110, 127
    structural weaknesses, 52
Bank Jakarta

liquidation, 133
bank loans
  increase, 53
Bank of Japan (BOJ)
  market intervention operation,
    89, 109
  rupiah stabilization, 97–103
Bank of Sweden, 198
bank owners
  corruption, suspicion of, 166
  governance, problem with, 135
  repayment of liquidity supports,
    182
bank runs
  big depositors, by, 226
banks
  capital deficiency, 94
  closure, 15, 90, 109, 117, 125–32,
    139, see also liquidated banks
    – alleged conspiracy, 137–39
    – public reaction, 132–37
  depositors, big, 226
  insolvent, 59, 81, 91
  lack of confidence, 100
  legal lending limit, 129
  liquidity support, 165–69, 177
  negative balance, increasing, 175
  non-compliance with prudential
    measures, 60, 61
  official information, lack of, 125
  re-capitalization, 179
  reserve requirement, 53, 205
  restructuring, 90–95, 110, 127,
    139, 140, 225
Bank Summa, 6, 27, 109, 130
BAPINDO, 94
bearer bonds
  planned issuance of, 102
Berg, Andrew, 30
blanket guarantee, 121–25, 159, 179
Bluestein, Paul, 72, 115

budget debacle, 153–56
Camdessus, Michel, 10, 65, 67, 161,
  162
capital
  influx, 31
  reversal, 32, 33, 34
cease and desist order (CDO), 94
cement
  marketing arrangements
    abolished, 158
  prices, liberalization, 82
Central bank, see Bank Indonesia
  calls for independence, 196–200
  independence in practice, 201–203
Central Bank Act
  powers of Bank Indonesia, 180
  independence for Bank Indonesia,
    209
  weaknesses, 213, 214
central bank intervention band
  widening, 37–43
Central Bank Law, see also Central
  Bank Act
  Article 17, 2
Central Bank of China-Taipei, 4
Chaiyawat Wibulswasdi, 8
Chamber of Commerce and
  Industry, 111, 146
classical economists, 22
Cloves Marketing Board
  dissolution, 158
Coffee Exporters Association, 6
Commander of the Armed Forces, 5
commercial banks' certificates
  (SBPU)
  discount facility, 62
Consultative Group on Indonesia,
  41, 220
Cooper, Richard N., 28, 29
corporate debts
  denominated in foreign

currencies, 45, 251
  ignored in IMF programmes
  no restructuring programmes,
    105
  policy, 225
  restructuring, 161
corporate ownership
  concentration in top 15 families,
    224
corruption
  high index, 116
Council for Enhancement of
  National Economics and
  Financial Resilience, 160
crony capitalism, 26, 251
Currency Board, 187, 188
possible motivation, 188–91
currency board system (CBS), 10,
  230
    aborting, 191, 192
    countries with hyperinflation, 189
    side effects, 192–96
current account deficit, 27, 36
debt instruments, 31
debt management, 25
debt repayment, 25
deposit holders
  small, 118
deposit insurance scheme, see also
  blanket guarantee
  absence, 117
deposit repayment
  small holders, 117
Development Cabinet VI, 1
directives
  liquidity support to banks, 177
dollar
  demand, 41
Don, Ahmad Muhammad 8
Economic and Finance
  Commission, 185

economic crisis
  inducing social and political
    crisis, 26
  social implications, 104
economy
  structural weaknesses, 14, 24
Emergency Finance Mechanism, 67
ersatz capitalism, 27
European exchange rate mechanism
  (ERM), 46
exchange rate
  collapse, 143
exchange rate management, 40,
  255–57
extended arrangement, (EA), 70
extended fund facility (EFF), 69, 77
Feldstein, Martin, 73
financial institutions
  weak but viable, 81
Fischer, Stanley, 64, 67, 197, 222, 242
fixed exchange system, 190
flexible exchange system, 35
  perceptions, 48
foreign debt
  private, 106
foreign exchange
  demand for, 39
  market, turmoil in, 24
  reserve management, 73
foreign investors
  ownership of companies, 163
Frankfurt Agreement, 179
garlic
  import monopoly, discarding of,
    82
Goldstein, Morris, 30, 130
governance
  problems with, 136
  weak, 229
Governor of Bank Indonesia, 8
  as cabinet member, 2

dismissal, 1–3, 9–12
   last meeting with President, 4–7
   power of President to dismiss, 2
   speculation as to dismissal, 11, 12
Greenspan, Alan, 10
Guitian, Manuel, 28, 29
Habibie government
   letters of intent, 233
Haggard, Stephan, 23
Hahm, Jooj-Ho 115
Hanke, Steven H., 188, 189
hedge funds
attack on Hong Kong dollar, 43
foreign, 32
hedging
   demand for, 89
Hong Kong
   reserves, ample, 74
highly indebted poor countries
   (HIPC), 77
IMF, 36
   crisis, role in, 234–46
   criticisms against, 237, 238
   general resource account (GRA),
     76
   Indonesia's financial position
     within, 245
   loans from, 84–90
   poverty reduction and growth
     facility (PRGF), 77
   seeking help from, 63–73
   staff, role of, 84
   structure, 83
   surveillance by, need for, 223
IMF Compensatory Financing
   Facility (CFF), 68
IMF-supported programmes, 15,
   76–103, 243, 244
   implementation, poor, 144–49
   issues ignored, 103–7
   limited success owing to inconsistent

   government, 227–32
   macroeconomic objectives, 80
   overview, 79–84
   outcome and reasons, 108–41
   safeguard measures, 70
income
   reduction, 34
Independent Evaluation Office, 231,
   243
Indonesian Bank Restructuring
   Agency (IBRA), 4, 124, 159, 171,
   182, 253, 254
Indonesian Chamber of Commerce
   and Industry (KADIN), 11
Indonesian crisis
   causes, 14
   chronology of event, 16–21
   comparison with Korea and
     Thailand, 218–21
   differing views, 23
   early policy responses, 37–75
   external and domestic factors,
     34–37
   issues arising, 14, 15
   liquidity support to banks, 169–72
   origin, 22–30
   programmes to address, 252–55
   protracted, 222, 250
Indonesian economy, see economy
Institute of International Finance
   (IIF), 33
inter-bank money market, 52, 58, 60
   interest rate, 40, 60
   segmentation, 119, 120
inter-bank rate, 60
interest rates
   high, 111
   argument of raising, 113
international ratings agencies, 32
International Reserve and Foreign
   Currency Liquidity (IRFCL), 86

international reserves management,
49, 73
intervention bands, 15, see also
central bank intervention band
Jakarta inter-bank offered rate
(Jibor), 100
J.J. Polak model, 240
Kalla, Jusuf 1
Kaminsky, L., 29
Keynesian economists, 22
Kim Dae-Hwan, 232
Kindleberger, Charles P., 23, 26
Korea
short-term corporate debt, 114
Kyung Shik Lee, 8
law enforcement
low index, 116
Law of Foreign Exchange System,
215
Law of the Republic of Indonesia
Number 13 of 1968 concerning
Central Bank, see
Central Bank Law
Lee Eik Tieng, 8
Letter of Intent
second, see Second Letter of Intent
licensing
import and export, 82, 96
Liem Sioe Liong, 126
Lindgren, Carl-Johan, 91
lines of credit
terms and conditions, 88, 89
liquidated banks
repayment to deposit holders,
175
liquidity
banking sector, 111
problems, 58
resolving mismatches, 168
support, controversy involving,
172–76

support during crisis, 169–72,
176–70
support, public debate regarding,
185–87
support, resolving problems
with, 179–85
tightened, 50, 51
types of support, 168, 169
local currency
panic selling, 23
Malaysia
non-reliance on IMF, 75
managed foreign exchange, 38
managed floating system, 14, 223
crawling band, with, 39
managed peg, 42
market sentiment
change in, 31–34
Master Refinancing and Note
Issuance Agreement (MRNIA),
182, 184
Master Settlement and Acquisition
Agreement (MSAA), 182
types, 183
McKinnon, Ronald, 199
McKinsey & Company, 135
Megawati government
letters of intent, 233
Memorandum of Economic and
Financial Policy (MEFP), 77, 79
Mexican crisis, 24
Minister for National Development
Planning, 25, 154
Minister for Public Enterprise, 1
Minister for Trade and Industry, 1
Minister of Finance, 10
Minister of State Secretary
Moerdiono, 9
monetary and banking policy
pre-crisis, 54–57
Monetary and Exchange Affairs

Department (MAE), 91, 127
Monetary Authority of Singapore (MAS)
  market intervention operation, 89, 109
  rupiah stablization, 97–103
Monetary Board, 46, 64, 123
  complying with President's instructions, 112
monopoly practices
  removal, promise of, 158
Moody's, 32
Muhammad, Mar'ie 10, 108
national banks
  letters of credit refused, 120
national payment system, 122
National Planning and Development Board, 63
Neiss, Hubert, 134
Net International Reserves (NIR), 49, 86
Nitisastro, Widjojo 63, 162
non-performing loans (NPLs), 59, 90
Official Reserves, 86
oil subsidy
  reduction, 104
Parliamentary Commission on Bank Indonesia Liquidity Support, 172
People's Consultative Assembly, 174
President Soeharto, see also Soeharto government
  favouring increasing liquidity, 148
  health, worsening, 148
  instruction to banks, 112
  lamenting currency speculators, 10
  power to dismiss Governor of Central Bank, 2, 3
  prohibiting raising of SBI rates, 99
  signing decree to dismiss Governor, 10
  working relations with officers, 147
Radalet, Steven, 28, 73
real sector
  structural problems, 29
regional development banks, 94
Reichsbank, 200
reserve requirement for banks, 53
reserves, 49
  prudent method of calculating, 86
  sufficiency, 64
rice
  removing monopoly on imports, 158
riots, Jakarta 25
Rubin, Robert, 10
rupiah
  appreciating, argument for, 35
  depreciation, argument for, 36
  free float, 43–51
  overvaluation, 26, 35
  pressure from dollar surging, 25
  stabilization, 80, 97–103, 222
rupiah note
  new 10,000 notes, 5
Sabirin, Syahril 5
Sachs, Jeffrey, 28, 73
SBI rates
  easing, 62
  prohibited from being raised, 99
Second Letter of Intent
  negotiation by President, 142, 162, 163
  limited results, cause of, 230
  programme, stronger, 156–61

Shaw, Edward, 199
Sheu, Yuan-Dong 4
short-term certificates, 51
short-term debts
    maturing, 89
    ratio to international reserves, 224
Singapore
    issue of loan from, 146
    reserves, ample, 73
small and medium enterprises
    state bank lending to, 112
social disintegration, 34
Soeharto government
    letters of intent, 234
Southeast Asia Central bank
    (SEACEN) Governors' meeting, 4
soybeans
    import monopoly, discarding of,
        82
Standard & Poor's, 32
stand-by arrangement, 64, see also
    stand-by loan
    acceptance by President, 72
    evaluation, 142–44
    implementing, 110, 111
    withdrawals, 113
stand-by loan, 68
    conditions not warranting, 71
    criticism, 235
    maximum amount, 84
state banks, 52
    problems, 81
structural reforms, 95–97
Sukardi, Laksamana 1
Supplementary Reserve Facility
    (SRF), 114, 258

Supreme Audit Board, 140, 141,
    166, 185
    investigations, 149
    report, 253
Taiwan
    reserves, ample, 73
tariff
    reduction, 82, 96
Thai baht
    rapid depreciation, 25, 26
Thailand, 30
    panic buying of dollar, 41
    reserves, 49
Thoenes, Sander, 16
Trihatmodjo, Bambang 133
unemployment rates, 34
U.S. Federal Reserve Bank, 198
vulnerability indicators, 219
Waigel, Theo, 10, 11
Wardhana, Ali 63
wheat flour
    import monopoly, discarding of,
        82, 96
Working Committee on Bank
    Indonesia Liquidity Supports,
    180
World Bank, 36, 242
    loans, disbursement of, 88, 259
yen
    effect of strengthening, 24
    reserves, 25

About the Author

J. Soedradjad Djiwandono is Emeritus Professor of Economics, the University of Indonesia, and Visiting Professor at the Institute of Defence and Strategic Studies (IDSS), Nanyang Technological University (NTU), Singapore. Previously he was a Visiting Senior Fellow, the Institute of Southeast Asian Studies (ISEAS), Singapore, and a Development Associate at the Harvard Institute for International Development (HIID), Harvard University, USA. He started his career as a researcher at the Institute of Economics and Social Research, Council for Sciences of Indonesia (LIPI) and ultimately lecturer and professor at the Faculty of Economics, the University of Indonesia. However, he also has had a long career in the government of Indonesia, working in different capacities, including Bureau Head in the National Development Planning Agency (Bappenas), Special Assistant to the Minister of Trade, and Assistant Minister Coordinator for Economics, Finance and Industry. He has also held cabinet posts in the Soeharto government, notably a five-year term as the Junior Minister of Trade and another five-year term as Governor of Bank Indonesia, Indonesia's central bank. Dr. Djiwandono earned a BA in Economics from Gajah Madah University (1963), and MSc in Economics (1966) from the University of Wisconsin-Madison, an MA in Political Economy (1978), and a PhD in Economics (1980) from Boston University, specializing in Monetary Economics, International Trade and Development Economics.